Architecture-Centric Software Project Management

Architecture-Centric Software Project Management

A Practical Guide

Daniel J. Paulish

✦Addison-Wesley

Boston • San Francisco • New York • Toronto • Montreal
London • Munich • Paris • Madrid
Capetown • Sydney • Tokyo • Singapore • Mexico City

CarnegieMellon
Software Engineering Institute

The SEI Series in Software Engineering

Many of the designations used by manufacturers and sellers to distinguish their products are claimed as trademarks. Where those designations appear in this book, and Addison-Wesley was aware of a trademark claim, the designations have been printed with initial capital letters or in all capitals.

CMM, Capability Maturity Model, Capability Maturity Modeling, Carnegie Mellon, CERT, and CERT Coordination Center are registered in the U.S. Patent and Trademark Office.

ATAM; Architecture Tradeoff Analysis Method; CMMI; CMM Integration; CURE; IDEAL; Interim Profile; OCTAVE; Operationally Critical Threat, Asset, and Vulnerability Evaluation; Personal Software Process; PSP; SCAMPI; SCAMPI Lead Assessor; SCE; Team Software Process; and TSP are service marks of Carnegie Mellon University.

ANY MATERIAL FURNISHED BY CARNEGIE MELLON UNIVERSITY AND THE SOFTWARE ENGINEERING INSTITUTE IS FURNISHED ON AN "AS IS" BASIS. CARNEGIE MELLON UNIVERSITY MAKES NO WARRANTIES OF ANY KIND, EITHER EXPRESSED OR IMPLIED AS TO ANY MATTER INCLUDING, BUT NOT LIMITED TO, WARRANTY OF FITNESS FOR PURPOSE OR MERCHANTABILITY, EXCLUSIVITY OR RESULTS OBTAINED FROM USE OF THE MATERIAL. CARNEGIE MELLON UNIVERSITY DOES NOT MAKE ANY WARRANTY OF ANY KIND WITH RESPECT TO FREEDOM FROM PATENT, TRADEMARK, OR COPYRIGHT INFRINGEMENT.

The authors and publisher have taken care in the preparation of this book, but make no expressed or implied warranty of any kind and assume no responsibility for errors or omissions. No liability is assumed for incidental or consequential damages in connection with or arising out of the use of the information or programs contained herein.

The publisher offers discounts on this book when ordered in quantity for special sales. For more information, please contact:

Pearson Education Corporate Sales Division
One Lake Street
Upper Saddle River, NJ 07458
(800) 382-3419
corpsales@pearsontechgroup.com

Visit Addison-Wesley on the Web: www.aw.com/cseng/

Library of Congress Cataloging-in-Publication Data

Paulish, D. J. (Daniel J.)
    Architecture-centric software project management : a practical guide / Daniel J. Paulish.
        p. cm.—(SEI series in software engineering)
    Includes bibliographical references and index.
    ISBN 0-201-73409-5
    1. Computer software—Development—Management. 2. Software architecture. I. Title.
II. Series.

QA76.76.D47 P378 2001
005.1'068—dc21

                                       2001051260

ISBN 0-201-73409-5
Text printed on recycled paper
1 2 3 4 5 6 7 8 9 10—CRS—0504030201
First printing, December 2001

To my family,
Ellen, Terry, and Nick,
for their love and support

Contents

Foreword

A FUNDAMENTAL assumption of my work in the area of software architecture is that the architecture is *the* crucial artifact in the development of software systems. The architecture is the basis for achieving business goals and the basis for achieving software quality attributes. This has led to my interest in the design of software architecture for quality and the evaluation of how well an architecture does achieve its quality goals.

Now, however, I see that this is a technology-centric perspective. If the architecture is central to the achievement of the business goals for which the system is being produced, then the architecture must become central to the project manager as well as to the architect. In this book, Dan Paulish explores what it means for an architecture to be central to the project manager. I knew that the architecture is the basis for the work breakdown structure and for work assignments, but the project manager must do much more than just assign teams to work on portions of a development and monitor their progress.

Since, as Dan says, "schedule and effort estimates produced in the absence of a high-level architecture have minimal value," then the project manager must occupy higher management with other business until the high-level architecture can be produced. The project manager must simultaneously ensure that the high-level architecture is produced within a specified time frame. Dan gives techniques and rules of thumb for accomplishing this.

His rule of thumb about estimation—that 40% of the development time of a project is for design (up to 3 months for high-level design and the remainder for low level), 20% is for coding, and 40% is for testing—should speak very strongly to the research community. What techniques can be developed to leverage the high-level design so that the need for low-level design and testing are reduced? Why are we spending so much research time on coding techniques?

Once a realistic schedule has been achieved, the project manager must manage expectations based on the schedule. The schedule is used to motivate the development team, since they own it, and to give other elements of the organization a basis on which to plan. Building a vertical slice through the architecture enables adding other functionality in increments and enables the adjustment of functionality to meet releases.

Dan points out that just as the architecture embodies trade-offs between various qualities, so too the schedule embodies trade-offs between delivery dates, quality, and functionality. He advocates making clear to the development team what the priorities are among these three and using schedule pressures to keep from overemphasizing quality and functionality. That is, with incremental deliveries in relatively short increments (eight weeks) it is possible to make marketing prioritize features and to choose those features that can be implemented within an increment with acceptable quality.

The schedule depends on the architecture, and the incremental delivery depends on the schedule. This type of control is an essential feature of architecture-based development.

Just as the techniques for designing an architecture borrow heavily from existing design techniques and the techniques for evaluating an architecture borrow heavily from existing review techniques, so, too, the techniques for managing an architecture-centric project are not divorced from existing management techniques. Making schedules explicit, getting buy-in from stakeholders, setting realistic expectations, being sensitive to the foibles of employees, and keeping cool in the midst of tempests are all hallmarks of a good manager in any environment. Still, it is useful to see them articulated.

I was an evaluator for one of the case studies Dan mentions (DPS2000), and it is interesting for me as an evaluator to see what happened to this system. As a consultant, I am always seeing a slice of a development effort, and it is uncommon to find out the end of the story. It is like reading the middle of a novel, with someone to tell you how it started but with no one to tell you how it ended. Although, as with some novels, this is often enough, with others I want to know how the story turned out. The DPS2000 system was one of those where the plot line was interesting and the characters were well developed, and so it is enjoyable to find out the end.

I also resonated with Dan's description of managing international development teams. The time differences among various locations of the team are often the least of the problems. Holidays, vacations, and different attitudes toward work are also problems that must be overcome to successfully build a team with international membership.

In summary, if architecture is to be the centerpiece of a development effort, then the project manager must treat it as the centerpiece, must use it to design schedules, generate estimates, manage people. Identifying the various aspects of project management and discussing them in a lively and personal fashion make this a book I enjoyed reading and one from which I learned a great deal.

Len Bass

Preface

As computer hardware provides more functionality at a lower cost, the need for new applications software is exploding. The World Wide Web is providing more information to more people at an ever-faster rate. Software products must be developed more quickly, with increased functionality, performance, and quality. The pressure on the software engineers who are developing new products and maintaining existing products is increasing.

This book provides some support to the software project managers who are attempting to juggle the demands of meeting their schedule while delivering features with good quality. My experience with observing and participating in many software development projects indicates that good design and project management skills go a long way in achieving successful projects. What is very clear is that it is unlikely that projects will be successful when the software architecture is not well designed or project management skills are missing. I have observed the connections between good software architecture and good project management on many projects, and I hope that some of the tips provided will result in better products.

Motivation

As an industry, we have not been very successful in managing successful software projects. Successful projects are those that meet their planned development schedule, provide the functionality promised, and deliver good-quality software. From the 1995 Standish Group CHAOS report, their research on software projects reported that 16% of projects were completed successfully, 31% were cancelled outright, and 53% were substantially over budget and schedule and delivered less functionality than specified. By 1998, more projects were successful, with 26% completed successfully, 28% cancelled, and 46% over budget and schedule with less functionality [Johnson 1999]. Thus, things are improving, but we still have a terrible track record in our industry for successfully completing software development projects.

Background

I gained the experience for writing this book while managing software design and development projects at Siemens. As part of the Siemens Software Architecture R&D Program, a large number of Siemens projects have been investigated in order to capture how Siemens software architects design software systems. The knowledge gained from this research has been embodied in the four-views architecture design approach described in the *Applied Software Architecture* book written by Christine Hofmeister, Rod Nord, and Dilip Soni [2000]. As the four-views approach was being developed, we had opportunities to participate as architecture design team members for new products being designed in various Siemens businesses. In some cases, we were also asked to plan and manage these new product developments and implement subsystems or components of the architecture. Thus, our project planning and management methods were developed in parallel with the four-views design approach.

A concrete example of this correlation between architecture design methods and project planning methods is the **architecture-centered software project planning (ACSPP)** approach described in Chapter 2. We used this approach to develop cost and schedule estimates for the development projects, based on the software architecture. Since we were heavily involved with participating in software architecture design teams, we began to believe in the advantages to be gained when project planning was done in parallel with design. We were also called into Siemens companies as reviewers, from time to time, and we consistently observed warning flags for projects that either were not planned well or were missing a software architecture that could be easily communicated to the reviewers or the development team.

Over this same time period, the importance of software products and good development practices increased. We began to observe that our project planning and management methods were having a significant business impact, in that they helped get software products to the market quicker and more predictably. Thus, our initial research interest was focused more on design methods and tools, but also we began to see the importance of good project management practices for meeting project goals.

As we became involved with real design and development projects, we realized that the key to effectively applying our methods rested with the working relationship between the project manager and the chief architect. These roles are described, respectively, within Chapter 8 of this book and Chapter 12 of Hofmeister, Nord, and Soni [2000]. When the chief architect and project manager work together as a decision-making team, it's much easier to introduce and tailor the methods I describe within a specific development project. We also got to observe the problems that can arise when one individual tries to fulfill both of these roles for development teams that are bigger than a few people.

Not all the project management tips I present in this book are directly related to architecture design. But enough of them are related, and I believe that a good software architect needs to understand some simple project management techniques in order to be successful within the chief architect/project manager leadership team. Good architects are involved primarily in making technical decisions, but they also appreciate the soft factors involved with leading projects. They often serve as sounding boards or critics of the project manager concerning any decisions that may affect the morale of the developers. Furthermore, I believe that project managers should provide a supportive environment to the chief architect and the entire development team so that good design practices are consistently applied.

The biggest benefit of working within an industrial laboratory is that you have opportunities to do both research and development. In my case, I've had the opportunity to research methods such as those described in this book. But I've also had the chance to apply the methods to real projects. As a result, the methods have been tweaked to be practical so that they are relatively easy to apply. Along the way, I've had the opportunity to design, plan, and develop Siemens software products that have been successfully sold in the market. I have attempted to conceal the real identity of these products in my examples and case studies, since I often describe real-world problems that we have had to overcome. But for the most part, the products that I have applied these design and project management methods to have been successfully developed and sold in the market.

The projects that I have worked on tend to be mid-sized projects. Typically, they have been on the order of 10–20 software engineers. I cannot claim that these project management methods will work for very large or very small projects, since I have limited experience. Furthermore, since software development projects can last a year or more, I have limited personal experience even for the types of projects that I have worked on. I will conveniently ignore these facts as I explain the various tips and methods as if they are great things that every project manager should do. However, there are no silver bullets within what I describe, although it may sound that way at times. A "leap of faith" will be required on your part to experiment with the methods I describe. Unfortunately, this is a persistent problem in most of software engineering, since real experimentation is often very limited. Thus, my tips are mostly anecdotal in nature.

How to Use This Book

The primary audience for this book is software project managers. The secondary audience is software architects who must work closely with project managers. The third audience is software developers who are looking for insights on how to work within a project team and who may be considering career changes to the first two groups. The book is mainly a collection of tips that could be used for software development projects. Each tip must be tailored to the unique circumstances of the project being worked on.

The tips are structured roughly in the sequence in which a project manager will be involved: planning, organizing, implementing, and measuring. However, there is no strict sequence of steps implied, since these management tasks will be iterated up to product release.

Once you've read the introductory material (Part One), it's probably best to read Part Two of the book, on planning, particularly the description of architecture centered software project planning (ACSPP) in Chapter 2. After you understand the steps involved with estimating the schedule for your project, you can read the other chapters. The case studies in Part Six should probably be read last. These may or may not interest you, depending on the type of software you develop. Examples from the case study projects are also included throughout the rest of the book.

Acknowledgments

This book would not have been possible without the many discussions with Siemens software architects and the support of the management at Siemens Corporate Research and the many Siemens companies we have worked with. At the risk of omitting someone, I would like to acknowledge the contributions of Tony Lanza, Jeff Melanson, Craig Kasulis, Christine Hofmeister, Rod Nord, Dilip Soni, Francois Bronsard, Peter Hess, Henk LaRoi, Sascha Lukic, Uli Syre, Ali Inan, Romie Ogbolu, Detlef Fischer, Michael Unkelbach, Ram Chintala, Wilfried Loeffler, Gerhard Lengtat, Gilberto Matos, Bill Sherman, Mike Greenberg, Paul Bruschi, Bill Hasling, Bill Landi, Jean Hartmann, Paul Drongowski, Bob Schwanke, Peter Spool, Steve Masticola, Bea Hwong, Bruce Ladendorf, Chris Darken, Fred Geheb, Len Bass, Paul Clements, Linda Northrop, Marcus Yoo, Xiping Song, and Brian Berenbach.

I am greatly indebted to Thomas Murphy and Thomas Grandke, who provided a supportive environment that made writing this book possible. The anonymous reviewers of the manuscript provided many valuable insights for improving its readability. Also, thank you to Debbie Lafferty and the staff at Addison-Wesley for providing encouragement and publishing expertise.

PART one

Overview

Introduction

THE rest of this book is divided into five parts, corresponding to the four tasks that the project manager performs—planning, organizing, implementing, and measuring—plus a fifth part on case studies. For architecture-centric software project management, the project manager works closely with a chief architect and uses and contributes to many of the artifacts that result from high-level architecture design. This chapter gives an overview of all the main activities that a project manager practicing an architecture-centric approach will be involved in.

1.1 What Is Project Management?

Project managers are involved in four primary activities:

- Planning
- Organizing
- Implementing
- Measuring

For software management, although these activities overlap a lot, they follow somewhat the sequence in which I present them. Projects are usually *planned* at their beginning. I envision a high-level design phase of a project, when much of the project planning is done while the architecture is being designed.

Planning will also occur again prior to every increment of development. I prefer to keep the increments shorter than eight weeks in duration.

Organizing is also done early in a project. The project team organization needs to be set up and the roles of the team members defined. In some cases, a project manager may be responsible for recruiting and selecting the members of the project team. In other cases, technical staff may be assigned to the project, and the project manager must then allocate the development team roles.

The project manager is responsible for *implementing* the project in accordance with the plans that have been developed. Often, the project manager will need to react to unforeseen situations, since plans are rarely implemented exactly as conceived earlier in the project. How the project manager reacts to these situations, the decisions that are made, the replanning that is done, and so on will affect the outcome of the project.

The project manager must *measure* the progress of the project and the characteristics of the product as it is being developed. He or she will also measure the performance of the project team, its members, and the effectiveness of the product they produced, both during and after the project is completed.

There are obviously many other tasks a project manager must be involved in, such as leading, controlling, setting customer expectations, innovating, deciding, directing, and mentoring, Some of these are described in more detail in Chapter 8. The **planning, organizing, implementing, and measuring (POIM)** definition of what a project manager does is simple to remember, and it functions as a convenient summary of major project management tasks.

How you spend your time will determine to a large extent how successful you are as a project manager. There is never enough time to get everything done, and you will need to carefully determine priorities among tasks to provide a successful balance. For example, in my experience, developing quarterly status reports has low priority, since very few people take time to read them. Their value is often limited, since you are reading about something in the past that you cannot affect. However, though writing quarterly reports is a requirement for many project managers, I myself try to spend as little time as possible writing them. Recognize the important action items, do those first, and push other, lower-priority tasks to the bottom of your personal queue. You will also have to balance the mix among the actions required of you by your development project and those demanded by your personal (non-work-related) life.

Good software project managers usually have a balanced mix of technical and people-handling skills. People management skills are often characterized in terms of communication, vision, leadership, empathy, teaching, charisma, and so on. These skills are often harder to learn than are technical skills. This book may not make you a better communicator, for example, but it can provide tips as to what types of information are important to communicate to the development team. Technical skills can often be augmented by a strong chief architect. Thus, people management skills are somewhat of a prerequisite for software project managers. Many of these skills have nothing to do with software architecture. They can also be developed outside of the project team and the work environment. I encourage new software project managers to build their people management skills at every possible opportunity. This could be done in other environments, such as while managing the company softball team or organizing an external speaker series, with less risk than in development projects.

1.2   What Is Software Architecture?

I will rely on the definition of software architecture found in Soni, Nord, and Hofmeister [1995]:

> Software architecture is concerned with capturing the structures of a system and the relationships among the elements. . . . The structures we found fell into several broad categories: conceptual architecture, module architecture, execution architecture, and code architecture.

The software architecture of a product serves both as a design plan and as an abstraction of the product envisioned to be implemented. I have seen within the past ten years a growing awareness of the importance of describing software architecture before implementing a product. This relates directly to software project management, since the project plan must support the creation and description of the architecture. Once created, the architecture must be described to every member of the development team. Quite simply, I have found that development teams with a good vision of what they are implementing have a better chance to successfully implement the product. For architecture-centric software project management, the project manager recognizes and supports the realization that a good software architecture is necessary for developing a good product.

1.3 Core Beliefs

The project management practices described in this book can be characterized as "middleweight" processes. This is somewhere between heavyweight processes such as those described within the **capability maturity model (CMM)** [Paulk 1995] and the **Rational Unified Process (RUP)** [Kruchten 1999; Royce 1998] and lightweight processes such as **extreme programming** [Beck 2000]. Basically I believe you should spend some time up front designing a software architecture for the envisioned product as well as planning the project. But use incremental development to get to the market quickly while incrementally updating your plan as you implement the architecture. These middleweight processes have the following fundamental characteristics.

- *Architecture design and description:* I believe that successful software development projects need a description of the architecture design that can be understood by all development team members. The architecture design should be done prior to writing large amounts of production code.
- *Project planning:* Projects should be planned while the software architecture is being designed. Schedules, effort estimates, and the project organization should be based on the architecture. Schedules developed prior to having an architecture design are likely to be very inaccurate.
- *Incremental development:* Software products should be developed incrementally, based on the software architecture and the set of desired features. The first increment, which I call a "vertical slice," should be used to prove major characteristics of the architecture.
- *Project manager/architect team:* The project manager and software architect should work closely together as a decision-making team. Responsibilities are roughly divided between management and technical decisions. Successful projects consisting of more than a few developers should have two different individuals in these roles.
- *Trade-off analysis:* Project management consists of a set of trade-off decisions. Thus, there are no right or wrong answers, and projects that

are implemented will never go exactly as planned. Project managers must be flexible to be able to best manage development risks.

- *Soft factors:* Soft factors will affect a project as much as or more than the technical issues. These soft factors include team building, morale, management influences, business influences, staff experience, and culture.

1.4   Project Management Process

The process a project manager uses to do his or her job will depend greatly on the software development process of the larger organization. It is *not* my intent to describe a rigorous procedure that every project manager should follow. Rather, to more easily introduce the book's concepts, I identify many of the steps the project manager is likely to follow when using an architecture-centric approach. This will help set the context for the practices described in the book and introduce what the project manager does and how that relates to architecture design activities.

Typically, a development process or work flow is set up as a sequence of steps with well-defined inputs and outputs along with roles and responsibilities. Project management is to a large extent an iterative process. Plans are formulated and an attempt made to follow them. But unexpected events arise, and plans must frequently be modified. These plan modifications are called *mid-course corrections*. Also, project managers sometimes make decisions based on partial information. Often, a straw-man plan will be made only to be refined or replaced as more information becomes available. Thus, I will not attempt to define precise processes or work flows for project managers. But I will attempt to list many of the steps the project manager should consider, in a rough sequence, as he or she attempts to plan, organize, implement, and measure a project working closely with the chief architect.

1.5   Architecture-Centric Project Management

I provide here an overview of how you could manage a software project that has architecture design at the center. Again, the specific sequence of tasks will depend on your software development process. But identifying the advantages and useful outputs of architecture design will help put the tips contained in later chapters of this book into a framework. You will perform many tasks as a project manager that have nothing to do with the design. But, very simply, over the course of managing a project you will need to make certain that you have an architecture design that represents the vision of the product that will be developed. Your software development plan will identify how you will achieve the vision that the architecture represents. As you manage the development, you will be guided by your plan as well as your progress in achieving the architecture. You will need to make many mid-course corrections to your development plan, but hopefully the architecture will remain more constant while it is being implemented.

Figure 1.1 identifies some of the major steps associated with implementing an entire project using an architecture-centric approach. The boxes represent the activities that will generally be done during the project, and the arrows represent some of the outputs that result from the activities and are inputs to other activities. This project management book will cover the period from when market requirements have been defined to when the software is delivered to the first customer. Thus, it does not focus on project management prac-

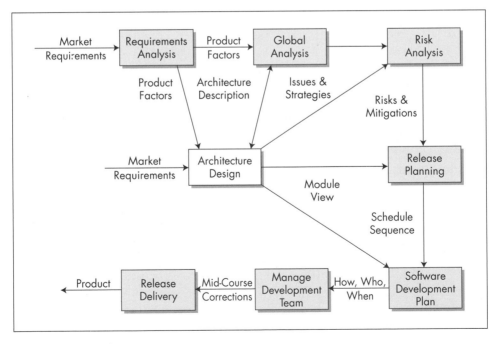

Figure 1.1 *Architecture-Centric Project.*

tices for software products that are mostly being maintained rather than developed. The following sections introduce these major and other steps in the project management activities of planning, organizing, implementing, and measuring.

Architecture-centric project management starts when an initial set of market requirements has been defined. The project manager and the architecture design team analyze the requirements. They analyze product factors and other influences as part of a global analysis. They analyze risks as part of the risk analysis. The module view of the architecture along with the feature list resulting from the requirements analysis become the basis for the release planning for the incremental development.

Once release planning is complete, a software development plan can be developed that also includes the schedule, estimated development costs, and project organization. The **software development plan (SDP)** is generally written for the entire project, with more detailed plans and specific tasks for the first incremental release. This document will be revised for each release increment as the build plan is developed in detail for each increment. I suggest keeping the increment duration small, to within eight weeks between releases. Once development starts, beginning with the detailed design of each software component identified within the module view of the architecture, you will be leading and managing the development team. You will use the schedule and organization identified in the software development plan as a guide. Mid-course corrections to the development plan are inevitable, since not everything will go as planned and unexpected events will occur (e.g., illness of a team member).

At the end of the development increment, the software will be released on the date agreed to in the release plan. You will then plan and implement a cycle of increments until the product functionality is sufficient for an initial product. This initial product will be delivered to users, possibly at first within some type of beta testing or for a lead customer. Within release delivery, you will review test results and data, in order to determine if the product quality is adequate for customer delivery. After the first increment is released, you will likely use a system-testing function to perform independent testing on the software while your development team is working on the next increment. You will plan the project so that you have test results available from the prior increment before you release the next increment. This helps improve product quality over time and avoids having to do all the testing and fixing at the end of the project.

1.6 Planning

The major steps involved with planning an architecture-centric software project are summarized in Figure 1.2.

Project planning starts when a first set of requirements is defined and ends with the software development plan. Project planning happens in parallel with the design of the software architecture in what I call the high-level design phase of the project. It will also happen before the development of each incremental release. The project manager works with and manages a small architecture design team during the high-level design phase. The chief architect is the technical leader of the design team. The project manager, along with the design team, contributes to the global analysis. The project manager focuses more on

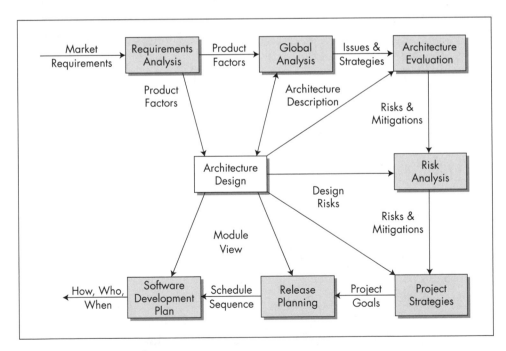

Figure 1.2 *Project Planning.*

organizational influencing factors, while the architects focus more on product and technological factors.

The project manager starts developing top-down schedule estimates in order to get a feel for the scope of the development that will be required to implement the architecture. Once the module view of the software architecture is defined, you can begin putting together bottom-up estimates for all the components of the architecture that will need to be developed. If possible, the members of the anticipated development team will develop the bottom-up estimates. When the architecture is described enough, you will schedule an architecture evaluation review, using both internal and external reviewers. You will keep track of the progress of the high-level design phase so that it is completed in a time frame consistent with the rules of thumb I suggest in Chapter 2.

As project manager you will begin release planning, based on the set of requirements, the bottom-up estimates, and the project milestones that should be reached. You will describe release feature content and define engineering releases and incremental builds within a build plan. You will be making key decisions with the chief architect concerning the technologies needed to implement the architecture.

Global analysis, the architecture design, and the architecture evaluation will help to identify the risks associated with implementing the architecture. As project manager you will further analyze these risks, propose possible risk mitigation actions, and identify project goals and strategies.

In addition to the architecture design specification, the other primary artifact resulting from the high-level design phase is the software development plan (SDP). The SDP contains the schedules and staffing plans for implementing the product. You will update the SDP for each successive release increment. The SDP will identify risk mitigation actions as project tasks. The SDP information is typically used for a management gate review at the end of the high-level design phase, prior to the beginning of development. Management is interested in learning how long the development will take and how much it will cost as an engineering investment. Depending on the results of the review, you may need to modify the SDP, which may also mean changing the architecture design. For example, if the required size of the proposed development team cannot be staffed, the SDP may need to extend the schedule or the architecture may need to be simplified to require less implementation. Clearly, you could also simplify the requirements. Project planning is a set of trade-offs that hopefully will result in a plan that can be staffed within an acceptable schedule, set of features, and quality level.

1.7 Organizing

The project manager will need to organize the architecture design team, the development team, and all the activities associated with project management. Project management activities include the interfaces to other functions within the organization, such as marketing, quality assurance, system testing, and documentation development. The major steps involved with organizing an architecture-centric software project are summarized in Figure 1.3.

At the at the beginning of the high-level design phase, you will need to establish the architecture design team and the chief architect. The development team members will first get involved with the project during the bottom-up estimation. Ideally, the engineer who is to implement a specific component prepares the estimate for that component. Thus, the project manager needs to

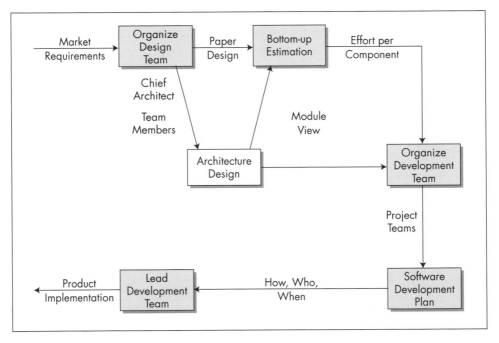

Figure 1.3 *Project Organizing.*

anticipate who the development team members will be and what their roles will be. Each team member will be given the architecture design specification and will have up to four hours to create a "paper design" and fill out a cost estimation form for each component he or she will be estimating.

The project manager will then start organizing the development team. Ideally, the architecture team members will become team leaders, and they will lead the development of each subsystem described in the architecture. Thus, the development team organization should look like the module architecture developed during high-level design.

The SDP will propose the organization, along with task assignments, schedule, and the definitions of the project team role. Most likely, at the end of the high-level design phase, you will hold a management review to determine the availability of each individual that the SDP identifies as needed to implement the product. In cases when key people are unavailable, you may need to modify the SDP or the architecture to accommodate the staffing plan.

After implementation begins, you, as project manager, will be the primary leader of the product development organization. You will need to refine the organization as the product is being developed. This may mean reassigning team members to specific tasks as they are being implemented. In general, critical tasks should be covered by the more experienced engineers. Engineers struggling with achieving their tasks may need support from a mentor or a more experienced engineer, or they may even be removed from the team if their skills or work habits are inconsistent with the needs of the project.

You will have a team of key contributors on whom you should be able to rely to implement the details of the project and make decisions. Foremost within this organization will be the chief architect, who will address many of the technical issues. Depending on the overall size of the project, you will also rely on the team leaders, who will direct the work of the engineers assigned to implement the major subsystems.

1.8   Implementing

The project manager is responsible for implementing the project in accordance with the software development plan. Often, you will need to react to unforeseen situations, since plans are rarely implemented as they were conceived earlier in the project. How you react to these situations, the decisions you make, what you replan, and so on will affect the outcome of the project. The major steps involved with implementing an architecture-centric software project are summarized in Figure 1.4.

The module view that comes from the architecture design provides inputs for organizing the development team. Risk analysis produces mitigation actions that are used to do the release planning, that is, the sequence in which the components and features will be implemented. The build plan, along with the effort estimates for each component, gives some of the inputs for creating the software development plan. The project manager implements the project in accordance with the development plan. Progress is monitored via weekly status meetings and other communications with team members. As the project is implemented, mid-course corrections will be made to meet the release dates. Release delivery will plan the details of each software release, including its functionality and quality. Each incremental release will be delivered to a system testing function. Later releases will be delivered as a product to customers from the time that a minimal useful set of features is implemented.

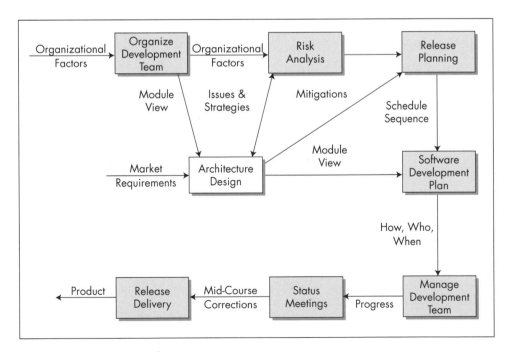

Figure 1.4 *Project Implementing.*

1.9 Measuring

The major steps involved with measuring an architecture-centric software project are summarized in Figure 1.5.

The architecture design will serve to drive the project planning to the point where a proposed software development plan can be written. From the software development plan, a number of metrics will be defined as target goals for the project. These target goals will include measures such as the development budget as calculated from the staffing plan, key milestone dates from the development schedule, size measures, and quality measures. These measures should be consistent with the overall project goals. Managing the project will involve making trade-offs among these goals, and the measures will yield insights with respect to achieving the goals. The goals and measures will likely require trade-offs among meeting the time schedule, providing desired functionality, achieving the quality of the resulting release, and the development costs.

As the software is developed, progress will be made and containing the measures tracked. An important measure for the overall project progress will be whether or not the incremental release dates are being met. After a release

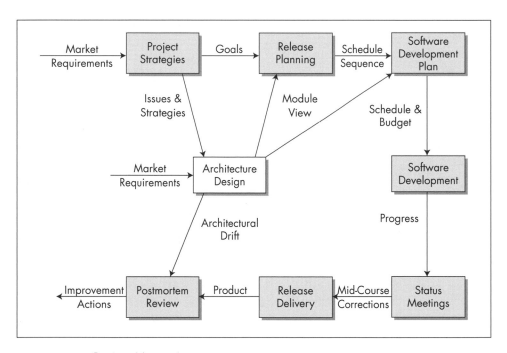

Figure 1.5 *Project Measuring.*

containing the last planned major set of features, you will likely perform a postmortem review on your project. Here you will compare the goals you set during planning with the measures tracked during development. The review will give you insights into how well the project went—such as whether you met your schedule, budget, quality, and functionality goals—and how you can better plan and manage your next project.

1.10 Summary

This chapter provides a broad overview of the major steps involved with architecture-centric software project management. The following chapters describe in more detail what the project manager can do and supply tips for achieving the project management activities.

PART two

Planning

CHAPTER 2

Architecture-Centered Software Project Planning

When we began working on the IS2000 project, our management was very nervous about the investment that might be required to implement the architecture that we were designing. Since we felt that estimates were being given too early, we asked the design team members not to communicate any preliminary estimates to management. By delaying our commitment to develop the product within a specified schedule and budget until after the software architecture design was completed, we were able to work on planning the project while the architecture was being worked on.

W ELL-MANAGED software projects usually start with good planning. I suggest that a good time for a project manager to plan the project is when the architecture is being designed. This chapter describes an approach for planning software projects, which I call architecture-centered software project planning (ACSPP). I'll describe the steps for this approach and how planning a software project is linked to architecture design.

2.1 Developing Realistic Schedules

It is well known that effort and schedule estimates given in the very early stages of a software development project can be very inaccurate [Boehm 1981; Boehm et al. 2000]. I believe that schedule and effort estimates produced in the absence of a high-level architecture design have minimal value. Milestone dates planned in the absence of a design will likely be missed. That is why I encourage software architects and project managers to complete the design of the architecture before committing to any development schedules. When the design is complete, then you can create a project plan, a schedule, and staff resource projections, all of which are dependent upon the software architecture of the product.

Architecture-centered software project planning is applied relatively early in the software development process. As illustrated in Figure 2.1, ACSPP is applied after the system requirements design is complete. Management often desires very early estimates of the time and effort required to develop a new software product. In some cases, these estimates may be needed to determine whether or not the development project should be undertaken. Business and product planning are often based on very early estimates that can be highly inaccurate. For example, according to Boehm [1981], actual effort expended can be 1.5 times the cost estimates given after requirements specifications are

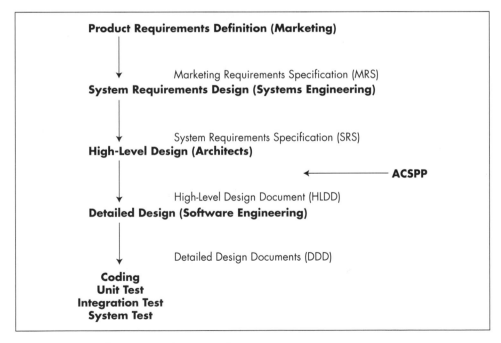

Figure 2.1 *Software Development Phases.*

complete. Actual effort expended can be four times the estimates given at the beginning of the project, before any feasibility analysis is done.

I believe that by applying ACSPP and estimating schedules after the high-level design is completed, the estimated schedules can be predicted within an accuracy range of 15% to 20%. This degree of accuracy is manageable by most project managers who track the progress of the development on a weekly basis. Using incremental development where the increments are small further helps the project manager keep the project on track. It's easier to manage a series of simpler plans of shorter duration than one that is large and complex.

Furthermore, I encourage software architects and project managers to resist committing to a development schedule until an estimate, based on the architecture, is completed. All too often, business managers are eager to accept a very early schedule, communicate the schedule to potential customers, and then attempt to hold the development team to shipping the software based on the very early estimate. This frequently creates unhappy customers whose delivery expectations haven't been met, poor-quality software for the initial release, or a burned-out development team. Often, the development team is not committed to meeting a delivery date based on very early estimates, and conflicts arise between the team and business and sales management. Many of these problems can be avoided if the software project manager and architect withhold any predictions and make no commitments as to how long it will take to develop the software until after the high-level design is completed and bottom-up estimates are generated by the development team members.

2.2 Approach

Figure 2.2 illustrates the approach used for ACSPP. The high-level design of the software architecture is initiated with a small design team. In parallel, the project manager launches top-down schedule planning, using preliminary estimates of lines of code as inputs to an estimation tool such as **Cocomo, the Constructive Cost Model** [Boehm 1981; Boehm et al. 2000]. The high-level design and top-down schedule estimates become the inputs for release planning. The software components identified in the high-level design are part of the bottom-up estimation process. The project manager then compares the sums of the effort and size estimates for each software source component with the top-down schedule. From all this information the project manager generates a project development

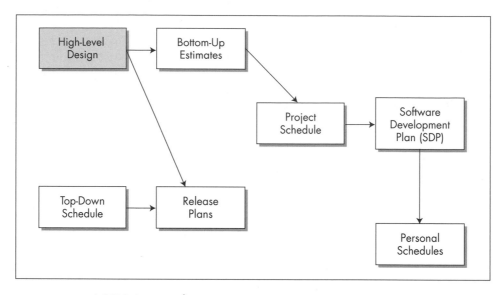

Figure 2.2 *ACSPP Approach.*

schedule. The schedule, along with the staff assignments and project organization, becomes part of the software development plan (SDP). Project team members use the SDP as a framework for developing their personal schedules. The following sections describe each step of ACSPP in more detail.

2.2.1 High-Level Design

The project manager begins working on a top-down schedule as the small design team is working on the high-level design of the architecture. While the software architecture is being developed, the chief architect explains it to the project team members through in-depth discussions. This is an iterative process that helps the development team members understand the high-level design and helps the design team (with their input) to improve it.

We describe the architecture using the four-views approach (Figure 2.3) [Hofmeister, Nord, and Soni, 2000]. A one-page layer diagram is generated as part of the *module architecture*. This artifact of the description of the software architecture will be extremely useful to the project manager when planning the project. Figure 2.4 presents an example of a simplified layer diagram for the

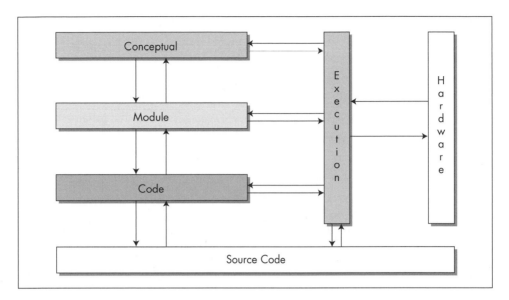

Figure 2.3 *Four Views of Software Architecture.*

module architecture. Modules within a layer can communicate with each other. Modules may communicate only with modules in the same or adjacent layers. Some type of **high-level design document (HLDD)** describes the architecture. Different organizations may call this document that describes the architecture by other names, e.g., design specification, system specification.

GUI		
Applications		
Application Services		
Probe Service	Image Processing	Database Services
Systems Services		
OS Layer		
Communication		
Hardware		

Figure 2.4 *Architecture Layer Diagram.*

Using the four views [Hofmeister, Nord, and Soni 2000]:

To describe the software architecture, we suggest using an architecture design approach such as the four-views. The project manager will use the description of the architecture for project planning, and it will help the entire development team to understand the structure of the software product they are building. " A software architecture has four distinct views: conceptual, module, execution, and code. . . . Separating different aspects into separate views helps people manage complexity. The conceptual view is tied most closely to the application domain. In this view, the functionality of the system is mapped to architecture elements called *conceptual components*, with coordination and data exchange handled by elements called *connectors*. In the module view, the components and connectors from the conceptual view are mapped to *subsystems* and *modules*. The execution view defines the system's *runtime entities* and their attributes, such as memory usage and hardware assignment. For the code view, the architect determines how runtime entities from the execution view are mapped to *deployment components* (for example, executables), how modules from the module view are mapped to source components, and how the deployment components are produced from the *source components*."

The architecture layer diagram provides stability and a point of reference for many aspects of the project, including technical coordination, assessment of alternative implementations, and project planning and scheduling. The diagram shows all the subsystems and components of the software system that will need to be developed or acquired. This diagram functions to identify all the modules that will be estimated during the bottom-up estimation process.

The project manager will rely mostly on the module view of the four-views for planning the work to be done for the project. Strictly using the four-views nomenclature, the project manager will identify the *modules* to be estimated from the architecture layer diagram. However, a module is a logical grouping of software functionality, so once the module is assigned to a software development engineer to be designed and estimated, the development team will immediately begin to think of the module as a *source component* or as components to be coded. Thus, per the four-views nomenclature, source components will be used strictly within the code view and should not be confused with the *conceptual components*, which go with the conceptual view. For the viewpoint of the project manager, I will relax the four-views nomenclature a little and talk about estimating the work to be done to design, code, and unit test each component to be developed.

It is useful if the layer diagram identifies all the *modules* or *subsystems* that will be estimated. This may require some grouping of smaller modules into larger modules or subsystems. We recommend that the diagram be drawn to limit the number of modules to be estimated to fewer than 150 and that they all fit on one page. This may require some fine-tuning by the architect. The goal is to balance the level of detail so that the estimate considers all pieces of the system to be developed and so that less than a few weeks is spent on the bottom-up estimates, using the available or anticipated team members. Following a guideline of less than four hours to achieve a component "paper design" and the bottom-up estimate, as described later, the architect can structure the layer diagram at the appropriate level of abstraction.

The architect should also keep in mind that the architecture layer diagram is a handy one-page representation of the entire system to be built. Thus, it should include the appropriate level of detail so that both top management and development team members can get, on a single piece of paper, an understandable representation of the module architecture of the system to be built.

The layer diagram is also useful to the project manager, since the project organization will often reflect the architecture of the product (Chapter 5). One approach to setting up the project development team organization is for key members of the high-level design team to assume responsibility for the major *subsystems* defined in the architecture. They will lead developers, who will have responsibility for selected source components within the subsystem. Again, for the viewpoint of the project manager, I will define a *subsystem* as a collection of source components with similar functionality, as loosely defined within the module view (e.g., the image-processing subsystem). The project team organization will likely also include other functions that are not involved with direct code development, such as integration and validation testing.

2.2.2 Top-Down Schedule

In parallel with the architecture design, the project manager begins investigating the top-down schedule and effort estimation using estimates of expected lines of code for each subsystem. The estimates of lines of code help in comparing the expected total lines of code for this project with the total for other, similar products or with that for competitive products, if such size estimates are available. These estimates become inputs to cost and schedule estimation model calculations (e.g., the Cocomo Model), which provide outputs of effort, schedule duration for major phases of development, and staff profile loading for various types of development skills (Figure 2.5).

Since the project manager will likely do the top-down estimate early during the high-level design phase of the project, the architecture design information will be sketchy at best. Thus, the estimates of lines of code will be rough and not very accurate. Such estimates are not easy to make, even when more design work is done. Sources for sizing the anticipated project could include the experience of the chief architect, estimates from prior projects with similar functionality (e.g., the current product), and even estimates from the products of your competitors. In general, it will be difficult to get size estimates from competing products, but you may know someone within a competitor's development team or may have read a published paper containing size data from a similar product.

The top-down approach is the more traditional way software project managers estimate new projects. There are many estimation models available to the project manager. In addition to Cocomo, commonly used models include SLIM, PRICE-S, and **function point analysis (FPA)** [Albrecht and Gaffney

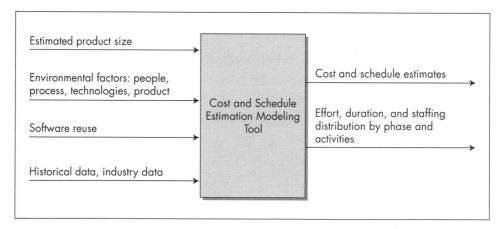

Figure 2.5 *Top-Down Schedule Overview.*

1983; Jones 1991; Putnam and Myers 1992; and Austin and Paulish 1993]. By themselves, the estimation models are usually not very accurate. This is because the models require calibration, and often the historical data on projects using similar technologies to do the calibration is lacking in many organizations. I suggest you select one estimation tool that is comfortable for you and then use that tool for all your project estimates.

The models do provide useful outputs, in that they help the project manager not to forget to consider any significant efforts when planning the project. For example, the models can provide useful estimates for activities such as documentation preparation, integration testing, and quality assurance. Another useful output for the project manager is a staffing profile over the life of the development and maintenance phases. This helps the project manager scope out the overall effort, identify the size of the team that will be needed, and estimate the time frame required before the first release. There is always a trade-off between the team size and the development time frame. Smaller teams are generally easier to manage and more productive, but sales advantages can be gained by getting to the market quickly. Also, given the rate at which technology is evolving, it's usually not a good idea to extend new-product development over many years, since both the requirements and implementation technologies are likely to change. The top-down schedule estimation efforts can be used to generate what-if scenarios about the trade-off between development team size and time frame. In some cases, it may also become obvious that the organization cannot afford or assemble the staff resources to develop the new product. That is when you initiate investigations into reuse, acquisition, outsourcing, licensing, and so on of certain subsystems/components.

An estimation model for the top-down schedule also helps educate management about the scope and risks associated with developing a new software product. Software engineering technology is getting better every year, so the actual development effort will likely be less than what a careful application of an older model predicts, given that the model usually lags technology advancements. However, many business managers, some with little or no experience with software development, may expect a software product to be produced easily by just putting some young software hackers in a room and periodically feeding them pizza and soft drinks. The architect and project manager can use the estimation model and top-down schedule to educate management and set appropriate expectations so that the time frame, risks, and team size are realistically considered before full-scale development begins.

2.2.3　Bottom-Up Estimates

When all the components have been defined in the high-level design, each team member does a "paper design" for her assigned components and generates estimates of the effort necessary to create the detailed design, code, and unit test for each component. Based on my experience, no more than four hours per component should be allocated to the paper design. As stated earlier, the architect needs to define the granularity of a component so that the number of components and the time frame for the estimation exercise are reasonable. The project manager should assign components to be estimated to the team member most likely to implement the component. This increases the overall ownership of the estimates, and links individuals with the parts of the system they are likely to be involved with. This is also the time that additional team members are brought into the project team, initially to work on the bottom-up estimates. Up to this point, the development team consisted mainly of the project manager and the high-level design team, headed by the chief software architect. The bottom-up estimation process helps team members understand the high-level design at a greater level of detail and provides more accurate estimates about the size and complexity of the components.

Each team member is responsible for the design of his or her assigned components, documenting the subcomponents and dependencies and filling out a template (Figure 2.6) that estimates the size, confidence, complexity, and design, coding, and testing effort involved. For each component, we ask the team member to estimate his confidence in the estimate, based on his experience with developing any similar components and any design or code he may consider reusing. The confidence column of the estimation form asks which inputs were considered in addition to the requirements specification and the high level design. The form entries for confidence are shown in Table 2.1.

The complexity column of the estimation form given in Figure 2.6 asks how difficult it will be to design, code, and unit-test the component. The complexity entries are defined in Table 2.2. The estimation form asks for code size, in estimated lines of code, for implementing the component. It asks for effort estimates, in staff-hours for detailed design, coding, and unit-testing from the engineer assigned to the component estimation and implementation.

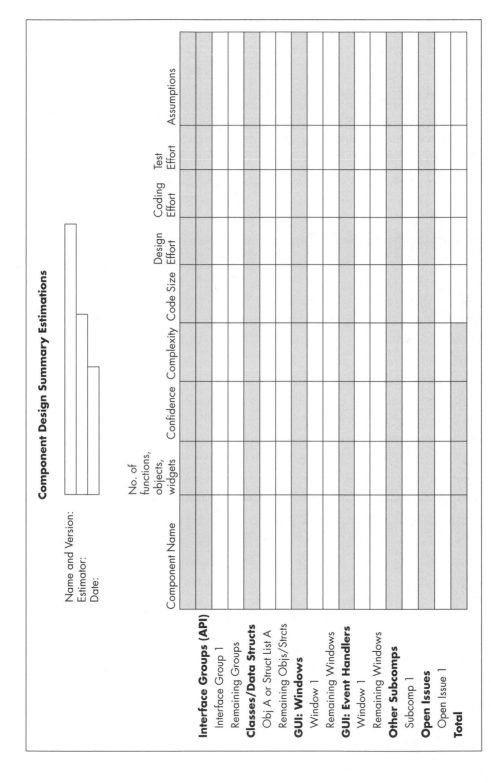

Figure 2.6 *Software Component Estimation Form.*

Table 2.1 *Confidence Column Entries.*

Entry	Meaning	Inputs Considered
1	Very low	None
2	Low	Design and code of similar components
3	Medium	Existing detailed design only
4	High	Existing code only
5	Very high	Existing detailed design and code

Adjustments will need to be made if someone with a much different background implements the component.

The estimates are compared with any estimates or historical data from any prior projects. The architect and design team members act as a type of review board, to review the estimates as they are generated, question any estimates that appear unreasonable, and form opinions about the degree of estimation optimism/conservatism of the developers. Final efforts per component are computed, reviewed, and used as inputs for the project scheduling. The sums of the estimated lines of code and the estimated development effort are then compared with the top-down Cocomo estimates.

It has been surprising to me how closely the top-down and bottom-up estimates have agreed for the projects that I have worked on. I suspect this is mainly coincidence. I tend to have more confidence in the bottom-up estimate, since the development team members generated it and they are more committed to the estimate. An example of a bottom-up estimation summary spread-

Table 2.2 *Complexity Column Entries.*

Entry	Meaning
1	Very low (straightforward, even for a beginner)
2	Low
3	Medium
4	High
5	Very high (needs a very experienced engineer)

sheet is given in Figure 2.7. Keep in mind that the estimates in the spreadsheet are only for detailed design, coding, and unit-level testing for each component identified in the software architecture. Thus, to get an estimate of total project effort, you must add in hours for other activities, such as configuration management, system testing, documentation, project management, and quality assurance. The top-down estimate would normally include such tasks. One approach is to insert the estimate of total lines of code from the bottom-up estimate into the top-down estimation tool to estimate the effort associated with the tasks not directly related to developing the components. Also keep in mind that your total estimates will depend on your software development process. For example, if your development process calls for code inspections, the coding effort column of the component estimation form should include the time to prepare and conduct the inspections, or you must add this additional effort to the total effort for the project.

The bottom-up estimation summary spreadsheet is also useful for doing cost-to-complete estimates. As design, coding, and unit-testing functions are

IS2000 Bottom-Up Cost Estimation
Major work packages

	Confidence	Complexity	Code Size	Total Effort (hours)	Total Effort (staff-years)
Versioned Object	3	5	2000	720	0.3938731
Study Management	3.2	3.4	600	1280	0.7002188
Check In and Check Out	3.7	3.3	1800	1320	0.7221007
Templates	3	5	1000	2400	1.3129103
Schedule Maker	1	5	19500	2920	1.5973742
GUI	2.8	3.6	18300	4960	2.7133479
Communication System	3	4	500	640	0.3501094
Probe Interface	3	3	11500	1580	0.8643326
HW Diagnostics	4	3	400	250	0.1367615
Flat Panel Display	4	3	700	800	0.4376368
All Other functions			20000	3500	1.9146608
Totals			76300	20370	11.143326

Figure 2.7   *Bottom-Up Estimation Spreadsheet.*

completed for specific components, they can be reduced to zero effort in the spreadsheet. Cost-to-completes are discussed in more detail in Chapter 13.

2.2.4   Release Plans

I propose that the software development be planned as a sequence of incremental engineering releases with increasing functionality. The first release will consist of a "vertical slice" through the architecture layer diagram, which will function as a prototype of the architecture. The last release will be the first set of functionality that can be sold as a package to a customer. You'll also plan alpha and/or beta releases to be tested either by your in-house testing function or by lead users. The project schedule will be structured so that while in-house testers or users are testing a release, the development team will be working on the next release. You should plan your release increments and testing such that test results will be available for your developers to include bug fixes in the next release. The cycle time defined for these incremental releases will depend on the times needed for testing and feature development as well as on business constraints such as when the first set of useful functionality is needed by customers. Often, these release plans are driven by the dates of industry trade shows, when a new release with the latest functionality is required. In most cases, I suggest fixing the release dates and release cycles and then fitting in the functionality for each release depending on the bottom-up estimates and what makes sense for functionally testing the software as a set of user-visible features. I suggest defining the target releases with a list of major features and a desired release date within a short document called a *release plan*.

With consultation from Marketing and Service, a **feature release specification (FRS)** document is completed detailing which product feature will be incorporated in which engineering release. A **component release specification (CRS)** document is also written to describe component releases necessary to implement the required features in each engineering release. Responsibilities for these component releases are assigned to team members. The team members create their own personal schedules from these documents. The FRS and CRS can be separate documents or can be combined into a single document, called a *build plan*, as illustrated in Figure 2.8. In this figure, Schedule Maker is an example component. The features listed are all implemented within the Schedule Maker component.

	ER1	ER2	ER3	R1	R2+
Schedule Maker					
Search Consumer Tree for Scheduled Events	✓			✓	
Create a Schedule	✓			✓	
Handle Report Events	✓			✓	
Handle Acquisition Events		✓		✓	
Optimize Acquisitions					✓
Handle Set Parameter Scheduled Events		✓		✓	
Display and Manual Update of Schedules			✓	✓	

Figure 2.8 *Example Build Plan Excerpt.*

In practice, the *release plan* usually identifies the target releases with a list of major features over the life of the development. The *build plan* concentrates more on describing the sequence of implementation for the detailed features in the next increment to be developed. You update these documents when planning each incremental release. You do this incremental planning along with the updating of the plans a week or two before the start of the next development increment.

You create a software integration strategy for the components and the features that will be implemented by partitioning them into internal engineering releases (build plan). You then review the component effort estimates, from the bottom-up estimation process, along with the desired availability of the features within an engineering release. From that, you can easily assign the component developments to a time schedule and identify the staff to design, code, and unit-test each component. You can also map the architecture into a development organization plan corresponding to the subsystems and components. The project manager can then assign at least one development team member to be responsible for each software component identified in the architecture.

> **TIP: Pick release milestone dates that are easy to remember.**
>
> Pick release dates that are easy for everyone on the development team to remember, e.g., the last Friday of the month or the Friday before a holiday

weekend. With incremental releases planned within 4-week to 8-week intervals, it's surprising how easy it is to forget when the next release is. Be careful when planning multisite development projects in different countries; you don't want to set release dates that conflict with the local holidays in other countries. Also, avoid picking release dates during weeks when key team members are on vacation.

2.2.5   Project Schedule

From the top-down schedule, bottom-up estimates, FRS, and CRS, you develop a schedule skeleton (Figure 2.9) for the project so that each of the internal engineering releases can be designed, coded, unit-tested, integrated, and system-tested within the desired milestones. Divide each component's development into subtasks according to the development phases (e.g., detailed design, coding, unit testing, bug fixing), as identified within the software development process of your organization, for each release. And repeat the development phases for each incremental engineering release. You plan the schedule for each component based on the effort estimates from the bottom-up estimation process. The schedule skeleton divides each component's development, depending on the total estimated effort, the staff resources available, and the FRS and CRS. For example, the design and coding tasks for a large component would start early even though the features it implements are not needed until later. In some cases, you implement partial functionality of a component and thus may distribute development across multiple engineering releases. It is also sometimes necessary to modify the FRS and CRS in order to fit the component development subtasks within the schedule skeleton using the available staff resources.

Note that the example schedule skeleton in Figure 2.9 is represented as a waterfall process model. As discussed with release planning, each engineering release increment will have its own development schedule. You may need to review requirements and high-level design at the beginning of each increment, but hopefully you will do most of this work when applying ACSPP during the high-level design phase. Avoiding too much requirements' churn is one reason to attempt to keep short the increment intervals and the delivery to the first customer.

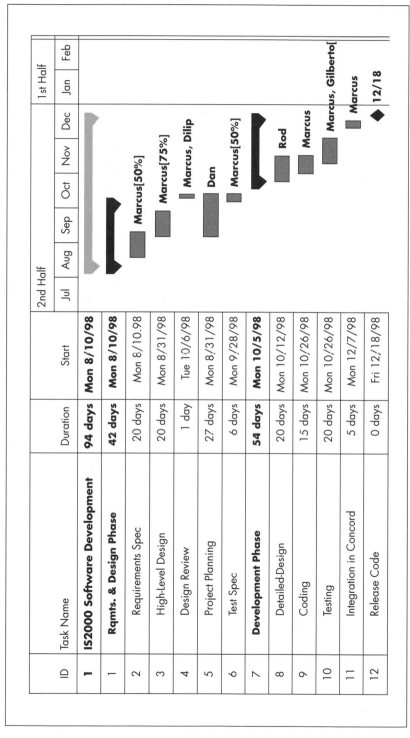

ID	Task Name	Duration	Start	2nd Half Jul Aug Sep Oct Nov Dec	1st Half Jan Feb
1	**IS2000 Software Development**	**94 days**	**Mon 8/10/98**		
1	**Rqmts. & Design Phase**	**42 days**	**Mon 8/10/98**		
2	Requirements Spec	20 days	Mon 8/10.98	Marcus[50%]	
3	High-Level Design	20 days	Mon 8/31/98	Marcus[75%]	
4	Design Review	1 day	Tue 10/6/98	Marcus, Dilip	
5	Project Planning	27 days	Mon 8/31/98	Dan	
6	Test Spec	6 days	Mon 9/28/98	Marcus[50%]	
7	**Development Phase**	**54 days**	**Mon 10/5/98**		
8	Detailed-Design	20 days	Mon 10/12/98	Rod	
9	Coding	15 days	Mon 10/26/98	Marcus	
10	Testing	20 days	Mon 10/26/98	Marcus, Gilberto[	
11	Integration in Concord	5 days	Mon 12/7/98	Marcus	
12	Release Code	0 days	Fri 12/18/98	12/18	

Figure 2.9 *High-Level Software Development Schedule Skeleton.*

Since you have effort estimates for each component to be developed, and the FRS and CRS identify when and in which release to develop the component, laying out the project development schedule is relatively straightforward. You'll likely use a project-scheduling tool such as Microsoft Project to help draw your schedules, produce reports, and check for inconsistencies. I suggest that you resist applying some of the more advanced features of the tool (e.g., load leveling) and keep your schedules at a high level of detail. Like the architecture, the project schedule is a communications vehicle, and thus it must be simple enough to be understood by everyone on the team. Also, it's better for the engineers to plan the details of their work within their personal schedules rather than for you to schedule everything for them.

The project schedule incorporates the subtasks for each component and their integration dependencies. In my experience, you can consider the resulting project schedule "high-confidence," in that the actual release date should be within 15% to 20% of the time estimated. Most project managers can handle a 15% to 20% deviation by tracking weekly progress on the project and making up missed milestones with evening or weekend efforts, if necessary.

TIP: Make your schedules highly visible so that everyone knows them.

I once worked on a project where all the development schedules were kept on the walls of a conference room we called the project war room. A hard-working project administrator updated the schedules weekly with colored dots to indicate which tasks were completed and which tasks were falling behind schedule. This worked very effectively, since red dots next to your task indicated that you were struggling with meeting the schedule and someone either from management or another team member would soon inquire how you could be helped to get your task back on schedule. I've also seen beautiful schedules put on a wall that no one updated or paid any attention to. Visible, updated schedules, although they may not be put on a wall, are more likely to be used, discussed, and monitored.

2.2.6   Software Development Plan

The software development plan (SDP) is a short document that includes the schedules, engineering release definitions, staffing requirements, subcontractor utilization, project organization, cost estimates, development tools and procedures, task assignments, risks, and hardware platform for the project. It references the organization's software development process, high-level design document (HLDD), feature release specification (FRS), and component release specification (CRS). The SDP summarizes when, how, and with whom the software product will be developed. An example outline for the SDP is given in Figure 2.10. But in order to keep the SDP short, feel free to move some information into other documents or appendices (e.g., software developer's handbook, risk analysis, release plan).

The SDP contains a description of the organizational structure for the project and a description of the roles and responsibilities of the team members. Often, the names of the development groups or teams are taken from the component names found on the module view architecture layer diagram (Figure 2.4). Components are usually grouped into subsystems. Responsibility for developing the subsystems rests with the team leaders. On my projects, I've sometimes used

```
1.0  Introduction                              5.0  Technical Process
     1.1 Project Overview                           5.1 Methods, Tools, and Techniques
     1.2 Project Deliverables                       5.2 Software Documentation
                                                    5.3 Project Support Functions
2.0  References
     2.1 Specifications                        6.0  Risk Management
     2.2 Standards
                                              7.0  Work Elements, Schedule, and Budget
3.0  Project Organization                          7.1 Work Packages
     3.1 Process Model                             7.2 Dependencies
     3.2 Organizational Structure                  7.3 Resource Requirements
     3.3 Organizational Boundaries and Interfaces  7.4 Budget and Resource Allocation
     3.4 Project Responsibilities                  7.5 High-Level Software Development
                                                       Schedule
4.0  Managerial Process
     4.1 Management Objectives and Priorities
     4.2 Assumptions, Dependencies, and Constraints
     4.3 Monitoring and Controlling Mechanisms
     4.4 Staffing Plan, Training
     4.5 Subcontractor Management
```

Figure 2.10   *Software Development Plan Outline.*

nicknames to describe team leader roles (e.g., Joe is the "GUI guy"). The subsystem teams consist of a number of software engineers who have responsibility for developing one or more components. The SDP represents a commitment by the project team to develop the software product within the schedule and staffing requirements described.

I have found that a description of the overall project goals is useful and should be stated within the software development plan. An example statement of project goals is "Quality will have higher priority than schedule, which will have higher priority than functionality." Such a statement of project goals will help the project manager make the trade-offs that inevitably must be decided right before a release. It will give some guidance in answering last-minute questions, such as "Should I slip schedule to put in a few more features?"

TIP: Do enough planning and project foresight so that you don't negatively impact the private lives of the development team members.

A project manager has an obligation to put enough time and effort into the next incremental release development plan so that people's private lives are not unduly impacted. This means not scheduling critical development tasks for people when they have planned vacation time. It also means not setting milestones so they fall after a holiday, e.g., the Monday after Thanksgiving. Don't overcommit key individuals' time. They likely will enjoy a challenging task assignment but will not appreciate being overworked or exploited.

2.2.7   Personal Schedules

Once the SDP is completed, including the project schedule, you should give it to all the development project team members. Using the project schedule, software development process, and task assignments, each team member develops a personal schedule. This schedule is detailed enough that you can monitor the weekly status of development activities for each person on the project team. The inputs from the personal schedules are used to provide more detail to the project schedule. At this point, there is usually good ownership of the project schedule among the team members, since their detailed activities are consistent with the tasks identified in the project schedule. It is then that you freeze the project schedule as a baseline schedule against which to monitor progress. I recommend that the project manager review personal schedules weekly and update the project schedule every two weeks or monthly, depending on the size and complexity of the project. I also suggest that you baseline the schedules at the end of each incremental release. If the releases are frequent enough (e.g., every 4–8 weeks), schedules are planned in detail and then tracked for only a couple months at a time.

2.3   Benefits

At the end of the ACSPP activities, each team member has a personal schedule with weekly milestones for the components that he is responsible for developing. In addition, there is an overall project schedule, monitored by the project manager, that identifies how the components are allocated to the incremental releases. The development project organization and schedule should be consistent with the high-level architecture design. The development team members have developed the schedules, and thus their ownership of these schedules should be relatively high. Business management, marketing, service, and sales can refer to the SDP to see when functionality becomes available within the various incremental releases.

The architecture layer diagram is a very valuable tool for the development team. Such a picture of all the major software components and their relationships gives the team a much better understanding of what has to be developed in order to implement the product. The layer diagram is helpful for deciding if components from other products could be reused to implement the new product. It is also helpful for planning and visualizing the integration steps and internal releases. It can define a "vertical slice" of the architecture for implementation for each integration step, with the first slice functioning as a prototype and learning vehicle for the architecture.

The architecture layer diagram helps define the components that are estimated for the bottom-up estimation process. Using both top-down and bottom-up approaches to estimation and comparing the results help increase the confidence for implementing the project schedule. As a result, the development team members have more ownership of the resulting project schedule than if only a top-down estimate using lines of code was done.

The high-level design serves as an education and training tool for increasing the overall team knowledge of the plans for developing the product. Many software architects underestimate the time and effort necessary for communicating and reviewing the high-level design with all the team members. However, once a good understanding of the high-level design is reached, the team members have a much better picture of what is necessary to implement the software product. The four-hour paper design and the estimates given become the basis for the project work packages. The sequence of component implementation is followed in accordance with the FRS and CRS. The software development plan provides enough information for team members to develop their own personal schedule.

Using both top-down and bottom-up approaches to estimation helps increase team members' confidence in and ownership of the resulting project schedule. Many software engineers do not believe the estimates that result from estimation modeling tools such as Cocomo. Often, this disbelief is masked by endless discussions and debates about the precise definition of line of code and how to count them. For many projects, the project schedule belongs to the project manager and not the development team. The developers should not be forced to believe the outputs of an estimation model. The project manager can make better use of the estimation model outputs as a framework for the schedule skeleton and as a means to educate management about all the activities required to develop the product. Bottom-up estimates that are based on the architecture and estimated by the team members are more likely to be accepted and followed. The project manager and architect can then better spend their time in monitoring progress and solving the inevitable unplanned problems that come up during product development. The end result is that the project manager and architect act as coaches to the development team rather than as taskmasters forcing a development schedule onto the team.

2.4   Experience

My colleagues and I have experience in applying this estimation process over the past five years, and we have been teaching it to other development teams. Our first experience was with a system already under development. Initially we created this approach to give engineers more objective data to help justify their scheduling decisions during discussions with their management. Another motivation was to foster team communication and buy-in for the high-level design and personal schedules. I calibrated the estimated effort against the existing actual project effort. There were 60 large-grain components to estimate, and the resulting calculations showed 45 staff-years of work left. This stimulated a major design change in the system, since management was not willing to make the required staffing investment.

We refined the approach during our second experience with a project that was carried through to completion. The system was made up of 130 components. Using the estimation process, we determined that there were 174 **KLOC (thousands of lines of code)** to be developed involving 17 staff-years. We planned the schedule for one year, which slipped about a month, or 8%. The product was successfully developed and has been a market leader since its introduction.

Other projects have used the estimation process. The architect of one of them reported that following the process has been "a great success." One benefit he reported was during a meeting with the customer. During discussions of what-if scenarios concerning schedule dates, the appropriate required staffing could easily be calculated from the bottom-up effort estimates. The architect could commit to the customer's milestones if the customer was willing to commit to the development funding for the required staffing scenario.

For another project, recently completed, we were working with a multinational development team. The high-level design and the estimation process have been very useful for estimating the effort, dividing the work, and building buy-in and a common project culture for a team geographically distributed across three different countries. This project has estimated 16 staff-years of effort for 140 KLOC over a 15-month development schedule. We defined six incremental releases with an average interval of 8 weeks. All planned release dates were met. The biggest complication in developing the schedules was to coordinate holiday and vacation times for development team members across the three countries. For example, development progress came to almost a complete stop at the end of 1999, when all countries were celebrating the new millennium. This pushed back an intermediate release milestone, which reduced the amount of time available for the development of the next release, which was needed for a trade show.

2.5 Rules of Thumb

From the projects in which we have used ACSPP, we have generated some rules of thumb (Table 2.3) concerning how long estimation-related tasks

Table 2.3 *Rules of Thumb for How Long Estimation-Related Tasks Should Take.*

High-level design duration: up to 3 months

Design team size: up to 6 architects

Number of components to be estimated: up to 150

"Paper design" time per component: up to 4 hours

Bottom-up estimate duration: up to 3 weeks

Time between engineering releases: up to 8 weeks

Schedule deviation: up to 20%

Overall project effort application
    Design: 40%
    Coding: 20%
    Testing: 40%

Milestone tracking: every week

Schedule update and risk assessment: every month or before each new engineering release

should take. Clearly, these values will depend on the size and complexity of the specific project. The guidelines are from our collective experience and are thus derived from anecdotal evidence rather than experiments.

Our experience with these rules of thumb has been applied to medium-sized projects for industrial and medical products within Siemens. These are typically projects with around 20 development team members (more than a couple of developers but less than a couple hundred). Applying the rules of thumb to these medium-sized projects, we estimate that the high-level design phase represents roughly 5% of the total development cost. This estimate assumes that the work of four to five people for a period of 3 months working on the high-level architecture design will have a big influence on a development team of 20 people who will be working for a year or more developing the product. Keep in mind that the development team of 20 people will also be doing design work for each component of the architecture, which we call detailed design. Thus, the effort applied to design-related activities will likely amount to 40% of the overall project effort, as indicated in Table 2.3. But the first 5% of effort invested in the software architecture will impact the development most significantly.

> **TIP: Stop high-level design when you've run out of time.**
>
> We are often asked what the boundary is between high-level design and detailed design. The architect's answer is that high-level design is complete when it is detailed enough such that a module can be given to another developer for detailed design. For the practical project manager these boundaries are fuzzier and should be milestone driven. Thus, I suggest that it is good practice to limit the amount of time allocated to high-level design roughly according to the rules of thumb given in Table 2.3. An architecture design is never fully complete, but identifying a date when it must be completed and reviewed will help guide the design team. Actions identified during the architecture design review will be used to update the high-level design document, but the development team will complete many other design-related tasks during the detailed design tasks.

2.6   Summary

This chapter provided some guidelines about how to estimate and plan the development project once the architecture exists. This activity heavily involves the software architect, working closely with the project manager. The result is not just a schedule. Hopefully, the estimation process will also produce an architecture that is understood and accepted by all the development team members. Once everyone understands how the components one must develop fit within the overall software architecture, the development of the components is made much easier and more predictable.

Global Analysis

I first applied global analysis on the DPS2000 project and immediately began to see its value. Although global analysis had been used primarily for developing design strategies, I also started to see its use for identifying project strategies. For the DPS2000 project, we were missing some key skills within the organization to be able to develop the product using the desired technologies. The analysis of influencing factors pushed us in the direction of doing development at multiple sites in different countries in order to find the skills we desired. The factor tables and issue cards we generated were useful artifacts of global analysis that I referred to at least once a month for the first six months of the project.

O<small>NE</small> of the few known certainties when embarking on designing a new software system architecture is that the design and its implementation will likely evolve over time as market requirements, technologies, hardware, and business factors change. Some of these influencing factors affect the entire system, and some directly contradict other factors. In order to avoid major potential rework, these factors must be addressed from the beginning of high-level design.

In this chapter you will learn how to use the technique of **global analysis (GA)** to develop issues and strategies for your project. The issues identified from global analysis as well as the risks resulting from architecture evaluation will provide inputs to your project risk analysis, determining the project goals, release planning, and the software development plan (SDP).

3.1 What Is Global Analysis?

Global analysis analyzes the organizational, technological, and product factors that globally influence the architecture design of a system. Applying global analysis during architecture design is described in Chapter 3 of Hofmeister, Nord, and Soni [2000]. Global analysis, an integral part of architecture design, is applied in the beginning of the design steps for each view of the architecture. The result of global analysis is a set of global strategies that you can use to guide the architecture design and improve its changeability with respect to the factors identified. Since the project manager will address some of these strategies during project planning, I focus here on using the results of global analysis for project management.

Using global analysis for architecture design [Hofmeister, Nord, and Soni 2000]:

The strategies resulting from global analysis will affect both the architecture design and your project planning. "Global analysis starts before the conceptual, module, execution, and code architecture views are defined, and it continues throughout the architecture design. There is a tension between factors that constrain the design and factors that make it more flexible. These factors have to be balanced so that the system is able to be implemented and adapted to future needs. During global analysis, you uncover the most influential of these factors, then develop strategies for designing the architecture so that it accommodates these factors and reflects global and future concerns. You should record the results of the analysis process as a part of the architecture so that individual developers can use these results while making decisions to address specific design problems. Without strategies that reflect global and future concerns, developers may choose a local solution that does not support anticipated changes. As the architecture design proceeds, the architect should monitor the efficacy and relevance of these strategies, and make changes when necessary."

Figure 3.1 illustrates the approach for doing global analysis. It analyzes three categories of *influencing factors* (organizational, technological, product)

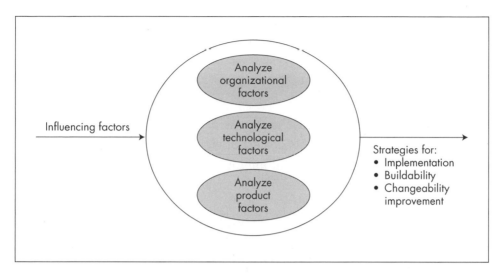

Figure 3.1 *Global Analysis Approach.*

with respect to their flexibility, changeability, and impact on the design or project. Analysis of the influencing factors gives rise to *issues* that are project problems you must solve in order to successfully implement the product. Issues are what often cause loss of sleep for dedicated project managers, since they often identify project risks that must be mitigated for project success. You propose *solutions* to address each issue and *strategies* to follow in both the design and the software development planning to keep the factors from influencing the project negatively.

In my experience, successful software architects and project managers prepare for the changes likely to occur as the product is developed, sold, and maintained. I'm always surprised at how much longer successful software products remain in the marketplace than originally planned. I regularly purchase gasoline at a service station that every day uses an embedded software product I worked on 16 years ago. The service attendants even seem to prefer it over newer products. Within global analysis, architects and project managers address potential changes by:

- Noting the flexibility of influencing factors and how likely they are to change
- Characterizing factor impact and how factors interact

- Using this information to prioritize and evaluate cost-effective strategies that enable the design to accommodate change
- Adjusting the project plan to accommodate the most likely changes
- Planning for change by analyzing project risks and developing mitigation approaches

Successful software products change as new features are added and existing ones evolve. Every few years, the software system will likely be ported to new software and hardware platforms. The product is configured within new environments. Its performance requirements will likely become more stringent over time. If the product is to remain successful in the market, it will inevitably need to change over time.

3.2   Global Analysis Activities

Figure 3.2 lists the steps involved in global analysis that should be tailored to fit your development process. The chief architect leading the high-level design team usually initiates global analysis. The project manager works with the team to produce the project-related strategies. Other key product stakeholders may provide inputs or become involved with global analysis (e.g., product management, marketing). Hofmeister, Nord, and Soni [2000] recommend two instruments to aid in following the steps of GA and for documenting the results: the *factor table* (Tables 3.1 and 3.2) and the *issue card* (Tables 3.3 and 3.4).

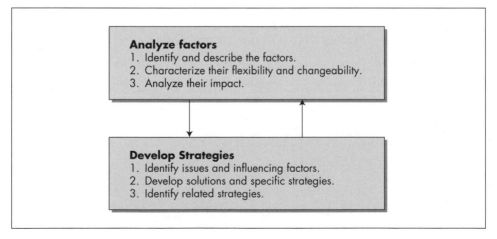

Figure 3.2 *Global Analysis Activities.*

Table 3.1 *Generic Factor Table: Organizational Factors.*

Organizational Factors	Flexibility and Changeabilty	Impact
O1: *<Factor category>*		
O1.1: *<Factor category>*		
<Description of factor>	*<What aspects of the factor are flexible or changeable?>*	*<Components affected by the factor or changes to it>*
O1.2: *<Factor category>*		
<Description of factor>	*<What aspects of the factor are flexible or changeable?>*	*<Components affected by the factor or changes to it>*
O2: *<Factor category>*		
O2.1: *<Factor category>*		
<Description of factor>	*<What aspects of the factor are flexible or changeable?>*	*<Components affected by the factor or changes to it>*
O2.2: *<Factor category>*		
<Description of factor>	*<What aspects of the factor are flexible or changeable?>*	*<Components affected by the factor or changes to it>*

Global analysis starts with identifying and describing the factors that could influence the design of the architecture and your project planning. In the factor table (Table 3.1) you list the factors in the leftmost column. The factors you analyze could have a significant global influence on your project; e.g., factors that could change during development, those that are difficult to satisfy, and those with which you may have little experience. In the middle column of the factor table, you indicate how each factor could change in the future and describe what may be flexible or negotiable about the factor. Can you control the factor, or is it more likely to be a constraint as you implement the project? Try to look into the future and assess what might change either during the development or after the product is released to the field. For example, Microsoft changes its operating systems roughly every two years. If your product has an expected lifetime of ten years, you may need five operating system upgrades. The rightmost column of the factor table documents the impact each factor might have on your project. Don't feel constrained to fit everything neatly within all the boxes. The factor table is a tool to guide your thinking about the major factors that can influence your project. It also helps provide documentation concerning the project decisions you may make and some of the potential risks associated with your project.

Table 3.2 gives an example segment from a factor table for the IS2000 project (described in Chapter 15). You give each factor a code for tracking purposes. Factor O1.1, new management, covers the changes due to the project

Table 3.2 *Factor Table for IS2000.*

Organizational Factors	Flexibility and Changeabilty	Impact
O1: Management		
O1.1: New management		
Project management is new to the IS2000 project.	The new management will likely change the project goals.	With new goals, the requirements and architecture design will likely change.
O2: Staff		
O2.1: Low morale		
The low morale of the team members is causing high turnover of the software staff.	The team makeup will change as people leave and are replaced.	The architecture design will need to be understood by the remaining and replacement team members. The high-level design document should be complete and easy to read.
O4: Development schedule		
O4.1: Time to market		
The required time to market is 2 years.	There's no flexibility to this time, since it's required by business needs.	This short development time will have a big impact on all design choices and project planning.

manager's newness to the project and to his inevitable rethinking of many of the decisions his predecessor made. These changes will likely affect both the product requirements and the architecture design. Factor O2.1 is the low morale of the current team. Some team members with low morale will likely find different jobs and leave the company. This means that you will need to document the software architecture design well so that new team members can read and understand it quickly. Factor O4.1, time to market, identifies that the maximum time available to develop the new product is two years. This is derived from a business analysis concerning how long the company can survive selling their existing products. Thus, this time is not negotiable, and this constraint will impact many design and project decisions.

Once you have analyzed the factors, the next steps of global analysis are to start developing the design and project strategies (Figure 3.2). The outputs of these activities are issue cards (Table 3.3). For the IS2000 project, a big problem is the very aggressive schedule for developing the new product. The factor table codes this as Pr1, and lists the influencing factors that are affecting this problem (Table 3.4). In the table I propose a possible solution to this problem of the aggressive schedule and then identify some applicable strategies (S1.1, S1.2, S1.3). Some people are more comfortable first defining strategies and then synthesizing solutions from the strategies. Again, I suggest using issue cards to analyze and document your strategies. But you should feel free to adapt them to your personal and organizational working styles. Since this is the first issue card developed for the IS2000, there is no need for step 3 of Figure 3.2 (identify related strategies), since there are no related strategies at this time.

Upon completing global analysis, you will need to consider what you have to do to realize these strategies. The strategies identified in the issue cards will have implications for both the architecture design and the project planning. For the IS2000 example, Table 3.5 summarizes the actions that will need to be planned for and initiated by the chief architect and the project manager. For example, if buying COTS is a strategy identified via global analysis, the chief architect will have to be concerned with fitting the COTS components into the software architecture. The project manager may have to worry about paying license fees for the COTS components or exploring other approaches to acquiring the components for the product. As an extreme example, the project manager may even get involved in purchasing the company that provides a key COTS component.

Table 3.3 *Generic Issue Card.*

<Name of the Architectural Design Issue>
<Description of the issue>
Influencing factors: <Influencing factors that affect this design issue, and how they influence it>
Solution: <Discussion of a general solution to the design issues, followed by a list of the associated strategies>
Strategy: <Name of Strategy> <Explanation of the strategy>   *Strategy: <Name of Strategy>* <Explanation of the strategy>
Related Strategies: <References to related strategies and a discussion of how they are related to this design issue>

3.2.1   Organizational Influencing Factors

Some organizational factors, such as schedule and budget, apply only to the product currently being designed. Other organizational factors, such as organizational attitudes, culture, development site location(s), and software development process, can impact every product developed by an organization. Some organizational factors can be controlled, but in many organizations they are fixed (e.g., software engineering head counts or fiscal year budgets), and thus the architecture design must accommodate them. In many cases, organizational factors

Table 3.4 *Issue Card for IS2000.*

Pr1: Aggressive Schedule
Given the estimated effort and available resources, it may not be possible to develop the software within 2 years.
Influencing factors: - O1.1: New management coming up to speed and changing goals will likely slow down the development. - O2.1: Low morale will likely cause staff to leave, thus further reducing the size of the development team. - O4.1: The 2-year time to market is derived from the business situation. The company may not survive if no new products can be developed.
Solution: Redesigning and reimplementing all the software will take longer than 2 years. Three possible strategies are to reuse software, buy **commercial off-the-shelf (COTS)** components, and use incremental development and feature releases.
Strategy: S1.1: Reuse S1.1: Reuse some in-house domain-specific components from existing products. *Strategy: S1.2: Buy COTS* S1.2: Buy commercially available software wherever possible, rather than build. *Strategy: S1.3: Incremental development* S1.3: Develop and release features incrementally so that lower-priority product features can be added later.

are what a project manager must accept and live with. Organizational factors such as the organization structure, development process, people, and environment are often not easily changed or will change only after a long period of time.

An example organizational influencing factor for the DPS2000 project (see Chapter 16) was the short supply of technical skills necessary to implement the application packages, since prior products had been Unix-based with local user interfaces, and marketing required new products to be Windows-based with

Table 3.5 *Implications of the Strategies.*

Strategy	Design	Project
S1.1: Reuse	See how existing product components can fit into the architecture.	Make existing product designers available to the new product design team.
S1.2: Buy COTS	Fit COTS components into the architecture.	License fees, mergers, acquisitions?
S1.3: Incremental development	Map features to components.	Build and release planning. Negotiate feature content and release sequence with marketing.

Web-based user interfaces. The resulting strategy to address this influence was to bootstrap and exploit expertise located at multiple development sites and to invest in training courses early in the development.

Another organizational factor was the company management's desire to get the product to the market as quickly as possible. Since the market was rapidly changing, they viewed it as critical to quickly get some limited features of the product to potential users so that their feedback could be solicited. Our strategy to address this factor was to develop the product incrementally so that scheduled release dates were met even if some features were missing from the release.

The factor tables (Tables 3.1 and 3.2) use the letter *O* to designate organizational factors. Some categories of organizational factors include: O1—management, O2—staff skills, interests, strengths, weaknesses, O3—process and development environment, O4—development schedule, and O5—development budget. You don't need to fit your influencing factors into these precise categories. Feel free to add other categories or even an "other" category as a catchall. There are thousands of factors, but you can't deal with them all. Pick the ones you think are most important, and concentrate on analyzing those. I suggest that you deal with the top 50 or so influencing factors for your analysis. It's often easier to look at existing lists of factors and see if they apply to your project rather than creating a list from scratch. This is why I provide some examples to help you get started on your analysis.

3.2.2   Technological Influencing Factors

Technological factors limit design choices to the hardware, software, architecture technology, and standards that are currently available. But technology changes over time and products must adapt, so the architecture should be designed with flexibility in mind. Technological factors and the decisions made concerning platform choices are a big issue today, due to rapid technological change and competing vendors' approaches.

An example of a technological influencing factor in the DPS2000 project was the necessity for a distributed object broker to meet the scalability and availability requirements within a distributed hardware configuration. To address this factor we elected to use Microsoft COM throughout the system development.

The letter *T* to designates technological factors. Categories of technological factors include: T1—general-purpose hardware; T2—domain-specific hardware; T3—software technology; T4—architecture technology; and T5-standards.

3.2.3   Product Influencing Factors

Product factors include features of a product as well as qualities like performance, dependability, security, and cost. These factors may be different in future versions of the product, so you should design the architecture to support the anticipated changes. Hopefully, many product factors that affect the functionality of the future product are described in some type of requirements specification, often initially generated by a marketing or systems engineering group. Many of the projects I have experienced often do not adequately specify the requirements up front, leaving that for later.

An example of a product influencing factor was, in order to support a product line architecture, the need for the DPS2000 **graphical user interface (GUI)** to be able to accommodate many different types of users for different applications. To address this factor, we implemented a Web-based GUI so that additional flexibility could be achieved as new applications are added and location independence could be achieved for the various user populations.

The letter *P* indicates product factors. Categories of product factors include: P1—functionality; P2—user interface; P3—performance; P4—dependability; P5—failure detection, reporting, recovery; P6—service; P7—product cost; and P8—maintainability.

3.3 Using Global Analysis for Project Planning

A project manager cannot deal with all of the thousands of factors that influence the design of a software system. Thus, it is critical to pick the ones that will have the greatest impact. Global analysis helps organize your evaluation of the factors and generate strategies to implement during the project. It often helps to look at lists of factors and the strategies that were used on prior projects. Some project strategies, such as incremental development, appear frequently enough to consider it a best practice and recommend it for most projects.

Experienced project managers should see if the strategies developed for prior projects would apply to their new projects. Having strategies to deal with adverse issues helps project managers get a good night's sleep and enhances their confidence. Furthermore, it's always good when all team members are concerned about the same issues as you. So I recommend developing a short list of key strategies for the project (e.g., top five or six) that all team members can easily remember. I will show later how you can use these *project strategy conclusions* during project planning.

Global analysis issues and strategies influence both the design and project planning activities. Figure 3.3 illustrates how global analysis fits into a typical development process during the high-level design and project planning phase of a project. In the figure, product, organizational, and technological influencing factors are illustrated as the inputs to global analysis, while issues and strategies and project strategy conclusions are the outputs. Product factors will tend to come from the set of requirements and their analysis, while organizational and technological factors will tend to come more from the environment in which you work.

The development process illustrated implies a set of sequential steps. In fact, the steps are highly iterative. During the project planning phase of most projects, there will be much feedback and iteration among the tasks, which is not shown in the figure. The global analysis issues, strategies, and mainly the project strategy conclusions are refined at each step of Figure 3.3, with the goal of addressing them in the software development plan.

As described earlier, global analysis is actually a part of the architecture high-level design task. I will focus here on how the outputs of global analysis

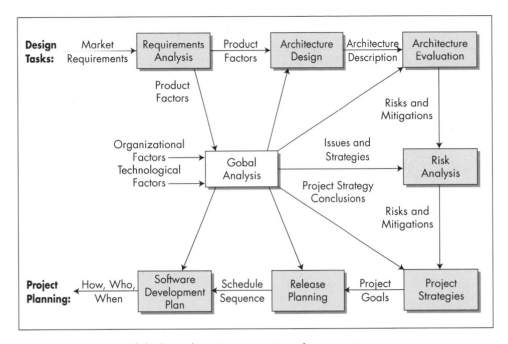

Figure 3.3 *How Global Analysis Fits into a Development Process.*

are used by the project manager for project planning. As shown in Figure 3.3 and just mentioned, product influencing factors tend to come from requirements analysis. Organizational and technological factors often come from external sources, such as your company management or development tools offered by outside vendors.

3.3.1 Project Strategy Conclusions

As a project manager, you can utilize the issues and strategies that result from global analysis as inputs to your software development plan. Your plan should address all the major risks you wish to pay attention to as the product is developed. Defining project strategy conclusions is a good way to set your project priorities and goals and to keep a short list of strategies that the entire development team is aware of. All the team members hopefully remember this short list. The strategies should become guiding principles for all the development team members. These project strategies help define the project goals and risks that must be mitigated for success.

Some example project strategy conclusions that were developed for the IS2000 project are as follows.

- Develop the IS2000 incrementally to be able to release some basic features within the desired development period to start a revenue stream.
- Make meeting the schedule the highest project priority. Trade off functionality to meet release dates, if necessary.
- Reuse components from the existing product, and buy rather than build to reduce the amount of new development necessary.

Design strategies determine the priorities and constraints of the architecture and help identify potential risks associated with the implementation of the software system. As a result of the DPS2000 global analysis, we identified 24 design strategies we believed could address the influencing factors. From these 24 design strategies, we derived six major project strategy conclusions as guiding principles for the DPS2000 architecture design and resulting development.

3.3.2   Architecture Evaluation

It's usually useful to explain your architecture design to a group of expert outsiders and attempt to defend your design decisions and strategies as a response to their questions. I've had good experience using the **Architecture Tradeoff Analysis Method (ATAM)**[1], which was developed at the **Software Engineering Institute (SEI)** of **Carnegie Mellon University (CMU)** in Pittsburgh [Kazman et al. 1999]. ATAM evaluates an architecture with respect to meeting nonfunctional requirements, such as scalability, security, and performance. These nonfunctional requirements or quality attributes are often the factors you have identified within the factor tables generated during global analysis.

---

1. ATAM is a service mark of Carnegie Mellon University.

The design and project strategies developed during global analysis are good inputs for the ATAM review team. As questions arise concerning different architecture styles, you can discuss these strategies and "validate" them during the review. During an ATAM review, you develop *scenarios* to analyze the architecture with respect to its intended use (use case scenarios), how it may change (growth scenarios), and the impact of unanticipated stresses (exploratory scenarios). The output of an ATAM review is a set of potential risks associated with realizing the architecture and some suggestions concerning possible strategies for mitigating the risks. Thus, the risks that result from ATAM should be compared with the issue cards developed during global analysis.

ATAM is *not* a design review. Your development process will probably have some other review meeting(s) aimed at finding potential defects in the architecture, where you will focus more on the functional requirements and exploring whether the architecture can support the features needed to serve the market. In this type of review, the product influencing factors you identified during global analysis will likely be scrutinized more than during an ATAM review, where the emphasis is on nonfunctional requirements. If the meeting is a **critical design review (CDR)**, there will also probably be some type of decision made, i.e., to continue the product development using the described architecture or go back and modify the design.

Regardless of the type of architecture evaluation methods your organization uses, you will hopefully become aware of some risks pointed out by the reviewers that you might not initially have been concerned about. You may also learn that you have focused on unimportant risks or those less likely to impact the project. These risks (and any corresponding mitigations), along with the issues and strategies from the global analysis, will be useful when you perform further risk analysis.

3.3.3 Risk Analysis

A risk, or "the possibility of suffering loss," consists of a condition, the resulting consequence, and the surrounding context. In terms of software project planning, risks are the things that project managers lose sleep over. They are the technical, political, business, resource, or other occurrences that can jeopardize either the product development, its market success, or meeting the goals of the project (e.g., schedule, budget, quality). Often, the way an organization perceives a project manager will be linked to the perception of the project, so project risks can also be potentially career threatening to the project manager. The skill of the project manager to plan for, anticipate, and react to risks will directly impact the project success. Risk mitigations are the tasks you will add to the software development plan to reduce the likelihood that a risk will have adverse consequences on the project.

Some organizations have formal risk analysis procedures for documenting and quantifying the risks. In some cases, the risk analysis is considered a deliverable artifact of the development process. Risk analysis may attempt to quantify the probability that a specific risk will occur. My approach has been to use a more middleweight process in which the risk analysis task collects and considers the issues from global analysis and an ATAM review or other type of architecture evaluation. The issue cards document the issues from global analysis. The ATAM outbrief documents the risks from ATAM, usually as presentation charts created by the review team. I also suggest that you document the risks and any planned mitigation actions (or strategies) in the software development plan and update them when the plan is revised prior to the next development increment.

An example of a project risk from the IS2000 project is the very aggressive development schedule. A possible project risk mitigation would be to closely track the schedule every week. If the schedule starts to slip, take aggressive actions to get back on track, such as reallocating staff or delaying vacations.

When you are developing a new product to replace an existing product, you will likely have a separate migration plan that addresses both the technical and market risks and their associated mitigations. For example, you may need to keep it a secret that you are developing a new product. If all your customers know about your project, they may decide to wait for the new product rather than investing in the current one. This could negatively impact current sales. Your marketing staff will need to determine many of these migration strategies, but those strategies will inevitably affect your project planning. For example, keeping your project secret from customers may lose you the opportunity to get feedback on any release increments until after the product is announced or introduced to the market. The product announcement may be tied to a trade show, which in turn may require an incremental release prior to the show so that the product can be demonstrated to potential customers.

> **TIP: Monitor your sleep patterns when doing risk analysis.**
>
> Good project managers often worry about what can go wrong with a project, especially important risks and risks without good mitigations. These issues will frequently bother the project manager while he is trying to sleep. Thus, I define risks as what the project manager loses sleep over. Keep a notepad on your nightstand so that you can write down and remember any new risks or risk mitigations you may have thought of during the night.

3.3.4   Developing Project Strategies

Analysis of the issues, risks, and mitigations will help you develop your project strategies and goals. Every project should have an explicit statement about the relative priorities among meeting schedule, quality, and functionality goals. It is not likely, in my experience, that every project will meet all goals. But if the priorities are clear, there's a good chance of meeting most of them. An example IS2000 project goal statement is that meeting *schedule* will have higher priority than *quality,* which will have higher priority than *functionality*. Such a project goal statement is very handy around release time, when decisions must be made by the project manager and others as to whether to release the software to users. When applying the IS2000 project goal statement a project manager may say something like, "I must meet the release schedule, and my software quality seems OK, but I'm missing a couple of minor features. Let's ship it anyway."

A project goal statement like the one used for the IS2000 is unusual, since for most projects, quality is thought to be the primary goal. For many projects, this equates to the practice of not shipping a product with any known serious defects. This is normally a good strategy; shipping *with* known defects is only asking for complaints from the first users. However, this may not always be the case, e.g., for situations where a small number of users are evaluating special features that will change based on their feedback.

Having a short statement of the project goals also helps the team members remember what they are trying to achieve. These goals should be documented in the software development plan and modified, if necessary, during the course of the development.

TIP: Bet half your money on red and the other half on black.

I have observed that project managers must aggressively attempt to mitigate all known risks as they plan and implement their projects. This is because plenty of additional unknown risks will pop up unexpectedly as development progresses. While planning one of our projects, we couldn't reach agreement on the style of the GUI. Product management wanted a rigorous style that left little room for user misunderstandings, while the design team wanted a more free-wheeling style with greater flexibility. Our mitigation approach was to implement both styles. This represented some additional development cost, although we reused a lot of code. But this reduced the risk of missing the market opportunity, and we learned that different classes of users indeed preferred different GUI styles, based on how they used the system.

3.3.5   Global Analysis and Release Planning

The previous chapter discussed release planning and the benefits of incremental development. Having a set of risks, mitigations, and project goals is a big help in developing the build plan. Since the build plan will be turned into a schedule of the development tasks, paying attention to the sequence of development tasks can further mitigate risks. For example, if a large perceived risk is associated with developing a particular interface between two subsystems, perhaps the design of this interface could occur early in the build plan. Then you could allocate additional time if difficulties surface during the design. Another useful approach is to develop a prototype made up of perceived risky components in the system. The prototype could explore a technical approach within an early build, and then you could refine it or redo it in later increments. In this case, the build plan will have multiple checks for a risky component or function within multiple increments, thus planning for the expected rework in order to get that component to work correctly. This is illustrated in Figure 3.4, where the feature *Create a Schedule* is reimplemented in each engineering release.

	FR1	FR2	FR3	R1	R2+
Schedule Maker					
Search Consumer Tree for Scheduled Events	✓			✓	
Create a Schedule	✓	✓	✓	✓	
Handle Report	✓			✓	
Handle Acquisition		✓		✓	
Optimize Acquisitions					✓
Handle Set Parameter Scheduled Events		✓		✓	
Display and Manual Update of Schedules			✓	✓	

Figure 3.4 *Build Plan with High-Risk Feature.*

Chapter 2 suggested that the first incremental release implement a vertical slice through the module layer diagram. This is, in fact, a risk mitigation strategy in which some of the design concepts that may have looked good on paper may not implement easily. Furthermore, the initial vertical slice is a mitigation against a project risk, since it can help train the development team and give them confidence and experience with the architecture.

Some prioritization of the features has already been done during global analysis. These surfaced as product factors, and they may have been constrained by the organizational factors. During release planning, you can map the features to engineering releases describing the plan for the sequence of implementing the features. In theory, if the release planning is done well, the project manager can walk around during the development and watch the features become visible as they are implemented per the plan. In practice, the features are never implemented exactly as planned, but their visibility gives the project manager (and his management) a way to compare the feature content planned and realized at the end of each incremental release. Furthermore, since I suggest that the incremental releases go through system testing, you also gain some measure (at least qualitative on the part of the testers) of the quality of the software as it is being developed.

Global analysis also helps show the traceability between features and design decisions. You may need to review these decisions as the release planning is done. Again, I'm describing a sequential process so that it can be more easily taught, but in practice the steps involved with planning a project based on the architecture being developed will be highly iterative. Typically, you will do your global analysis during high-level design. You will also do the initial incremental release planning during high-level design. But you will do the detailed planning for each successive release at the end of the development of the release currently being worked on, as described in the SDP. For each incremental release, you will likely create new versions of the release, build, and software development plans.

3.3.6 Global Analysis and the Software Development Plan

As we discussed in Chapter 2, the software development plan is a primary artifact used for planning development, and it is updated by the project manager prior to each development increment. The issues, strategies, and project strategy conclusions from global analysis and the list of risks and possible mitigations are documented in the SDP. The SDP is a living document, since engineering releases are not very far apart, and every team member reviews it before the project manager commits the team to develop the next increment by the release date specified. When reviewing the SDP, the team members will often immediately skip to the schedule to see what their proposed task assignment is for the next increment. But regular updating of the document allows the project manager to modify, augment, or better communicate the important risks and strategies.

3.4 Using Global Analysis for Test Planning

The primary artifact used for system test planning, in my experience, is the system requirements specification. The system testing team is mainly interested in testing for the successful implementation of functional requirements. Thus, their interest will focus mainly on the product influencing factors. I have found, however, that the system test people find the issue cards from GA useful in providing valuable inputs to test planning. If there are key issues that are related to the functionality of the product, these are the areas where system testing should put their emphasis, e.g., by developing more thorough test procedures for the parts perceived as riskier. In the DPS2000 project, an area identified as an issue during GA (as well as the ATAM review) was the interface between the acquisition and data-processing subsystems. The system test team was aware of this concern, and they made special efforts to test the functions supported across this interface earlier and more thoroughly than if the issue had not been well documented and understood.

3.5 Benefits

Global analysis helps provide a link between the design of the architecture and the planning of the development project. There is a close correlation between the issues that arise from global analysis and the risks the project manager must track to achieve project success.

CHAPTER 4

Managing Expectations

On the IS2000 project we had a management team that was very nervous about the potential development cost associated with the software architecture we were designing. We had to manage the architecture team's communications with management, since several times a day we would be asked how much effort the implementation would require. To provide an estimate that was too high would depress our management. To provide an estimate that was too low would set expectations too high and put extra pressure on the development team. The "correct" answer was a realistic estimate, which we could communicate only after we had had some time to analyze the requirements and propose a software architecture that we were confident could be implemented.

Project managers should be given adequate time to plan their projects. Unplanned software projects are less likely to be completed successfully. Project planning activities should occur during the time frame I informally describe as the high-level design phase of the project. Chapter 2 gave some rules of thumb for the time duration and effort for the high-level design phase. I suggest a time limit of approximately three months for this phase; this has been adequate for the medium sized projects I have worked on.

This chapter suggests ways to manage expectations while a project is being planned. If your management's expectations are set correctly during the early phases of the project, it is more likely that a realistic plan will be developed and supported throughout the development.

4.1   When to Plan and When to Commit

Project planning looks at different scenarios for implementing the product, before it is developed. Schedules, budgets, staffing assignments, risks, and strategies have to be considered, as discussed in Chapters 2 and 3.

For architecture-centered software project planning, I suggest that project planning occurs in parallel with the design of the architecture. For the projects I have worked on, and using the rules of thumb presented in Chapter 2, I estimate that roughly 5% of the development cost or 20% of the development time will be spent on the high-level design phase. This is a reasonable business investment to help ensure that your project is well planned.

There will often be great pressure on the project manager to give an early estimate of schedule and development cost. Budgets are often planned within fiscal year boundaries, which may not correlate well with the project plan. You must make trade-offs among cost, quality, schedule, and staffing. To get products to the market quicker, there is a tendency to add more people to the project team. However, bigger teams tend to be less efficient than smaller teams, so the project manager must consider many trade-offs and scenarios for selecting the "best" plan to meet the business needs. From an unscientific observation of projects within Siemens, a one-year development schedule seems to be most common. This may be driven by fiscal-year planning cycles, but more likely by the marketing desire to get new products, or enhancements to current products, to customers every year. The annual cycle of trade shows and sales forecasts also holds many development schedules to one year. Obviously, very large projects will require more than one year of development time, since there is often an upper limit to the size of the development team and engineering investment that the organization can support.

These time pressures will often push a project manager to propose a larger development team than he is comfortable leading, or he may have to shorten the planning time or restrict development budgets and head count. What often happens in this situation is that management "wishes" for a development plan that is consistent with their planned investment scenario. This is why the project manager must take some time to explore various scenarios about how to implement the product.

The top-down schedule estimate in Chapter 2 is a good way to establish rough parameters for the development plan and thus to establish some initial expectations. If you generate the top-down schedule using an estimation tool based on conservative parameters, it likely will result in a schedule, development cost, and staff loading profile larger than from the bottom-up estimate. Thus, initial expectations can be set, at least to the rough scope of the project. Furthermore, most estimation tools will provide a range of estimates with varying staff size, schedule, and development cost possibilities. What the top-down schedule can do is help make some of management's wishful thinking more realistic. The estimation tools enable one to remember all the diverse costs associated with developing a product. The plans generated by the tools remind management that the resulting software development plan also has to consider who will test the product, write the user's manual, support the configuration management system, and so on.

The high-level design phase is when the project manager explores with the architecture design team members various scenarios concerning the trade-offs among team size, schedule, and development cost. The project manager can also explore with his management the business and organizational constraints concerning the development, but he should only identify scenarios, not discuss specific plans, while the architecture is being designed.

Once the initial architecture design is developed, documented, and reviewed, the project manager can start thinking about committing to a development plan. This he can do by following the architecture-centered software project planning (ACSPP) steps discussed in Chapter 2. The software development plan (SDP) documents the proposed and committed plans. The commitment to a development plan by the project manager and the development team is a significant event that should be reviewed and discussed upward, downward, and sideways within the organization. The commitment is critical to getting the best effort from the development team as well as the management support to complete the development. Thus, the commitment is multidimensional: Management agrees to support the project with resources, the project manager agrees to manage according to the plan, and the development team agrees to produce the product. Of course, real life can upset even the best plans. Unexpected events such as the departure of key staff members, unforeseen business situations, changed market conditions, and natural disasters can hit any project. Uncontrollable events do not lessen the commitment of the team. But it is harder to excuse projects that fall badly behind schedule due to poor or nonexistent planning.

In today's Web-time-based business climate, project managers usually do not get a second chance to commit to a schedule and then miss it. This is similar to the professional sports team manager who is let go at the end of the season if his team fails to have a winning record. However, the best managers often have made planning or project controlling mistakes in earlier projects but learned from their mistakes. It is unfortunate if they don't get a second chance, at least with their current organizations.

TIP: Tip: Never include a project's release date in its title.

Management once had the bright idea to include the release date in the project name; that is, the P90 product will be released to customers during calendar year 1990. The problem was that the project name was selected before the project was planned. Years 1990, 1991, and 1992 came and went before the product was released to market. This was of concern to the project manager and his management, and he eventually left the company. We offer this tip, despite Microsoft's tendency to include years in the names of their operating systems. In Siemens, most software projects created in the 1990s included "2000" in their title, e.g., IS2000, DPS2000.

4.2 Managing Upward

While the project manager is considering the various scenarios and strategies for developing the product and the architecture team is working on the architecture design, management is usually waiting impatiently to learn what the development will cost and when the product will be available. In particular, the marketing and sales managers will be attempting to get any product functionality and availability information they can share with their key customers. In this environment, it is important to restrict communicating any details of the various project development scenarios the team is considering. The project manager has to serve as the gatekeeper and be willing to say, "Sorry, I can't speculate on the development schedule, since we haven't completed the architecture design yet." Perhaps for this reason, architecture teams that are physically isolated from their management often seem to have better plans and be better supported by their management.

If the project manager has a boss who can be trusted, it is desirable to review and discuss the most likely scenarios before they are proposed or committed to. You will also need to discuss certain business conditions, such as when the development estimates indicate a team that is bigger than the current organization or the delivery dates are much further out than when the product is needed.

Even with a trusted boss, there may be business pressures that push the project manager to attempt to commit to an impossible plan. In this situation, the project manager must play what I call *hardball*,[1] meaning the project manager must be willing to walk away from a project plan that either he or his team believes cannot be achieved. There will be doubts and risks associated with any plan, but in my experience the project manager and chief architect must truly believe they can substantially achieve the development plan, i.e., meet the schedule, cost, and functionality goals of the project within a small deviation of the plan. If either the project manager or chief architect lacks this basic confidence, the project is doomed to fail. All the team members must also share this faith to some extent, but they will often follow the lead of the project manager and the chief architect.

A project manager must be willing to leave a project if he believes he is being pressured to commit to a plan he doesn't think can be achieved. It's much better to recognize this before beginning the development than to begin the development and then fail to meet the project goals. Unfortunately, many project managers do not feel they have the option to refuse to accept an unrealistic plan. But this is the power the project manager must exert. If one's management is not accepting of the proposed plan, it's better to leave the project at the conclusion of the high-level design phase and propose that some other project manager be assigned to handle the development. If management realizes that the project manager is willing to put his job on the line and take his commitments seriously, often they will accept the proposed plan.

Certain business situations may demand an impossible development, such as when the business has only one product or needs a new product to shore up declining market share. In these cases, the project manager can accept the challenge of doing something impossible. But his management better recognize it as such, and all should discuss the consequences of failure prior to the

---

1. The term *hardball* comes from baseball, where it refers to the most serious variety of the sport, when a small hard ball is used. This is different from *whiffleball,* where a plastic ball is used, and *softball,* where a large ball is used that is usually also quite hard.

development. Sometimes such arrangements are implemented using time-based bonuses. For example, management can state that they know this is a very difficult job and if it is done with good intentions until a specified date, the project manager will receive a financial bonus (or severance package) regardless of the outcome. Such impossible developments or time-based bonus situations should also include the development team members as well as the project manager.

As discussed later, the setting of project goals and measuring the success of the project in achieving the goals will vary depending on company and country culture. Most American project managers that I've worked with strive to reach the project goals within a small deviation. They often view goals that are not challenging as too easy or boring. Most American managers seem to want to challenge themselves and their teams with aggressive goals, and they want a feeling of satisfaction when they try to meet the goals. This may not be the case with non-American managers. For example, some of the European managers I have worked with only measure success when the goals are precisely met. Thus, American project managers with non-American bosses should discuss how project success or failure is determined when the goals are set and met.

Unfortunately, new project managers can best learn these approaches to managing upward over time across multiple projects. Thus, experience is a primary factor as to whether project managers set expectations correctly and meet their project commitments consistently. It is the responsibility of the neophyte project manager's boss, usually a director of **research and development (R&D)**, to determine whether the proposed software development plan is realistic. If the proposed project plan calls for hiring six new software engineers in two months and the R&D manager knows that the job market is tight in their area, he must relax or modify the proposed software development plan. In this way, hopefully the neophyte project manager will avoid some of the planning mistakes that an experienced R&D manager has insights into.

4.3 Managing Sideways

The project manager must also set expectations with the management of the peer level organizations that he will deal with during the development. This includes functions like system testing, software quality assurance, user documentation, product management, marketing, and sales. In many cases the software project manager needs the cooperation and support of these sideways functions, but he has no direct control or power over their activities. Thus, the project manager must compensate for this lack of power by communicating clearly what the project requirements are and what expectations he has.

Probably the most visible and frequent communications a project manager will have with a support function is system testing. With an incremental development approach, the project manager will plan system testing of the incremental releases every 4–8 weeks. In most organizations, system testing is a function that is independent from development, with a separate reporting relationship. Often, system testing will test multiple products. Thus, the project manager has to state very clearly his expectations of system testing and the dates he expects the incremental releases to be tested. Ideally, the development plan should identify a release milestone date that can be met with a high degree of certainty. After some level of functional testing, the system testers report defects to the development team, which fixes the defects in time for the next incremental release. For example, for the DPS2000 project, system testing a new incremental release required two weeks, but our minimum interval between releases was four weeks, so we had sufficient time to fix most defects by the next release. This obviously requires a high degree of coordination and communication between the project manager and the test team, as well as much joint planning concerning the content of each incremental release, so that the test team can develop test procedures in advance of the incremental release date. The incremental build plan is a good artifact to facilitate such communication. But again, via close coordination you will need to handle the discrepancies between the actual implementation and the plan. The development team will likely do their own testing prior to more formal system testing, but many a good test manager has saved a project by uncovering major defects before any customers discover them.

Another highly visible and important interface for the software project manager is the person(s) responsible for determining the functional content of the product. This usually is someone with a product management, marketing, or system engineering function. If we call this person the product manager, the software project manager will need to establish a close working relationship with him, one that includes frequent discussion and refinement of the features that are planned and implemented for the product. In the planning phase this includes definition of features and identification of their relative importance. As development commences, it includes discussions concerning the sequence of feature implementation and initial feedback on their implementation, for example, the look and feel of a feature to a potential user of the system. As testing progresses, the discussions center on the quality and functionality of implemented features, such as which should be dropped, modified, or deferred. Prior to a release, discussions will focus on which defects must be fixed, the relative priorities of fixes, and which fixes can be deferred. Thus, in addition to the relationship with the chief architect (discussed later), the project manager's relationship with the product manager is critical to the success of the product development.

4.4   Information Flow

For the project manager to manage expectations concerning his project, both upward and sideways, during the high-level design phase, it is important to manage the information flow. The project manager and chief architect should be the only sources of information during this phase. This is because the project manager and the architecture team are exploring many design and project scenarios. Incomplete or preliminary information can negatively impact or confuse the expectations the project manager is trying to establish. For this reason, the architecture team should be left alone for a predetermined period of time. Sometimes this can be best achieved if the architecture team is isolated from their management or offsite.

Figure 4.1 summarizes the suggested information flow. Project information should come from the project manager. Technical information should come from the chief architect. I prefer a reporting relationship in which the chief architect works for the project manager. But they work very closely as a team and jointly make all the important decisions concerning the proposed software development plan. The architecture team members will also likely report to the project manager, but their daily direction and interaction concerning the architecture design will come from the chief architect.

> **TIP: As a project manager, always try to do what you say.**
>
> Consistency between words and actions is very important for a successful project manager. Management wants project managers to meet their

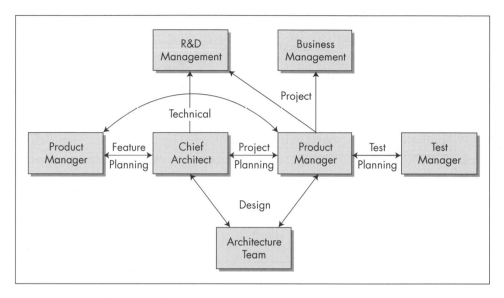

Figure 4.1 *Information Flow.*

commitments and not to introduce many unexpected changes to the development plan. Once I saw the impact of not doing what I had said while working on a project in a small German town. I needed to visit this town to attend meetings over the course of a few days. I would arrive in town by train and then take a taxi to the local office, on the other side of town. Noticing only one taxi at the station and realizing the remoteness of the meeting site, I arranged for the taxi driver to pick me up after the meeting. At the conclusion of the meeting, one of my colleagues offered to drive me back to the city, and I forgot about my arrangement with the taxi driver. The next morning when I got off the train, the same taxi driver was there and he was furious with me. He said, "I waited to pick you up yesterday and you didn't show; today you can walk to your meeting because I refuse to drive you."

4.5 Using the Software Development Plan

The software development plan (SDP) is the primary artifact for communicating proposed project plans. I envision versions of the SDP being released in pairs. The first version is a proposed plan. After negotiation with upward and sideward partners and review downward with the architecture team, you update the SDP to a second version, which becomes the plan for the next incremental engineering release of the project. At this point, the SDP represents a committed plan that the project manager implements, and each development and support team member agrees to achieve the plan in accordance with the baseline schedule. Thus, the initial version of the SDP functions as a proposal to management and as a proposed plan to everyone involved with the development. I typically allocate a few days so everyone can provide feedback on the proposed plan to the project manager. Anyone who fails to respond with feedback loses the chance to modify the proposed plan. It is best to keep the SDP to a limited number of pages to encourage everyone to review it, although the proposed schedule with the assigned staff members is carefully scrutinized.

The SDP commits the project team to the development activities for the next incremental release. Since I recommend that incremental releases be approximately 4–8 weeks apart, the plan does not cover a very long time period. To address the planning for future increments, I generate a release plan document that identifies the highly visible features associated with each increment and the target release dates (to system testing). In my experience, developing two versions of the SDP for each incremental release—the first being a proposal and the second being a committed plan for the development increment—is an effective way to manage the expectations of the product stakeholders.

As discussed earlier, if the project manager receives pressure to modify the proposed plan to the point where he doesn't believe it is realistic, he will likely need to walk away from the project. Usually, this is not the situation, and positive discussions and solutions about reducing the schedule using experienced staff members, likely risks, and so on, can occur as part of the negotiations between the project manager and the various stakeholders.

TIP: Be ready to walk away if things don't "feel right."

One spring evening on the way to my nephew's graduation I was driving through some Philadelphia suburbs I hadn't been to in a long time. On the way, I realized that I would be driving past the research center where I had first worked after getting out of college. I alerted my wife and children to get ready to see where Daddy had worked for his first job. This particular company has merged and been acquired to the point where the original company name no longer exists. Expecting to see the rather attractive research campus facility I remembered, I was surprised to see instead some newer buildings and a sign identifying my former research center site was how a "managed community for adults." In retrospect, it was probably a good idea to leave this particular company, even though I had worked there for six years and had built up many good relationships with the staff.

4.6 Summary

The primary artifact for managing expectations is the first, or proposed, version of the SDP for each development increment. It is here that you identify the proposed schedule, feature content, and staffing assignments for everyone to comment on. I have found that 4- to 8-week increments are easier to plan than multiyear projects. The release plan identifies how the increments will eventually be developed to implement the usable product functionality. The build plan, generated prior to the SDP for each increment, identifies the relative development order for each feature for each software component.

Managing expectations during the high-level design phase is usually handled better by experienced project managers dealing with experienced R&D managers. Project management is a lot like playing pinball. If you do well at it, your reward is to get to play another game. This creates a problem for the neophyte project manager, who may never get a chance to do a second project if the first one doesn't go well. Like the professional baseball team manager who has a losing season, the unsuccessful project manager may not get a chance at planning another project. This is why the planning part of project management is so important. The proposed development plan has to be challenging enough to make everyone stretch themselves to meet it, but it cannot be unrealistic. This balance between challenge and avoiding risk makes project planning interesting.

Despite the best planning, projects seldom progress as anticipated. Later chapters will discuss how to handle some of these issues. But if the SDP is reviewed and accepted and the architecture is designed, documented, and understood, the project manager has a good chance to succeed at developing the product in accordance with the stated project goals. With success, the project manager will have opportunities to plan future projects. If things do not go well or if the project manager is coerced to implement a plan he doesn't support, the project manager is well advised to return to the more technical work he likely did before becoming a project manager.

PART three

Organizing

The Project Organization

When we were organizing the development team for the IS2000 project, we observed that we selected the names for the various project teams from the subsystem names identified in the architecture layer diagram. People who had worked on the high-level design of the various subsystems became the team leaders for their respective subsystems. The team size was set according to the bottom-up development estimates we had for each subsystem from ACSPP and whom we had available.

PROJECTS that are more than a few people in size will need to be organized so that the team members have specific roles and communication paths. Team members will vary in their skills. Some will be specialists, some generalists. Some will be experienced software developers, some will be novices.

The project manager must set up the project organization so it functions well in achieving its task—the development of the product. There is a convenient way to define the project organization in accordance with the software architecture of the product being developed. This chapter explores how to organize the development team in order to best meet the goals of the project.

5.1 Using Software Architecture to Define the Project Organization

The module architecture view, described in Chapter 4, not only gives the project manager the list of components that have to be estimated for development, but also provides insights into how to organize the development team. When using architecture-centered software project planning (ACSPP) it is desirable for the team member who will work on developing a component to also work on its paper design and bottom-up estimate. This helps build ownership and commitment into the estimate, and it helps factor in the experience levels of the individuals on the team. This is based on the assumption that if you have done a similar task before, it should be easier to do it again as compared to someone doing it for the first time.

The module view describes the way the software system is decomposed into subsystems and modules. We can use this view to map the project organization so that it reflects the architecture. This helps reinforce the architecture within the project, and it helps partition team members' roles with respect to what parts of the system they need to become experts in. A useful artifact of the architecture design activity is the architecture layer diagram that is generated while designing the module view. Figure 5.1 repeats the architecture layer diagram presented in Chapter 2 as Figure 2.4.

Figure 5.2 presents a possible development team organization created from the architecture layer diagram of Figure 5.1. In addition to the structural information contained in the architecture layer diagram, it uses the component estimates developed during the bottom-up estimation (Section 2.2.3). Since we have a bottom-up estimate for each component, we can size the teams on the project organization chart to be consistent with the relative amount of effort anticipated for each component. We assume that a team leader should direct

GUI		
Applications		
Application Services		
Probe Service	Image Processing	Database Services
Systems Services		
OS Layer		
Communication		
Hardware		

Figure 5.1 *Architecture Layer Diagram.*

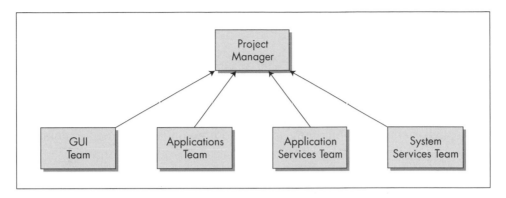

Figure 5.2 *Development Project Team Organization.*

no more than approximately seven software engineers. Keeping in mind these span-of-control restrictions, we can size the teams based on the anticipated work and break them down into smaller teams or combine them into larger teams, consistent with the layer diagram and the module partitioning of the architecture.

This example is simplistic, since we are attempting to clearly explain it. In real projects, a simple one-to-one correspondence between the architecture layer diagram and your proposed organization is unlikely. Furthermore, you will have to consider interpersonal issues, such as since Joe and Fred don't work well together, they shouldn't be on the same team; and that Fred as the head of the graphical user interface (GUI) team will upset Frank, who will probably quit and leave, and so on. But correlating the project organization with the software architecture is a good starting point. Furthermore, I encourage you to use this first proposal as a straw-man organization that can be communicated informally to the team members. Ideally, you want to avoid any major surprises when you announce the organization, like someone who used to work for me is now my team leader.

The project manager typically combines the results of the bottom-up estimation into a spreadsheet that summarizes the effort estimates and possibly groups them into subsystems. This spreadsheet can be helpful in setting up the sizes of the teams and partitioning the organization chart until the teams are within span-of-control restrictions. Figure 5.3 shows a bottom-up estimation summary spreadsheet from the IS2000 project. If this spreadsheet were used to size the GUI team in the organization chart of Figure 5.2 and the development schedule were approximately one year in duration, then the expected GUI team size would be three people. This is from Figure 5.3's estimate of 2.7 staff-years (4,960 hours) development effort. This three-person GUI team would have a leader and two more junior level software engineers. Be careful however, when converting estimated effort hours to staff-years. Figure 5.3 divides the number of hours by 1,828, which is the number of average work hours per year for an employee at our facility in Princeton, New Jersey. If the work is being done in different locations, the average applied work hours per year will vary. For example, in Germany the numbers of hours worked per year is substantially less, mainly because each employee receives six weeks of vacation per year.

When determining the sizes for the project teams, also be aware of the issues associated with part-time team member assignments within your orga-

IS2000 Bottom-Up Cost Estimation
Major work packages

	Confidence	Complexity	Code Size	Total Effort (hours)	Total Effort (staff-years)
Versioned Object	3	5	2000	720	0.3938731
Study Management	3.2	3.4	600	1280	0.7002188
Check In and Check Out	3.7	3.3	1800	1320	0.7221007
Templates	3	5	1000	2400	1.3129103
Schedule Maker	1	5	19500	2920	1.5973742
GUI	2.8	3.6	18300	4960	2.7133479
Communication System	3	4	500	640	0.3501094
Problem Interface	3	3	11500	1580	0.8643326
HW Diagnostics	4	3	400	250	0.1367615
Flat Panel Display	4	3	700	800	0.4376368
All Other functions			20000	3500	1.9146608
Totals			76300	20370	11.143326

Figure 5.3 *Bottom-Up Estimate Summary Spreadsheet.*

nization. For example, a staff member assigned to a specific project team may also have responsibility for maintaining an older product. Thus, he will not likely be able to work full time on your project during the course of a fiscal year. In this case, even though the effort estimates in the bottom-up summary spreadsheet represent the total hours required to implement the component, part-time staffing may require you to increase the project team sizes in order to meet the desired schedule.

5.2 Architecture Team Roles During Development

During the high-level design phase of the project, the development team is limited mainly to the architecture design team and the project manager. Per the rules of thumb in Section 2.5 for setting up the high-level design phase, I suggest that you limit the architecture design team to roughly five designers. Thus, the development team during this phase is limited to six people. Toward the end of the high-level design phase, assuming that a larger team will be necessary to develop the product, additional team members are brought in to participate in the bottom-up estimation. It is at this time that the project manager begins to form the project organization. Again, it is desirable for the team members that will likely work on designing and developing a specific component to prepare the estimate for that component. This brings additional accuracy and commitment to the schedule estimate, since it helps compensate for the various experience levels of team members.

One approach for setting up the project organization is to use the architecture design team members as leaders of the development teams within the project organization. The architecture team members will likely have a good understanding of the architecture, having jointly designed it with the other design team members. They can help the chief architect transfer the knowledge of the architecture design to the additional development team members within their team. Since the project organization will reflect the structure of the architecture, assigning design team members as team leaders helps reinforce the architecture, which allows everyone on the development team to see where their components fit into the product.

Using the example organization shown in Figure 5.2, we can assign team leaders as given in Figure 5.4. If Mike led our architecture design team, and

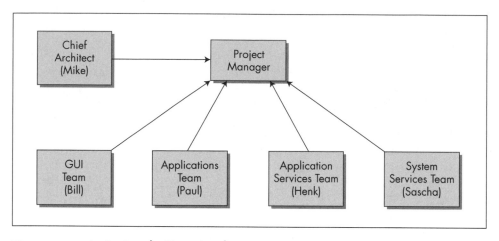

Figure 5.4 *Assigning the Team Leaders.*

the team members were Bill, Paul, Henk, and Sascha, then we could assign the team leaders as shown in Figure 5.4. In this example, Mike, as the chief architect, would not have responsibility for a specific team. But as the chief architect, he would make the key technical decisions for the project, mentor the team members, when necessary, and be the primary maintainer of the architecture. The role of the software architect is summarized in the box nearby. The role of the project manager and his relationship to the chief architect is described in Chapter 8.

Unfortunately, not all project team assignments will be as easy as our simple example. Good architects do not always make good team leaders. Some organizations share their architects so that after they finish designing one product they move onto a design team for another product. The size of the project or the sizes of the teams (as determined from the bottom-up estimates) may require additional levels of hierarchy or management support. But in my experience, having substantial continuity of staff members that worked on the architecture design also be involved in the development of the product is a good way to transfer the architecture to additional team members and to help ensure that it is followed during the development. This is also a good way for the project manager to easily propose an organization structure that is consistent with the design and best utilizes the design team members.

> **Role of the Software Architect [Hofmeister, Nord, and Soni 2000]:**
>
> The architect:
>
> - Creates a vision of the architecture to be implemented as a product
> - Is the key technical consultant for the project
> - Makes technical decisions
> - Coaches the team members
> - Coordinates the team members
> - Implements the product

I have been involved in considerable discussion over the years concerning how much code the chief architect should write for the product and how much leadership and mentoring must be given to the development team members. I believe that good architects generally also have good programming skills and that they should have the opportunity to contribute some of their code to the product. This will depend, of course, on the individual skills of the architect and the characteristics of the development team members. But what I try to avoid is putting the chief architect in the critical path of the schedule with respect to development tasks or leading large teams of developers. I want our chief architects to be available to all the team members when questions arise throughout the development. You'll know the project is going well, as far as the chief architect assignment, when development team members are continually raising technical issues for the chief architect to provide guidance on or resolve. If the technical issues are queuing up waiting for resolution, then perhaps the chief architect is spending too much time writing code or directing the work of team members.

I also prefer our project managers not to write code or function as chief architects or development team members. In my experience, for only very small projects (1–3 people) can the roles of the project manager, chief architect, and developer be combined in one person. Ideally, the chief architect is concerned with technical decisions and the project manager worries about everything else.

5.3   Project Functions That Support Development

Up to this point, I have discussed organizing the development team based on the architecture design (from the module architecture view) and using the architecture design team members as technical leaders for the development team. However, there will be other functions that must be put into place and covered as the product is developed. These functions are identified when developing the top-down schedule, and they include support functions such as quality assurance, system testing, user documentation, training, integration, configuration management, and software process improvement. The project manager must remember to account for these functions and to add their contribution to the project costs determined from the bottom-up estimates. The following sections provide some suggestions for organizing and dealing with these support functions.

5.3.1   Working Through a Matrix

In many organizations, the support functions associated with product development will be matrixed to the specific project development team, often because many of these functions will be used for multiple project teams that may be developing products in parallel. This is especially true for an organization that is attempting to design and implement a product line architecture. The matrix of these support functions represents a special challenge to the project manager. In most cases, the project manager will have minimal control or power over these matrixed functions. He will often be competing with other project managers to allocate enough time to his project while the matrixed resources are also working on other projects. These matrixed functions are often the ones that are understaffed and underfunded to begin with, and timesharing across multiple projects makes things worse. This is most obvious when two software products are released at approximately the same time and both of them end up waiting for test results, since the organization's development process calls for system-testing to validate releases before they can be given to users.

Most project managers, if given their preference, would have all support functions report directly into the project organization rather than be matrixed. The best way for the project manager to deal with the matrixed functions and their management is through good planning. If the system-test manager knows when the release is coming and what its likely functionality will be, he will more likely be ready to test it when it is released. Consistently meeting your release dates, providing good-quality code, and supplying clear release notes helps the test manager prepare for the release. Thus, the project manager must go out of his way to provide the support function managers with the plans for the development, estimations of the complexity and size of what needs to be supported, and likely events that could go wrong along the way. The project manager must inform all the support functions about the details of the software development plan that affect them. This is not a simple task for the project manager, and you will see in Chapter 6 that it is even more complicated when the support functions are at physically remote sites, e.g., when you are developing code in one country but it is system-tested in another country. But if the project is to succeed, the project manager must establish rapport and credibility with all the matrixed support functions.

5.3.2   Power

In a matrix organization, project managers may be viewed as more of a staff function, as compared to a line management function, where the engineers report directly. Even more general technical competence centers, like software engineering, may matrix their staff to your project. Thus, even though you are the project manager, you may have no one reporting directly to you.

Such an organizational arrangement could create problems for you with respect to how much power you are perceived to have and how you wield what power you do possess. From a simplistic point of view, the only real influence you have over the members of your development team is when you can affect their income or their future with the organization. Although most software engineers I've worked with are highly professional, the only tangible threat you can apply (either real or perceived) to get your team members to do a better job is to withhold approval of their next raise or to remove them from the organization if performance is unsatisfactory.

If you are dealt a weak hand with regard to the competence of the people assigned to your project team and you have no real or perceived power, you may have difficulty achieving the goals of your project. Thus, it is important to get yourself into project management situations where you have direct inputs into the next salary adjustments of team members, and you have some control over who is assigned to your project, at least in key leadership roles. This can be achieved through your relationship with line management, as long as it is well known throughout the organization that you can potentially reject or remove engineers from your project team and that you will be the primary source of performance information come salary review time.

Some project managers mistake their perceived power with the size of the development team they are managing. It is clear that smaller teams are more efficient, since there are fewer communication paths. Thus, to make your job easier and to increase the chances of meeting your project goals, it is desirable to reduce your team to its smallest possible size. Of course, if you take too long to develop the product, you may miss the market window. This is one of the key trade-offs, along with functionality and quality, that we will discuss further in Chapter 9. But having a large team made up of individuals you did not select and whose performance you have no power to influence is not likely to lead to a successful or rewarding project.

5.3.3 Constructive Testing and Quality Assurance

Ideally, software products would be designed and developed defect free so that they never need to be tested. But defects are introduced as the product is being developed. Sometimes, defects are introduced very early in the development process, as incorrect requirements. Thus, competent **quality assurance (QA)** and system-testing functions can often help the project manager to identify defects in the product before users discover them. At Siemens we often refer to the "four-eyes principle," by which it sometimes is easier for someone else to find a defect in a developer's work.

It is thus in the best interests of the project manager to fully collaborate with software testing and QA functions. The project manager and the managers of these support functions must back each other up and work toward common goals. After all, top management doesn't really want to hear about all the problems that have been found. They prefer to know when the product will be shipped and have some confidence that the users will not complain too much about newly discovered defects.

I have sometimes observed organizational behavior where the system-testing and development functions are antagonistic with each other. The developer's pride sometimes gets in the way: "How can he find something wrong with my code when he doesn't understand it?" The tester complains that the developer surely hasn't done quality work when defects are so easy to discover. Finger pointing is done by both sides, especially for defects that are difficult to reproduce.

The project manager and the test manager need to work together to set examples so that testing is constructive rather than destructive. Every defect that testing identifies is one less that the users will discover. Testers have an obligation to communicate the test results effectively to the developers, such as describing or showing how a particular defect is reproduced. Developers have a responsibility to review and address every defect so that every defect has some resolution, even if that it is to keep it in the product without being fixed.

I have seen a recent trend with effective software project managers where their role changes as the development progresses. One recommended practice for the project manager is to actively participate in the testing of the product. This could include conducting some of the testing as a member of the test team, but it also means carefully reviewing the test results and defect reports. In this way, the project manager can gather information for when the difficult decisions must be made, e.g., whether to release the product to users. No product is ever perfect. The project manager will need to feel (via data and intuition) whether a product has sufficient quality to expose it to the critical review of users who have paid for it.

Project managers also have to establish a good working relationship with the software quality assurance function. In some organizations, QA serves as the "quality police" to ensure that development processes are being properly followed. Again, QA is acting in the best interests of the project manager, although antagonistic relationships can develop where the QA person feels the project manager is hiding information or the project manager's pride is hurt if he believes that the QA person is persecuting his project. Again, good planning and the clear communication of project goals are necessary to ensure that everyone is working toward the goals. If the project goal is to develop quickly a low-quality prototype for some preliminary customer feedback, the QA function should be informed and they should adjust their procedures accordingly.

5.3.4 Dealing with Marketing

Dealing with marketing is often difficult for the project manager. A marketing manager, a product manager, or a lead sales person sometimes represents this function. Marketing deals with representing the voice of the user or customer for the product. Thus, marketing should describe the requirements so that the developers understand them and can provide technical solutions. However, for today's software products, the requirements are often fuzzy, and market conditions are subject to dramatic changes, such as those resulting from deregulation. Also, there's a tendency for marketing to ask for every conceivable feature without regard to the development cost. In theory, products that are feature rich are easier to sell. Products that are sold as part of a tender process often have required base features that must be satisfied for a vendor to be qualified to bid on the request for quotation. In such situations, having a particular feature is something that must be checked off if the product is to be considered for purchase.

Project managers must strive for precision when dealing with marketing. This will take much of the project manager's time. But it is important for the project manager to understand and document the relative priorities of certain features and to constantly remind marketing of the implementation costs. This results in many discussions, along the lines of "If you want that feature by that date, then we can't do these features instead." After a while, the project manager and marketing will reach a working relationship, one of constant negotiation and trade-off.

The project manager must also strike a balance between responsiveness and sticking to the plan when dealing with marketing. Every development plan will change as the product is developed, and new features and their priorities are shuffled to best meet market needs. However, too much change will frustrate the development team members, especially if they start work on features that are later changed. Thus, the project manager must be willing to say no and identify when a change request will create significant problems for the development team. This is often best discussed with some quantitative representation of the effort involved, i.e., the cost to change direction. You can usually obtain these feature efforts from the bottom-up estimation data. On the other hand, a project manager who sticks to the plan, even when there is strong evidence that users will not buy the product with its implemented functionality, is just delaying the eventual failure of the product. In such a give-and-take relationship, it helps considerably if marketing and the product manager fundamentally trust each other. This trust is often built up by spending time together, during working hours and sometimes after work.

5.3.5 Buildmeister

A key project role that I have found useful on our projects is what I call the *buildmeister*. The buildmeister is responsible for integrating the system as it is built up from its individual components. Within incremental development, where builds are being made frequently as the system functionality is continually increased, the buildmeister is the point person through whom all changes must be integrated and backed off when they don't work or negatively impact other parts of the system. The buildmeister is responsible for generating the system for each build. In most cases, builds will be done every day, incorporating the changes that individual developers have introduced into the source code checked into the configuration management repository. Organizationally, it is best if such a key role reports directly to the project manager. Of course, the buildmeister must work very closely with the chief architect, since he is integrating the code to implement the architecture and functionality envisioned during high-level design.

TIP: Use nicknames to help clarify development team member roles.

We were working on a project that used a three-tiered architecture: presentation layer, business object layer, and database layer. When we set up the project team organization, we identified three development teams led by three members of the architecture design team. The development teams corresponded to the three layers of the architecture, and we named the team leaders: *GUI guy*, *com kid*, and *schema boy*.

5.4   Responsibilities, Roles, Authority, and Ownership

The software development project team has several key roles and responsibilities. In addition to the chief architect and project manager, some of the important roles are summarized here.

- *Team leader:* Each team leader is responsible for assigning and monitoring tasks for developers working within a particular software subsystem, as defined in the module view of the architecture. The team leader is responsible for determining which bugs to fix and how to develop new features for the particular subsystem(s) or modules assigned to that team.

- *Developer:* A developer is responsible for designing subsystem components and developing code. He is responsible for performing component tests to ensure that the code is correct. A developer submits code, using the configuration management system, to be integrated into the product.

- *Buildmeister:* The buildmeister is responsible for building the system from source code and also for performing integration tests. He is responsible for integrating the changes submitted by the developers into the builds. The buildmeister is often also responsible for **configuration management (CM)** and determines the policy of how software changes are accepted from the developers. The buildmeister can accept or reject submitted changes from the developers and is ultimately responsible for creating builds for the entire product. He is responsible for ensuring that each build successfully passes the regression test suite. The buildmeister is also often responsible for performance testing.

- *System test manager:* The system test manager is responsible for the system acceptance or validation testing. Often, this is a GUI-level test. The system test manager uses the use cases and marketing requirements specification to develop the acceptance test suite. The system test manager is also responsible for ensuring that the software and documentation are consistent. The system test manager ensures that bugs are finally fixed and correctly integrated.

- *Marketing or product manager:* The marketing manager is responsible for defining the functionality of the product being developed. The marketing manager will often contribute to the marketing requirements specification and provide guidance on the definition of features. The marketing manager also specifies the nonfunctional requirements, such as performance, security, and availability. The marketing manager reviews defects as they are discovered during system testing, and helps set the priorities concerned with defect corrections.

5.5 Summary

This chapter has shown how the architecture can be used for setting up the organization of the product development team. The members of the architecture design team likely will move into roles of team leaders as the project team size is increased during the development. The chief architect and the project manager work together to provide technical and project leadership. There are also support functions required for any software product development that the project manager must deal with.

CHAPTER 6

Global Development

On the DPS2000 project, it was clear from the beginning that the product would be developed at two development sites in Germany and Switzerland. The teams at both sites were small, skills associated with new technologies were missing, domain knowledge was split between the two sites, and there was a natural partitioning of subsystem know-how that mapped to the software architecture. Since both sites spoke German and were within the same time zone, the risks associated with using two development sites were viewed as manageable. However, when the project development team was expanded to two additional sites in the United States, the project complexity and the number of risks grew larger, and a good architecture description that defined subsystem interfaces became critical to our success.

In today's world, business is becoming more global and software development projects are more often being done across collaborating development sites, often in different continents, countries, and time zones. This trend toward global software development creates special challenges for project managers. It's difficult enough to organize the work of a development team within a single facility. Miscommunications among team members and the project manager are more likely to occur during multisite development when people are used to working in their native languages in time zones that may limit overlap in working hours.

Often, global development projects are initiated primarily for reducing development costs. Software engineers in certain countries are paid less than in others, and utilizing cheaper labor, in theory, can reduce the cost associated with developing the software. These cost savings are often lost, since global development can introduce large inefficiencies during the development. On the other hand, products that are developed with diverse development teams from multiple countries often are better suited for the world market, since the developers often have special knowledge of technologies or local requirements. This chapter explores some of the issues associated with global development and provides some suggestions for the project manager to use the architecture and other methods to get the most contribution and output from the distributed project team.

6.1   Why Global Development?

There are many influencing factors that may push a project manager to consider global development. The decision to do global development should come from a global analysis, as described in Chapter 3, in which you systematically look at influencing factors and the resulting project strategies. The analysis can result in a global development project strategy, for example, when no single site has a full set of necessary development skills. In that case, a project strategy may emerge where global development is undertaken in order to assemble the required skills using team members from around the world to develop the product.

Multisite development may be globally distributed or may occur within a single time zone. This creates complexity for the project manager, since it is more difficult to track the status of the development when it's multisite. For products that are to be sold in global markets, global development often has positive benefits, since the developers have unique knowledge about local requirements.

6.1.1   Global Analysis

The global analysis done for the DPS2000 project resulted in a set of design strategies that we used to guide both the product line architecture design and implementation of the application packages. The organizational influencing factors very much pushed us toward a design strategy of using a global development team for the DPS2000 design and implementation. This was primarily because a critical mass of necessary technical, product, and domain skills were not present in any single location.

6.1.2 Organizational Influencing Factors

Organizational influencing factors most often are the ones that tend to push development projects toward global development or not. An example of an organizational influencing factor for the DPS2000 project was the short supply of technical skills necessary to implement the application packages, since prior products had been Unix-based with local user interfaces and marketing required new products to be Windows-based with Web-based user interfaces. The resulting strategy to address this influence was to bootstrap and exploit expertise located at multiple development sites, to invest in training courses early in the development, and to make use of consultants. Also, we developed a second level of design specification documentation at a level lower than the high-level design. This system design specification concentrated on describing the interfaces between major subsystems of the architecture so that it was easier to parcel out a subsystem development to a remote software engineering site.

Another organizational factor was that company management wanted to get the product to the market as quickly as possible. Since the market was rapidly changing, it was viewed as critical to quickly get some limited features of the product to potential users so their feedback could be solicited. Our strategy to address this factor was to develop the product incrementally so that scheduled release dates could be met even if some features were missing from the release. Thus, for the DPS2000, project schedule took priority over functionality. We developed a build plan for each engineering release, identifying the sequence for adding functionality. The project functionality and schedule were baselined after each engineering release. We found that a 6- to 8-week development cycle for each engineering release worked well for the development team to provide a reasonable set of features that could be tested and evaluated. With such a strong emphasis on speed to market, we needed to acquire development resources wherever we could find them, which resulted in distributing the development team to four locations in three countries.

6.1.3 Design Strategies

Design strategies determine the priorities and constraints of the architecture and help identify potential risks associated with the implementation of the software system. As a result of the DPS2000 global analysis, we identified 24 design strategies that we believed could address the influencing factors. From these 24 design strategies, we derived six major conclusions for use as guiding principles for the DPS2000 architecture design and resulting development. One of the major conclusions of the global analysis was to set up a global development team.

The lack of sufficient technical skills at a single location was an influencing factor that was addressed by setting up a global development at four sites within three countries. This put constraints on the design so that components could be more easily distributed for development at multiple locations, and the development environment and tooling were set up for multiple locations.

6.2 Architectures for Supporting Global Development

It's important to recognize that global development is being considered for use around the time the architecture is being designed. Certain architectures will be more suitable to global development than others, and it is important for the architecture design team to realize this. For example, architectures in which subsystems are loosely coupled lend themselves more to global development, since interfaces can be defined and each site can take responsibility for developing each subsystem and its interface to the other subsystem. For the DPS2000, we developed the acquisition subsystem and the data-processing subsystem in different countries and jointly defined a loosely coupled interface between them. Also, in this case the second level of design specification documentation or system design specification concentrated on describing these interfaces between major subsystems of the architecture, so it was easier to parcel out a subsystem development to a remote software engineering site.

Another approach to parceling out the development work for each site is to use the layers defined in the module view. For example, the presentation layer of a three-tiered architecture could be developed at a single site. In this way, that site can specialize in obtaining or training for the expertise needed to implement efficient and useful graphical user interfaces (GUIs).

6.3 Development Processes for Global Development

Global development requires changes to the development processes at each site. For example, configuration management must be distributed in some way if development team members in different sites need to access the same code.

6.3.1 Distributed Project Management

Distributed project management requires a team approach to managing the project in multiple locations with much communications and coordination. It is important for each team member to have some type of local management support with which to interact on a daily basis. The project will also have an overall leader located at a primary site. It's important for the project manager to work with the local support managers to discuss staffing assignments, compare development progress, and evaluate the performance of individuals working on the project. Thus, distributed project management will function as a team, with overlapping responsibilities concerning the support of the development team members at the various sites.

An example of how such distributed project management can work is the case where a developer is slipping behind schedule. The project manager likely first notices the slip during the weekly teleconferences (described later). The project manager may determine that the rate of progress is too slow, notice when unplanned absences occur, or indicate that unexpected problems are hindering progress. If the project manager is sitting remote from the developer who is slipping his personal schedule, it's difficult for the project manager to provide support to the remote developer. At this point, the project manager has to rely on the local manager for that site to provide such support. He could ask the local manager to spend time with the lagging developer to gather information, propose schedule catch-up actions, explore alternate staffing scenarios, and so on. Either the local manager works with the developer to reduce the schedule slip or he will discuss alternative solutions with the project manager. These alternatives could include actions like removing a feature from the incremental release, rearranging staffing assignments, and, in the worst case, slipping the overall development schedule.

In many cases, the local manager will be able to resolve the problem causing the personal schedule slip without affecting the overall schedule or discussing alternative solutions with the project manager. But what is most important is that the local manager and the project manager (assumed to be remotely located for our example) work as a team to resolve the issue. In some unfortunate cases, one of the development sites may be waiting for another of the development sites to slip schedule so that they are not the first site to slip. These problems must be resolved at the project level, and the local managers must be willing to put the good of the project ahead of individual sites' reputations. It is particularly important for all the developers to view the local managers and the project manager as a united team striving to do the best for the project.

In some cases, the project manager may also be the local manager for the site. This will depend on the size of the development team for that site and the organizational structure of the company. In Siemens, these project managers, often with the responsibility for the entire product line, are called *global development managers*. My observation concerning the success of such distributed project management is that it depends greatly on the skills and motivation of the local managers. The local managers will more likely recognize development problems with their staff, and they can provide the face-to-face support required to resolve emerging schedule slips. The local manager can also handle any communication problems associated with differences between the project and native (local) languages.

6.3.2 Project Tracking

Project tracking for the global development should be done weekly and conducted using teleconferences. It is very important for each team member to report his status every week. Projects slip their schedule a week at a time, and if a couple of weeks go by without adequate project tracking, the project will inevitably slip. There will be some time periods when a weekly teleconference will not occur. For example, a teleconference may not be scheduled when a majority of the team members are together at a site for review meetings or when important holidays occur and one or more sites are not expected to progress with the development since they are not working.

Table 6.1 presents the goals and schedule for a typical teleconference to track schedule progress. Each development team member should be able to communicate weekly status in accordance with their personal schedule and the

Table 6.1   *Development Status Teleconference Goals and Agenda.*

Purpose: To review weekly development status by individual per personal schedule and project schedule. To exchange problems of general interest to team members that require follow-up. To raise information that is of general interest to team members (e.g., upcoming meetings, ideas for developer's handbook).

Outcome vision: Team members are informed about overall development status.

Customer: Project management and all team members.

Success Criteria: Team members are better informed about project status and common development problems.

Timeline:

- Start and agenda review: 15.30
- Site A status: 15:35
- Site B status: 15.55
- Site C status: 16.15
- Wrap-up and feedback: 16.25
- Complete: 16.30

Agenda items:

- ER 1.0.1 development and release status

overall project schedule and release milestones. In some cases the project manager will review the personal schedule of a development team member, and in some cases he will not. This will depend on the experience, competence, and motivation of the team member. In my experience, it is better to let the development team members develop and track their own personal schedules and to let the project manager track the progress of the overall project schedule.

There are obvious logistical constraints associated with such a teleconference meeting. If the team is larger than approximately 15–20 members, and the meeting is limited to one hour, you should plan a hierarchy of meetings to avoid long meetings with many people. This hierarchy can be task, location, or organizationally based.

The project manager can also use the teleconference to distribute information of general interest to team members, e.g., key milestones, results of management reviews, promising new customers. Team members often prefer to keep informed about the overall status of the project, even when this doesn't directly affect their specific work task. One hour per week seems to be a reasonable time investment for individuals to report their status, identify common problems, and keep up to date with the overall progress of the project. Even for projects not geographically distributed, you can arrange project team meetings on a weekly basis where every team member has the opportunity to report his progress. Note items requiring significant discussion for resolution as follow-up actions, rather than bogging down the teleconference. The project manager should follow up important information in writing, usually in the form of e-mail messages for the distributed team.

6.3.3   Configuration Management

One of the key success factors for any software development project consisting of a team of more than a couple of people is a good configuration management system tool. This is especially true for projects that are distributed. As code is developed and modified by multiple developers in multiple sites, it is important to keep it under control. Nothing is more frustrating to the development team than code that is lost, modified unexpectedly, no longer builds, or the like. Such situations decrease productivity throughout the entire team. In severe cases, development progress may appear to be moving backward rather than forward.

Many books and papers have been written on configuration management (CM), and I will not repeat this information here [see White 2000]. Commercial CM tools are available, and there is much heated discussion among developers and vendors about which are the "best" tools. Suffice it to say that for the global development project, CM tools and the associated data communications support across the development sites represent a critical success factor. Avoid shortcuts with respect to training CM support staff, for this is not an area to attempt to reduce development environment investment costs. Mistakes in CM adversely affect the productivity of the entire team. Poor planning and execution in this area will hurt development team productivity and overall morale when developers lack the tools to do their jobs.

For the DPS2000, project we set up the main source code repository in Switzerland, and all the other development sites had networked access to this repository. We also used subsystem owners who mainly worked on code within the subsystems that they had responsibility for. The buildmeister had a major role in accepting or rejecting newly checked-in code, as the system was built frequently during development.

6.3.4 Meetings

Meetings will make or break a project. Meeting time is often misused, especially when meeting goals are not clear, meetings do not start on time or finish late, and the wrong people attend. Rules for conducting project meetings are the first goals and actions for defining the project culture within the global team. Is it important to start on time? Should the size of the meeting be limited? Such questions must be answered at the beginning of the project.

In general, you should plan a meeting prior to scheduling it. This means determining the meeting's goals, participants, and time schedule in advance. For the DPS2000 project, part of our team training was to learn a standard way to plan and conduct meetings. You can see this in Table 6.1, through which the facilitator, prior to each meeting, determines and communicates the purpose, outcome, customer, success criteria, and timeline. We attempted to apply these guidelines whether the meeting was at a single site or at multiple sites as a teleconference.

You should also plan a wrap-up and feedback section for the end of each meeting. During our team training, we were taught a meeting feedback process that uses "smiley faces." The meeting facilitator draws a happy face, a neutral face, and a sad face on the whiteboard (Figure 6.1). Each meeting participant then makes a voting mark to express his summary level of satisfaction with the meeting. Participants vote on the perceived outcome/result of the meeting; i.e., did the meeting achieve its purpose? They also vote on the process used for the meeting; i.e., how effective was the meeting while achieving its results? The feedback helps in the planning of future meetings.

```
        :=)            :=|            :=(

        | | | |          | |             |
```

Figure 6.1 *Meeting Feedback Process.*

6.3.5 Distributed Code Inspections

Code inspections are a software development practice that has been observed over time to improve product quality [Austin and Paulish 1993]. Fagan inspections for reviewing code originated from Michael Fagan's work at IBM, as cited in the 1976 paper "Design and Code Inspections to Reduce Errors in Program Development" in the *IBM Systems Journal*. *Fagan inspections*, taught only by Fagan himself or licensees, are a formal process with rules of thumb concerning how many lines of code to inspect per time, the roles of the participants, return-on-investment for time spent, and so on. Formal inspections are used widely throughout Siemens companies, adapted from Fagan's process and usually taught by in-house trainers within the various companies. *Code walkthroughs* are a more informal process, often referring to any situation where someone visually reviews or reads code to find defects. Walkthroughs can be done by a group, where the reviewers have defined roles, or by an individual reviewing her own or others' code.

Within the distance constraints of multisite projects it's impractical to do formal inspections across multiple locations. We have experimented with a semiformal inspection process that uses telephone communications to inspect code that may need additional review either for meeting quality goals or to educate team members on important coding styles or functions.

6.3.5.1 Why Do Code Inspections?

A number of published studies have identified the cost benefits of doing code inspections. Within the overall software development process, the cost of correcting a defect increases for later process steps as compared to earlier steps. For example, the cost to correct a defect discovered during testing is much greater than that for a defect found during design reviews. Furthermore, certain types of bugs (or defects) are difficult to detect through testing and often are easier to spot via visual inspection of the code. Thus, it makes good economic sense to include code inspections as a development practice.

6.3.5.2 Goals of a Code Inspection

The primary purpose of a code inspection is to discover software defects. A secondary purpose is to spread the knowledge of certain software components to additional team members (training). Thus, the selection criteria for code to be reviewed should include modules that need to exhibit high quality or performance or modules that other team members are likely to reuse.

A code inspection should not address solutions for fixing the defects that have been identified. Corrections are the responsibility of the author of the code and the team member responsible for that subsystem. If solution-related discussions or brainstorming are desired, it should be the responsibility of the author to set up follow-up meetings with other team members or the chief architect prior to correcting the code. Thus, discussions on how to fix defects are beyond the scope of a code inspection.

The goal of a code inspection is to attack the code for the purpose of uncovering defects. This implies that the attack not focus on the author of the code (egoless programming). Any attempts to link the quality of the code to the quality of the coder can be destructive to the quality improvement goals and team morale of projects. Thus, reviewers are strongly encouraged to focus on finding defects.

6.3.5.3   Process Steps for Distributed Code Inspections

Any development project team member can propose code to be inspected that they view as being important for quality, reuse, or training reasons. If it is the code author who proposes that the code be reviewed, he will approach another team member to function as the moderator of the code inspection. If someone proposes code to be reviewed that has been written by someone else, the proposer will likely function as the moderator. More information concerning the roles of the team members involved in a code inspection is given in Section 6.3.5.4.

The moderator will schedule a code inspection meeting (at least a few days in advance) and identify up to three reviewers. A code inspection can also be done with only the author and moderator. Thus, the inspection team can range in size from two to five members.

The moderator will notify the other inspection team members of the repository location of the code to be reviewed and the time of the inspection. Prior to the notification, the author will ensure that the code to be inspected compiles correctly. In addition, I strongly recommend that all code to be inspected be run through an automated convention checker by the author prior to the notification so that the inspection will focus on discovering defects rather than on identifying coding standard violations.

Advance notice is necessary so that each reviewer and the moderator can individually review the code prior to the inspection meeting. Thus, each reviewer and moderator should come to the inspection meeting prepared with lists of potential defects discovered from their personal review.

The inspection meeting is scheduled for a specific date and time, and it is organized as a conference call when the team members are spread over multiple locations. If the review team members are all located at a single location, the moderator will schedule a conference room for the inspection.

At the beginning of the inspection, the author will give an overview of the requirements, features, structure, and design approach for the code to be reviewed. The author will then "walk through" the code in sequence, and the moderator and reviewer(s) will attempt to identify potential defects based on their prior personal review and their current understanding of the code. The moderator will keep a list of defects to be e-mailed to the author shortly after the completion of the inspection. The moderator will assign an impact priority to each defect (high, medium, low). The author will be responsible for making corrections to the code. The moderator will facilitate the inspection, taking care to avoid discussions about potential fixes for defects, alternate implementations, and style/convention issues.

The distributed code inspection process steps are as follows.

1. A team member proposes code to be inspected.
2. Author, moderator, and up to three reviewers are identified.
3. The author ensures a clean compile and convention checking of the code to be inspected.
4. The moderator schedules the inspection meeting and notifies the reviewers of the location of the code to be inspected.
5. The moderator and reviewers personally review the code to be inspected.
6. At the beginning of the inspection, the author gives an overview of the code to be inspected.
7. The author walks through the code to be inspected.
8. The moderator keeps a list of defects and assigns an impact priority to each defect.
9. After the inspection, the moderator e-mails the list of defects to the author.
10. The author makes the corrections to the code.

6.3.5.4   Inspection Team Roles

Author: The author is responsible for ensuring that the code is ready to be inspected, giving an overview of the code to the reviewers, walking through the code, and making the corrections.

Moderator: The moderator schedules the inspection and identifies the reviewers. The moderator facilitates the inspection and generates the list of identified defects.

Reviewer(s): Reviewers personally review the code to identify defects prior to the inspection, and then they participate in the inspection.

Project Manager: Although not usually a member of the inspection team, the project manager will assist the moderator in identifying the appropriate reviewers. The project manager will also plan for the impact of code inspections on the current and future tasks within the software development schedule.

6.3.5.5   Effort, Size, and Time Guidelines

Table 6.2 presents effort, size, and time guidelines for preparing for and conducting distributed code inspections, including a comparison with the guidelines for Fagan inspections. In general, the times for the distributed inspections have been reduced in order to accommodate the logistics issues associated with multisite development in multiple time zones.

The primary difference between distributed inspections and Fagan inspections is that Fagan inspections use a code reader other than the author to walk

Table 6.2 *Distributed Inspection Guidelines.*

Activity	Distributed Inspection	Fagan Inspection
Amount of code to be reviewed	<300 lines of code	<300 lines of code
Number of inspection team members	2–5	3–5
Preparation time (personal review)	<30 minutes	<3 hours
Overview presentation time	<10 minutes	<30 minutes
Inspection meeting time	<1 hour	<2 hours

through the code. Inspections that occur within a single site could use Fagan-like procedures and time guidelines if the moderator desires. In no cases, however, should the Fagan inspection meeting time guidelines be exceeded, since the efficiency of defect discovery is substantially reduced after two hours of meeting time.

On the DPS2000 project, we had some success applying this approach across multiple sites. Potential defects were found when we applied the process steps listed earlier. We also noticed that different styles of coding or design were applied at the various sites. For example, some developers provided many comments versus fewer comments, and some developers used more iterative styles (e.g., trial and error) versus more planned approaches (more formal designs). Some of these styles could be culturally biased, but different individual developers within a location can also have differing styles, especially concerning the number of comments. The biggest difficulties we faced concerned the logistics of the distributed inspections. Due to time zone differences, scheduling the inspection meetings was more difficult because of the limited time overlap in the normal working day. Also, teleconferences tended to be more physically tiring than face-to-face meetings. However, these types of constraints apply to any type of distributed meeting, and the guidelines of Tables 6.1 and 6.2 help to limit the duration of such meetings.

6.3.6 Holidays and Vacations

The biggest headache for the global project manager is planning for and keeping track of the holidays and vacation days of team members in different countries. More often than not, a project manager in one country will forget to consider the important holidays in another country. This always creates confusion and sometimes resentment for the development team members.

Vacations can also vary among different development sites. Development team members sometimes synchronize vacations to coincide with their children's school vacations. This can require considerable advanced personal life planning on the part of the team member. The project manager must take care to factor these personal schedules into the overall project schedule. United States–based project managers are often surprised by the amount of vacation taken in other countries. For example, our German colleagues typically receive six weeks of vacation per year. This can seem like an excessive amount to the new project manager in a United States–based company who starts out with two weeks of vacation a year.

One rule of thumb that generally seems to hold for all projects for all countries is to avoid releases or major milestones during the end of December or early January. (This was particularly true during the new millennium celebrations of 1999/2000.) Software development productivity during this time of the year seems to be low, and you should avoid important tasks in your project plan. Thus, it's better to schedule releases around this time of the year for, say, December 15th, and then don't plan the next release until the end of January, at the earliest.

6.3.7 Travel

Face-to-face meetings will always be necessary for global development projects. Plan sufficient travel expense budgets and time for such meetings. In some cases, more junior members of the development team will be traveling to foreign countries for the first time. The project manager has an obligation to provide whatever support is available to reduce the potential hardships for these first-time travelers. After all, the meetings will not be very productive if team members are overly jet-lagged or uncomfortable in a foreign culture. Local hosts should go out of their way to support these guests and should plan some personal time to host evening dinners or social events, without tiring out the visitors. Experienced travelers should share their tips concerning flight class upgrades using frequent flyer programs, where to stay and eat, and the like. These details may seem extraneous to the project manager when compared to the many bigger problems to worry about, but a little support or consideration for these issues will pay a return with increased meeting or work efficiency at the remote sites.

6.4 Multicultural Variables

Multicultural variables are a factor for projects developed in multiple countries [Kopper 1993]. These variables can be exploited as strengths for the development, or they can get in the way, depending on how they are handled. Our projects were not only multisite but also multinational. There were also strong multicompany cultural variables, since part of the development team came from a company that had recently been acquired by Siemens.

Having gone through team training and multicultural training for Americans, Swiss, and Germans, we were very aware of the role of multicultural variables on the DPS2000 project, although we sometimes didn't know what to do about them. For example, we observed that there are culturally biased attitudes concerning basic qualities such as punctuality. These biases often indirectly affect project schedule planning and execution concerning meeting deadlines. This can frustrate certain team members. Knowing that the frustration is culturally based sometimes helped us better accept our team members' perceived strengths and weaknesses and may have reduced the frustration.

Some of the very basic project decisions that are taken for granted by single-site development teams could have highly significant meaning for multinational teams. For example, writing design documentation in English is usually taken for granted by a United States–based team. For a multinational team with members who are not native English speakers, this can affect the task time estimates of team members with less experience writing specifications in English. This can frustrate American team members, who may think, "Why are those Europeans so slow?"

Language can also affect the way that design meetings and reviews are conducted. In an environment where design alternatives are expected to be "argued" until a consensus is reached, the non-native English speakers can feel disadvantaged. They may be less skilled in communicating their preferred design approach. Sometimes in such design meetings, the designer who speaks the most and the loudest will bias the team to pursue a specific approach.

Software engineering is usually concerned with the management of trade-offs. Project managers and development team members constantly wrestle with concerns such as "If I had a few more weeks to perfect my design, the resulting code would be higher quality, but the product will take longer to get to the market." Cultural biases concerning such things as perfectionism, quality, work ethic, and teamwork will often color the trade-offs that are selected. In a project with a tight schedule and limited staff, trade-offs among quality, schedule, and functionality are made every day.

One of the more difficult cultural differences addressed in the DPS2000 project was the frequency of interaction and collaboration among the team members. We observed that the European colleagues preferred to be assigned a task and then to pursue that task with minimal interaction with their colleagues. Americans tended to ask more questions of each other after they had initiated a task, sometimes changing the task characteristics as new information became available. This sometimes made it difficult for project management to measure the progress of development tasks or the relative productivity of team members. A project rule was instituted that after an individual had spent a predefined amount of time on a task, he was encouraged to ask questions of a colleague to help move the task along. Setting up a chief architect was important to support this rule, since most of the time the team members would direct their questions to him.

TIP: Carefully select the working language for meetings.

For any meetings you are organizing, give careful consideration to the working language. Usually, this will be the language selected for the project documentation. But depending on their native languages, attendees may prefer to work in another language during the meeting. I once attended a meeting in Nuremberg with a few Swiss colleagues where the working language was German. This did not surprise me, since they came from a German-speaking part of Switzerland. What did surprise me, however, was learning later that the Swiss would have preferred to work in English for this meeting, since they believed that their local Swiss accents put them at a disadvantage when negotiating with Germans in Germany.

6.5 Recommendations for Global Development Teams

Based on my experience with global software development teams split across the United States, Germany, and Switzerland I offer the following recommendations. The suggestions and lessons learned are probably most applicable to medium-sized software development projects rather than to very small or very large projects.

- *Develop a project culture:* In order to reduce cultural variables, explicitly build a unique project culture. This project culture can select norms from a single culture or mix the "best" characteristics of multiple cultures. You should establish this project culture from the very beginning of the project. For example, from the outset, will team members address each other by their family names or by their given names? By explicitly developing this project culture, the comfort level of individual team members should increase. A skilled project manager can recognize the cultural differences while setting the norms for the project. For example, a project manager can state, "We realize that you normally don't spend so much time in design meetings, but for this project we will meet for another couple of days before we break off to write specifications."

- *Set project goals:* Within a multicultural environment it is important to set clear project goals and to define the criteria that must be satisfied for project success. This means putting relative priorities on project characteristics that must be traded off, such as quality, schedule, and functionality. For the DPS2000 project, we decided during global analysis that the project schedule would take priority over functionality. Such goal definition at the beginning of the project helps the team later recognize when it has achieved success.

- *Overcommunicate:* For global development, it is necessary to overcommunicate. This helps overcome communications problems associated with language understanding. Avoid abbreviations and slang. And follow up in writing any decisions made during spoken communications.

- *Put as much as possible in writing:* This is related to overcommunicating, it is important to put as much project information in written form as possible. This includes technical information, such as specifications, as well as project information, such as the software development plan. For project team members who are working in non-native languages, put as much technical information as possible in diagrams that are easier to read than words. For software architecture descriptions, **Unified Modeling Language** (UML) notation has been helpful [Hofmeister, Nord and Soni 2000]. It's also helpful to have a native speaker on the design team for the language being used for documenting the architecture. For long documents, include a brief summary to help struggling readers.

- *Practice patience:* Issues will not be resolved as quickly for a global development team as for a team located at a single site. In our case, with a six-hour time difference between the European and U.S. sites, the common workday was limited to a couple of hours. Many issues were not resolved until the next day. Thus, all team members and their management must practice patience.

- *Identify team roles:* Attempt to identify each development team member's role in the project. For the DPS2000 project, we defined roles and named the roles with titles we thought would help in understanding the role. In some cases, we needed to communicate and describe the roles a few times before team members understood them.

- *Build consensus:* Different cultures have different ways of indicating agreement and resolving conflicts. Within global development teams, consensus should be built at every opportunity. The European colleagues often were more comfortable with hierarchical decision making, but the power of a diverse multinational team with differing viewpoints can be tapped only when team members are actively solicited for their opinions.

- *Invest in team building and multicultural training:* This training helped us to formulate our project culture. Particularly important were the meeting management skills that we learned during the team-building training. The training also gave us an opportunity to learn more about the various team members and some of their cultural biases and stereotypes. The group exercises performed during the training can address real project issues, such as defining practices within the software development process.

- *Get to know each other outside the work environment:* Common meals and outings after working hours helped form personal as well as professional relationships among the team members. The personal relationships often helped bridge the gap when communications broke down during the workday. The personal relationships were also helpful for handling logistics and information issues that resulted from traveling: where to stay, shop, eat, relax, and so on, when away from home.

- *Don't be reluctant to travel:* It is extremely important for key players to work together in person. We have consistently found that a day of face-to-face communication is more effective than a couple of weeks of communication by telephone and e-mail. This is especially true with team members from different countries, where nonverbal communication often plays a much larger role in the exchange of information. Show hospitality to foreign team members who visit your site.

- *Provide management support:* Project management for global development must be both centralized and localized. Overall project leadership must be centralized, but every development team member needs a local manager for day-to-day support. Thus, multisite collaboration and cooperation is necessary for the management team. Nevertheless, team members who are highly self-directed seem to perform better on global teams. If the project manager has a choice, he should attempt to staff the global development project with as many self-directed team members as possible.

6.6 Conclusions

Team members of multisite projects must, because of geography, be highly self-directed. Assigned tasks must be flexible enough to resolve the trade-offs that arise without waiting for the next business day. Team members must collaborate with their technical interface counterparts frequently, especially when stuck on design issues. Face-to-face meetings still work best.

From our experience on the DPS2000 project it appears that global development is not as fast or efficient as when a team is located in one place. Often, questions must wait a day to be answered, since they usually do not arise during the limited common working times of team members in different time zones. However, the overall strength of global development is the flexibility and modifiability of the resulting design. Different views of the product colored by cultural biases, knowledge of local market conditions, experience with differing technologies, and the like, produce a design that is more adaptable to changing markets than when the design is created by a single location team with less cultural and technical diversity.

The system design specification is critical for partitioning work packages across multiple development sites. We have observed that integration of the various subsystems has gone remarkably smoothly when subsystem leaders are brought together in one location.

In the beginning of the DPS2000 project, project meetings were held monthly, rotating among the development sites. Later, meetings were held mainly for major subsystem integrations or when training and/or detailed design work was necessary to get someone started on a new development task. We had weekly teleconference meetings to track schedule status and to bring up common problems the developers needed to be aware of. We published the goals of the teleconference in advance, using the techniques we had learned to plan and conduct meetings during team-building training.

Despite our best efforts at communicating among the four development sites of the DPS2000 project and our emphasis on design documentation with well-defined interfaces, that experience showed that global development is clearly more difficult than single-site development. This is a result of occasional miscommunications caused by different vacations and holidays in the three countries, time zone differences, and occasional network or computer outages. For example, if questions arise for colleagues in Europe during their evening hours while the United States–based teams are working, they likely will need to wait until the next day before the issues can be resolved. To compensate for the unexpected on the DSP2000 project, team members often used the home telephone numbers of their colleagues in the other countries, and the software system was rebuilt almost every day in multiple locations using the latest checked-in source code. We also invested in technical training, team building, and multicultural training for the development team members.

The DPS2000 software product line architecture was designed to be very flexible and expandable to handle a wide variety of applications. We believe that the diversity of our development team members, with their differing skills and experience, has helped us better achieve a flexible design.

CHAPTER 7

Building a Project Culture and Team

While performing an audit of a Siemens software development organization, I was surprised how consistent everyone throughout the organization was when they said that the best thing about working there was the good team spirit. This organization was clearly at level 1 on the capability maturity model (CMM) process scale. But their products were well regarded by their customers, their software quality was good, and they were relatively productive. We concluded that their team spirit was a key success factor in explaining their organizational competence.

As in professional sports, the skills and abilities of your software development team will likely make or break your success as a project manager. It is thus very important to a project manager's personal career success to assemble the best possible team. Professional sports managers are often replaced at the end of a losing season. In many cases, such losing teams do not have the best players. But in many sports as well as software projects, teamwork is often a major success factor. Teams where everyone understands their role and the members work well together can often achieve greater success, assuming that the basic skills are present to accomplish the work. This chapter explores how to organize and build your software development team over time so that they can achieve success.

When we look at factors that influence the performance of a software development organization, we typically look into four related areas: development process maturity, quality of the people in the organization, the work environment, and technologies applied. Good software architecture design methods are one of the technologies that can be applied. You can define and control your development process, but changing people's work habits within an existing organization often may take longer than is available to develop your product. You may even have less control over who is assigned to your project and the environment they work in (e.g., your facility). But you can immediately start to build a strong development team and provide a supportive culture for the people on your project.

7.1   Establishing Project Goals

One of the key factors for a software development team to achieve success is for them to recognize what they must do and what the criteria for success are. This means setting project goals for the team that every team member understands and believes will be achieved. By setting challenging goals you help to energize the team, and it gives the members a sense of accomplishment when the goals are achieved. However, it is often difficult in software engineering to distinguish a challenging goal from an impossible or unrealistic goal.

Clearly communicate project goals so that all the team members understand them. This is not always easy, since cultural biases strongly affect the way goals are set and then worked toward. Some cultures are very literal with respect to the language used to set goals. If a project goal is to ship a product with no known defects and the cultural bias is toward a literal interpretation, the team will not ship until they have corrected every defect. It may disturb some team members or reflect negatively on the credibility of the project manager if fixing certain defects is deferred to a later time or they are not fixed at all. An American project team might also have as a goal to ship with no known defects, but this may be interpreted as shipping with no known *serious* defects. For these reasons, I suggest that project goals also include example success criteria with some quantitative meaning. For example, a more quantitative project goals statement might say, "We will always meet our delivery dates (i.e., by the Monday following a release done on Friday), and we will attempt to implement all the features identified in the release plan (i.e., we will ship at least 90% of the features identified)."

Project goals usually address the trade-offs and priorities of schedule (time), effort (cost), quality, and functionality. It is unrealistic to ask for everything possible; i.e., the product must be delivered on schedule, under budget, with excellent quality, and a complete set of features. It is better to understand what are the most important priorities and then to set goals where at least one of the trade-off variables (time, cost, quality, or functionality) can have less restrictive goals.

For example, a more realistic project goal statement would be: "We will absolutely meet our release date with good quality, but we will strive to add most features discussed in advance and not be overly concerned with the development costs," or "If we can productively invest more in the development in order to ensure good quality or meeting our release dates, we'll consider increasing the budget." Once such a project goals statement is communicated, additional discussion or quantification can occur about what is meant by words like *absolutely*, *more*, *excellent*, and *complete*. The primary purpose of the project goals statement is to help all team members understand what the project is striving to achieve and to help set their individual priorities as they make their own trade-off decisions. A secondary purpose of the project goals statement is to help the project team (and their management) recognize success when they have achieved it. If an important goal is to absolutely meet delivery dates, and the team consistently achieves this, then everyone can recognize the project team as being successful.

7.2   Characteristics of Good Teams

Having done software project audits and postmortems, and having been involved with good and bad teams as both a manager and a member, I have developed a list of the characteristics of good teams. Some of these are taken from the world of sports, but I believe most of them also apply to software development teams.

- Within good teams, whenever one team member is struggling a bit with a task, other team members automatically help out to take up the slack.
- Good teams are generally loose and comfortable in their interactions with each other. This is observed by frequent joking and playfully poking fun at each other's idiosyncrasies.
- Good teams enjoy a give-and-take communication style where conflicting ideas are immediately dealt with and usually resolved.

- Members of good teams know each other well and can usually predict each other's reactions to proposed ideas.
- Good teams will sometimes share activities not related to their primary tasks such as meals and social activities.
- Members of good teams pull their own weight and feel an obligation to other team members to successfully complete their tasks.
- Members of good teams are committed to achieving the overall goals of the team.
- Members of good teams usually use *we* rather than *I* when describing their accomplishments.
- Good teams take some time to form. Changing team members sets back their progress, and new team members need time to be accepted and integrated. Once the team understands a new member's role, it will again make progress.
- Teams need leadership in the beginning in order to learn to become a good team. But over time this leadership becomes less critical and the team becomes more self-directing. The team leader then becomes more of a "coach" than a "director."
- Members of good teams have different but synergistic skills, attitudes, backgrounds, value systems, and so on. The members usually understand and can describe their roles and responsibilities.
- Good teams have had some successes as they develop, which become a source of pride and build the team's self-confidence.
- Members of good teams have usually previously made mistakes on other teams and have been members of bad teams.
- Good teams collectively and generally believe that their tasks will likely be successfully accomplished.

Although it's fairly easy to recognize good teams, it's much more difficult to build them. Organizing a software development team to be a potentially good team requires careful attention to building the appropriate project culture.

7.3 Building a Project Culture

In Chapter 6, we discussed the cultural influences that affect the performance of global development teams. These cultural influences can be either exploited or minimized by setting an appropriate project culture. This project culture can be created anew, can be borrowed from existing project cultures, or can be mixed and matched from the best practices of the various cultures of the team members. What are most important is that the team members know the characteristics of the project culture and that the culture be consistent with achieving the project goals. For example, a team member may respond when asked about the project culture, "Communications amongst ourselves are very casual, but we all understand the importance of meeting our release dates."

7.3.1 Trust, Openness, and Communication

Trust, openness, and communication must be present among the team members and the project manager in order for the project to succeed. Trust can only be built over time. This is achieved by doing what you say, accepting responsibility, and meeting commitments.

There should be very few secrets or hidden information in the project team. By knowing all the various parameters and information concerning the project environment, team members can better make the trade-offs necessary to accomplish their tasks. Some information, however, must not be communicated, including personal information, such as individual salaries, and information restricted by law, such as advance information concerning acquisitions and mergers that can affect stock prices. Keeping such information confidential helps to build trust. But project-related information that is not restricted by law or morals should be openly communicated. For example, feedback from early users of software should be openly communicated so that team members can orient their work toward providing functionality that may be better appreciated by future users.

7.3.2 Breaking Down Resistance and Cultural Barriers

As discussed in Chapter 6, there are cultural barriers that can get in the way of achieving the project goals. In any new team, there will be resistance by the team members to commit to achieving the project goals. Many people will take a wait-and-see approach before they engage in meeting the team's goals. This resistance is part of every organization and can be found especially in teams that have not yet committed to achieving success.

There are many techniques to help break down the resistance; these tend to be mainly communications approaches. In theory, a team member, given enough time and information, will commit to the goals of the project once he feels comfortable with the other team members and the project manager and is convinced that achieving the goals is realistic. One recommendation for new teams consisting of new members who do not know each other or the project manager well is to plan some team-building training or workshops early in the project. Such team-building training with a professional facilitator will help the team members get to know and trust each other, will help to reinforce project goals, and possibly expose some of the current or future problems the team will face. One practical outcome of team-building training is the emergence of tools to organize and conduct team meetings. This helps build the project culture and helps make people's time more efficient when they understand the structure and expected outcomes of project meetings.

A good way to break down resistance, discussed earlier in the context of cultural issues, is for the project manager to overcommunicate. This means that the project manager will provide information about the project (e.g., the next release delivery date) multiple times in different forums. Spoken information will often be followed up with written information and vice versa. Different people receive information better using differing approaches (e.g., visual, audio). Furthermore, many software development teams will have staff members with differing native languages. With respect to breaking down resistance, overcommunicating gives the team members multiple opportunities to challenge or question information given by the project manager. Once the information is challenged, a dialog can occur in which resistance can be identified and potentially dissipated either through clarifying communications or modification to the current working plan. For example, despite extensive planning, a project manager's plan may have a flaw that surfaces (to him) only when someone is willing to point it out. A simple example is when a release date is set, but key staff members are already committed to attending a team-building workshop the week before the release.

A useful technique for helping to break down cultural barriers and resistance that is often used during team-building workshops is called the *walkaround*. In a walkaround, the team members pair off in discussion pairs while walking around outside as a group. The pairs reform after a specified period (e.g., 10 minutes) until all members have been paired off again. If there is an odd number of members in the walkaround group, the person who is not paired can serve as timekeeper for one specified time period. Within the specified time period, the time is divided into half for each pair member. During this time, the team member tells what she likes and dislikes about the other team member, in the context of the project team. Since each team member is both giving and receiving possible criticism, the discussions tend to be constructive and supportive in nature. An example discussion could be: "I don't understand the details of your design; if you were to put more information into the design specification, that may help me understand." Team members who have not worked together much on project tasks can use the specified time to introduce themselves. After the walkaround is completed, each team member will have given and received feedback from every other team member. The insights gained from this experience often have immediate effects for the project and a longer-lasting impact on the team members. Variations of this exercise can also be done indoors by having people pair off in a conference room for the purpose of exchanging feedback.

7.3.3 Handling Personality Conflicts

In many cases, team members find themselves having to work on project teams with people they don't know well or have conflicts with. Clearly, teams of people who like and respect each other are more likely to work well together. Project managers should consider these factors when making task assignments. People who have worked well with each other on earlier projects are more likely to work well together on new projects. This is one reason for engineering managers to manage their staff attrition so that teams or people that have worked together in the past can work together again.

In today's world of highly specialized software engineering skills, engineers will likely be forced to work with someone they don't always get along with. The project manager will earn his pay trying to support the effective collaboration among such individuals. The project manager has to communicate and reinforce the project goals so that the individuals involved can focus on achieving their tasks for the overall good of the team. The project manager must provide strong support (see Section 7.5) to help the team members work well together. With extreme personality conflicts, the project manager should consider other staffing and teaming alternatives.

To some extent, every time you change a team member diminishes the productivity of the entire team. New team members must fit in and learn their roles. Removing team members sometimes creates resentment among the remaining team members, since they may feel like they have to take on the work of the departing team member. Still, project managers have an obligation to remove team members who are not fulfilling their role or are undercutting the productivity of other team members due to personality conflicts or other social problems.

I've observed that a key job satisfaction factor is how much you enjoy working with the people on your team. People will often enjoy their jobs more when they enjoy working with other team members. Conversely, very interesting tasks can lose their appeal when they must be done with people you don't like or respect. I've often observed people leave a project team or even the entire organization when either their reporting relationship or work group members have been changed.

Project managers should be aware of these interpersonal relationships when assigning tasks to individuals or setting up work teams. Sometimes, you cannot avoid having two people who do not like each other work on a common task. In this case, you must support both team members and ask for their contributions to achieve the common project goals.

7.3.4   "Getting to Know You" Meeting

One way the project manager can communicate goals and set expectations is through what I call a "getting to know you" meeting, with either an individual or part of or the entire team. The project manager calls the meeting to discuss his expectations and some of the values that are important to him. Team members, when they understand these expectations, can often accommodate the project manager and spend their time solving the more important project problems. The meeting also gives the project manager an idea of the skills and the type of work preferences of the team members for when he must make task assignments.

When the project manager meets with an individual team member, one of his primary goals is to gather information that can help him pick future task assignments for the team member. Thus, the meeting is similar to a job interview, where the project manager tries to gather information about the skills of the team member and the types of tasks the team member enjoys doing the most.

When meeting with a group of team members, there is less emphasis on gathering information about skills and task interests and more emphasis on discussing values. While discussing values, the project manager tries to describe the soft values that are most important to him. These include an identification and definition of values that are important to the project manager and to the success of the project. Table 7.1 lists example values that can be discussed during such a meeting.

Discussion of values often helps team members adjust their behavior so they can avoid smaller interaction problems on the project. For example, if the project manager explains that punctuality is very important to him, team members may put more emphasis on attending, starting, and finishing meetings on time. Furthermore, if the project goals set a high priority on meeting milestone dates, then punctuality can be reinforced as both a personal value and a desirable project cultural characteristic. For this example, the project manager can explain at the personal level that being late for meetings will irritate him, but from the project's viewpoint being late on milestone dates gets in the way of meeting the project goals. Such discussions of values and their relation to project goals help define the project culture.

7.3.5 Building Confidence

Team members must believe that they can achieve success for the team to be able to achieve success. The project manager must nurture the building of this self-confidence, and he must plan actions both to help achieve the project goals and to grow team members' confidence to achieve the goals.

Part Two described some of the actions that help build confidence. For example, incremental development is a great confidence builder, since everyone can see the product functionality grow nearly every day. The initial incremental release that is defined is actually a prototype implementation (vertical

Table 7.1 *Example Values.*

Honesty	Integrity	Openness	Punctuality
High quality	Productivity	Efficiency	Speed
Commitment	Passion	Fun	Empathy
Respect	Detailed	Social	Supportive

slice) to prove the feasibility of the architecture. This helps build confidence in the architecture design.

Visible risk analysis and aggressive risk mitigation also help build the confidence of the project team. Many developers will increase their confidence in meeting the project goals when they know that the project manager is aware of the risks and is planning actions to minimize the risks. In general, responsiveness and quick decision making on the part of the project manager will also help build team members' confidence. The team will have confidence that if something does go wrong, the project manager will take quick corrective actions.

Having been involved in project and architecture design reviews and audits, I can often predict the outcome of a project based on the degree of confidence exhibited by the project team. Project teams that are likely to succeed usually have a good understanding of the potential risks and unresolved issues. Despite the risks, they usually have confidence that the risks can be overcome, and they can describe specific actions to take to minimize the risks. However, as stressed throughout this book, you must also be careful of over-optimism or overconfidence, where the plans and goals are unrealistic and are either wished for or dictated by the development team's management. Thus, teams with minimal experience developing products and who cannot articulate the risks and possible mitigation plans are suspect.

TIP: Build an upbeat project culture that supports good morale.

I once worked on a project in an organization where the staff had a "morale problem." The effect was that the staff didn't enjoy working there. Every Monday morning a group of team members would be lined up in front of my office waiting to hand in letters of resignation. This clearly had a negative impact on achieving our project goals. Do whatever you can to build a project culture that encourages openness, respect, trust, and all the other values you consider important. Spend your time and effort on facilitating the things that can affect team members' attitudes concerning your project and the company they work for. This includes getting them the best possible tools to do their jobs, making new team members feel comfortable on the project team, planning social events after work, and anything else you can think of to build a good work environment for your project team.

7.4 Building Consensus

One of the strengths of global development teams where the team members are from diverse cultures, countries, backgrounds, and skill sets is that each member has the opportunity to contribute unique capabilities to the team. For example, team members may have special knowledge concerning product requirements for localized markets. This knowledge can produce software systems that exhibit greater flexibility or functionality because they are driven by local requirements. It is thus important for the project manager to build consensus as a way of drawing out ideas and suggestions from each team member. This takes advantage of the diversity of ideas from team members. This consensus building can in some cases go against the native cultural practices of some of the team members. In some cultures, exchange of ideas may be foreign, and team members may be reluctant to express their individual ideas to the overall team. But if the project manager does not solve such problems, he will essentially have a team with diverse ideas that never surface.

The project manager has two challenges when building consensus among diverse team members. He must first establish a project culture in which new ideas are solicited so that every team member contributes freely and is forthcoming with potential solutions to project or technical problems. Once the ideas are flowing, the project manager must act on them. Here the project manager will build consensus so that the ideas are discussed and conflicting suggestions decided on. This obviously is not achieved overnight, but if the project culture values ideas and proposed solutions, the consensus-building and decision-making processes are more likely to succeed. A few suggestions and practices to accomplish this are given next.

7.4.1 Architecture

Building consensus on the software architecture design is key to the success of the development. This is why it's important to communicate the architecture design to all team members and also to apply the architecture evaluation or design review techniques identified in Chapter 3. You have to communicate the architecture so that team members can understand how their development components fit in the overall structure of the product. Such training or communication of the architecture should also build consensus and give each team member the opportunity to question the design.

The chief software architect is an advocate for the software architecture. This includes communicating with team members, answering their questions about the architecture, and building their confidence in implementing it. Thus, for technology issues concerned with the architecture, the chief software architect should be building consensus among project team members.

7.4.2 Project Plan

The project manager's job becomes easier if everyone on the project team is committed to achieving similar goals. Building consensus on the project plan involves getting everyone to contribute to the plan, giving team members an opportunity to change the plan before it's committed to, and then getting all team members to commit to achieving it.

The project plan or the software development plan (SDP), as described in Chapter 2, is an important artifact to help build consensus. I suggest that the project plan be released twice, with a short time period between releases for project team members to question and contribute to the plan. This is important to building consensus concerning the project plan and to soliciting every team member's commitment to achieve the plan. Since you do planning before every release increment development cycle, it is necessary to keep the time short between the proposed and committed-to versions of the SDP. Thus, the project manager must be building consensus continually so that the details of the proposed plan are not a big surprise. The project manager must also be cautious when assuming that no response to the proposed plan implies commitment. Although this quick response process can be established as part of the project culture (speak up, or forever hold your peace), sometimes the project manager should communicate directly with key project team members to establish whether consensus is continually being built or whether people are being railroaded into accepting the manager's plan.

7.5 Setting the Amount of Direction

Newer teams will need more direction in the beginning and will likely require less direction over time as the team builds its technical and interaction skills. This also applies to individuals. In general, newer or less experienced employees will require more management direction than very experienced employees.

In addition, newer employees and teams will likely require more support from their managers. For this discussion, I define *management direction* as the amount of instructions that a manager gives either the team or specific team members. This direction will take the form of commands, e.g., "Do this task first, come back to me when you are finished, and then I'll tell you what to do next." *Management support* is defined as the amount of problem solving the manager does with the team or team members when they raise issues that need to be decided on. More experienced teams or team members will often solve their own problems and then decide on actions without raising them as issues to their project manager. Assuming they make mostly good decisions, this simplifies the work of the project manager. Inexperienced teams and members will often expect their project managers to make many decisions for them. In these cases, support may also result in direction, e.g., "Now that we have decided to take this course of action, you must do these actions in order to solve our problem."

I have known managers who try to avoid having many team members who require lots of management support. These managers view these employees as "high-maintenance" team members who require large amounts of the manager's time. Unfortunately, it is impossible to staff a team entirely with very experienced members, especially when working with new technologies, where very few people have much experience. Many managers appreciate team members who may not have much experience but are quick learners who will try to obtain support from many sources. Often, these team members will consult with others before bringing a set of alternatives to the manager for a decision. This tends to streamline communications, and the manager may spend less overall time on support-related tasks.

To a large extent being a good project manager is recognizing how much support and direction the team and all its members require. Managers that give too much support and direction to team members not needing it will be viewed as "micro-managers." Managers that give too little support and direction to team members who do require it will be viewed as apathetic, aloof, or not engaged enough with the project or people. Thus, the project manager must be aware of the amount of support and direction that he will provide for every situation that the team faces. In general, the degree of direction and support the project manager provides will depend on the experience level of the team members, but even very experienced teams can become stuck with very difficult problems that the project manager must help resolve. However, such experienced teams likely will recognize which are the difficult problems and what type of support they will need from their management. In some cases, the manager's unique perspective is what will be needed to resolve the issue, e.g., changing business needs, political issues, unexpected scenarios. With such experienced teams, the manager may serve as a decision facilitator or a source of information to give the complete picture.

Figure 7.1 identifies the degree of support and direction that a manager gives as part of the experience maturity of the project team or individual team member. Such a representation is obviously not a continuum of maturity progression, since it is task and situation dependent, and even very experienced team members will sometimes be given problems to solve for which they have no relevant experience. But Figure 7.1 may help the project manager recognize and be aware of how much support and direction is appropriate to a specific situation. Too much support and direction to a team member who does not need it are as damaging as too little support and direction to a team member who really does need help. The diagram can also be a basis for discussion between the project manager and the team member to help establish the rela-

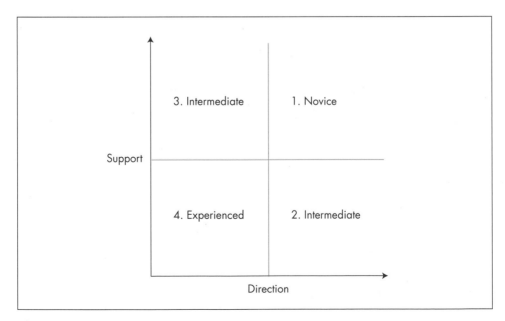

Figure 7.1 *Management Direction and Support.*

tive amount of direction and support desired by both of them for specific tasks. Such a model can be discussed during the getting-to-know-you meeting described earlier.

> **TIP: Try to organize your team around self-starters.**
>
> Sometimes the project manager's job feels like you are a highly paid baby-sitter. Staff members who make up teams that are mainly in the novice category of Figure 7.1 require high degrees of direction and support. Too many people in this category on your project team means that you will work much harder than a team with more experienced members who are willing to make their own decisions. Always try to staff your project with the best possible people you can find. Self-starters are usually easier and more rewarding to manage. Make sure that at least the key people in leadership roles of your project are experienced self-starters rather than novices.

7.6   Summary

This chapter provided some tips on how to build a good project team and a project culture to support the team. Project managers should be aware that such highly functioning teams take time to build, and sometimes such working relationships form only over multiple projects. However, in today's world of ever-shorter development schedules, the project manager is well advised to try out many alternatives to build a good team. Selecting good people for the team certainly helps make the project manager's job easier. But, many project managers do not have the luxury of selecting the team members, and distinguishing good software engineers from those not so good is not always easy. Furthermore, team personalities must mesh so that the project roles are understood and accepted and so that personality conflicts are avoided or defused. However, despite the difficulty, there is a reward for the manager (and the team members) who experiences the culture and accomplishments of a high-performance team that has been built over time. The output of such a team far exceeds the sum of the individual contributions, or at least it appears this way. Furthermore, working with such teams is often a lot of fun.

Attracting and keeping good employees help an organization achieve its goals. This is particularly true for the software project manager. Find good software engineers to work on your project, train them to fit into the team quickly, keep them on your team for the duration of the development, don't give them too much work so they burn out, and don't give them too little work so they get bored. If you make a sincere effort to support the well-being of the people on your development team, they in turn will contribute well to meeting the goals of the project.

CHAPTER 8

The Role of the
Software Project Manager

When performing audits of projects that typically have gone off track, I always feel sorry for the current project manager. In many cases, he is overworked, has minimal control over the staff and budget given to his project, and may be a replacement for some departed manager who began the project. Unfortunately, project managers themselves are judged by the success or problems of their projects. The skills of successful software project managers are very broad. Project managers must be good engineers, leaders, politicians, team players, coaches, communicators, and so on. It is difficult to learn this broad set of skills in a classroom. In most cases, the best way to learn is on the job, by managing smaller projects. Software engineers who are considering becoming project managers should read this chapter carefully to help determine if they would be comfortable in this role.

PREVIOUS chapters have discussed organizing the software development project team, stressing the importance of building a good team in which everyone knows their role. This chapter discusses the role of the software project manager and how he relates to the other team members. As a project manager, you will interact with many other people in the organization: architects, lead engineers, developers, testers, product managers, quality assurance experts, and customers. To be successful as a project manager, you must understand what these various people expect of you and what you should expect of them.

8.1   Creating a Vision

Like the software architect with his vision of the successful architecture, the project manager should create a vision of the successful project—not just a sugarcoated vision that everything will go totally as planned for the entire project. The project manager should have a basic belief that the major risks will be adequately addressed as they arise and that the project has a good chance to be completed successfully. Not only must the project manager create this vision, he must also believe that the vision is generally achievable. His self-confidence in the eventual success of the project will provide leadership to the entire project team. If the project manager does not believe that the schedule, budget, and functionality can generally be met, it is unlikely that the team will believe it.

In this role, a project manager with successful experience developing earlier products will have more credibility as a visionary leader. However, in the software industry, newer products often do not look like prior products, and they may employ technologies and processes that were unavailable on earlier projects. Thus, it may be more valuable for the project manager to have a basic understanding of the business requirements and the faith that the product being implemented will generally meet user requirements.

As project manager, you will need to think globally and to consider the many different influencing factors that could conflict with one another as you form your vision for the project. Chapter 3 discussed the role of global analysis in defining project goals and strategies. These influencing factors can also be used to help form your overall vision for the project.

8.2   Coaching

As project teams become more experienced, the amount of direction the project manager must provide to team members decreases. When this starts to occur, the role of the project manager switches from director to coach. As a coach, you will need to ensure that each team member understands the goals of the project. To do this you will establish a dialog with each team member, depending on her experience and degree of skepticism. Chapter 7 discussed how the getting to know you meeting helps communicate the goals and desired culture of the project. But coaching discussions must be ongoing, and you will need to obtain the buy-in of each project team member for the project to be ultimately successful.

The project manager will also participate in mentoring. This is a form of coaching or support that must be given to the more inexperienced team members. Coaching as mentoring is needed to guide the work of very inexperienced team members to the point where they can make reasonable decisions on their own.

8.3 Making Decisions

The project manager will make decisions concerning the directions the project will take. The chief architect will likely make technical decisions. The project manager will make decisions that affect the project, i.e., the schedule, cost, quality, or functionality. In many cases, there will be project dependencies concerning technical decisions, and vice versa. This is why, in most cases, the project manager and chief architect will make decisions jointly. In certain situations, the project manager may wish to build consensus either before or after making an important project decision.

What is most important to the project team is that decisions be made in a timely fashion. You won't always have all the information you need to make a decision, nor will you always have time to build team consensus. Sometimes, making no decision is worse than making a wrong decision. A wrong decision can often be corrected later, at some rework cost, but delayed decisions can hold up the progress of the entire development team. Thus, it is important for project managers to make timely decisions when team members are waiting for direction or problem-solving support.

The most important decision the project manager is likely to make is whether or not to release a new software product for customer use. All known defects are never corrected nor all functionality in place on the target release date. And a Murphy's Law effect often occurs when the testers discover a fairly serious bug the day before the target release date. The project manager (or, in some organizations, the product manager) would very much like to declare the work finished and release the product. But this usually requires a careful decision about trade-offs that must be made concerning functionality, quality, customer needs, and the market or business situation. Most organizations establish *release criteria* that help support the manager's decision. These can even mean that no product will be released if known defects within certain severity levels remain unresolved. However, these criteria can be very situational and subject to interpretation and thus may be modified if necessary.

As an example of tough decision making, let's imagine a key customer who is demanding to have a product by a specified date. Very late in their test cycle, system-testing finds a fairly serious defect that will take a couple of weeks to fix. As it happens, the defect is in a feature this customer is not likely to use. What should the project manager do? He should release the product, but minus the feature containing the defect. In this way, the need date and release criteria are met, but with a feature missing. In my experience, there almost always will be future releases when the corrected feature can be included. This is especially true when the update approach may be to upgrade a Web-based server versus replacing **programmable read-only memories (PROMs)** in the field for an embedded product with many installations (e.g., automobile controllers). The decision is situational, but if the project manager carefully considers and documents the reasons for his decision, then the project manager is fulfilling his role.

8.4   Coordinating

The software project manager spends much of his time coordinating. This includes getting the right information to the team members who need it and linking team members together to accomplish tasks for which they must communicate. In this sense, part of the project manager's role is as a communications broker who attempts to get the right information at the right time to team members so that they can make their own decisions. If there's any doubt about the usefulness of the information, the project manager should err on the side of overcommunicating. Team members will be more effective at filtering out information they perceive as irrelevant to their current tasks.

The project manager will also spend much of his time coordinating logistics. This can range from how to deliver software releases to the best hotels to stay at during remote project meetings. Clearly, good organization skills and attention to details are important to the successful project manager. When logistics are not well coordinated, project team members run the risk of wasting time, thereby lowering their productivity.

8.5   Working with Your Project Team

As said earlier, the project manager's career success will depend on the capabilities and accomplishments of his development team. The success of the manager is often tied to the success of the team in meeting its goals. Thus, it is important for the project manager to work well with the members of the project team. Success characteristics include the ability to work well with various types of personalities, effective communications, development process knowledge, and teamwork. Simply stated, the project manager must be a valued project team member as well as the leader of the team.

8.5.1   Working with the Chief Architect

The project manager/chief architect team is critical to the success of the project. In general, the chief architect makes technical decisions and the project manager makes decisions that affect the project. Since most decisions have implications affecting both technical approaches and the project direction, the project manager and chief architect must work effectively as a team.

Table 8.1, reproduced from Hofmeister, Nord, and Soni [2000], summarizes the division of responsibilities between the project manager and chief architect for various tasks. As the project manager, you are generally responsible for the organization of the project, and you'll manage the resources,

Table 8.1 *Software Project Manager/Architect Roles. [Source: Hofmeister, Nord, and Soni 2000.]*

Task	Project Manager	Software Architect
Software development	Organize project, manage resources, budgets, and schedules	Organize team around design, manage dependencies
Requirements	Negotiate with marketing	Review requirements
Technology	Introduce new technology	Recommend technology, training, tools
Quality	Ensure quality of the product	Track quality of the design
Metrics	Productivity, size, and quality measures	Design measures

budgets, and schedules. The architect knows the technical details, and he should advise the project manager concerning work assignments and needed skills. Having a partner to help make project decisions will help minimize the isolation that some project managers experience, especially on larger projects.

As already stated, the project manager must have a good working relationship with the chief architect. But it's likely that the chief architect will have a reporting relationship to you, the project manager. This means that the two of you are not exactly peers, and you may have to overrule the architect from time to time, since you are ultimately responsible for the successful delivery of the product. This is why you should trust your chief architect's abilities and give him the technical authority needed to succeed.

TIP: Be willing to change the chief architect, if vision and confidence are absent.

We were asked to work with a chief architect for a new product line and review some of his ideas for its architecture. We realized after a while that the architect didn't have much confidence that a product could be implemented within a reasonable time frame to meet the business requirements. We shared our observations with the project manager, and suggested that he consider assigning another chief architect, one with a more optimistic viewpoint and more confidence. This suggestion was rejected by the project manager; as a result the project stagnated and didn't progress until a new architect was assigned, one with a different architecture vision. The architect needs to have confidence in meeting the architecture vision, and the project manager confidence in meeting the project vision, for the project team to have the leadership to succeed.

The project manager/chief architect relationship is fundamental to my view of succeeding with architecture-centric software project management. I have observed too many projects where one individual was doing both roles, a situation I believe that can produce subpar technical or project decisions. As an architect or project manager, you may have difficulty convincing your management to support both roles on your project. Some of this difficulty may be cost related, since it's cheaper to have one person do two jobs. But some of the resistance may be due to your corporate culture. For example, perhaps your organization views desirable project managers as being technically competent and always "on top of things." Thus, as a project manager you may need to fight to get a chief architect assigned to your project, or vice versa. I suggest that you resolve this before you take on the project. If you have to perform both roles, you will probably work very long hours.

8.5.2 Roles of the Team Members

The members of the high-level design team will likely assume responsibility for major subsystems as the project enters the implementation phase. Developers have responsibility for implementing selected components within the subsystems. They will also have responsibility for project functions other than code development, such as integration and testing. Chapter 5 describes some of these more specialized roles.

TIP: Communicate the obligations of the development team members.

As already discussed, the project manager needs to do a reasonable amount of planning and organizing so as not to waste the time of team members. The chief architect has an obligation to make technical decisions and communicate the architecture. The project manager should communicate to the development team members their obligations so that his expectations are more likely to be met. These obligations will depend on the environment and situation, but in general the project manager should expect the development team members to take their commitments seriously. This means that each team member is willing to do whatever is necessary to develop his assigned components per the project schedule and with reasonable quality. For meeting serious commitments, each team member should do what he can to meet delivery dates, except for events that cannot be controlled (e.g., snowstorms, hurricanes, computer or communications failures) or when environmental situations change (e.g., competitor reaches market first, layoffs, staff turnover, new management).

8.6 Software Project Management as a Career

Software project management can be a rewarding career to engineers who enjoy being in control, are willing to accept the unknown risks associated with any project, and are not easily frustrated by detail work, such as developing schedules, managing release criteria, coordinating, and handling logistics. A potential negative to becoming a project manager is that you will likely become less technically skilled over time as you assume more responsibility and spend more time organizing tasks. This is why I suggest a division of responsibilities and resulting career paths for project managers and architects. These roles must be separated for projects consisting of more than a few developers. Every project manager should have some technical work to do that either fills a hole within the project (e.g., one of the system testers) or is personally enjoyable, but project managers who interfere with the technical work of their team members will likely be resented. Furthermore, coordinating a reasonably sized project team so that everyone is striving to achieve the project goals requires lots of the project manager's time. Isolating yourself from the coordination tasks for a week to bang out some product code will likely have an adverse effect on the entire team as communications are missed, decisions are delayed, and logistics become tangled.

This book focuses on the problems a project manager must solve. Reading it all at once may make the software engineer considering moving into a project management role apprehensive that the job is more hassles than rewards. But there are rewards associated with having responsibility for a successful project that delivers a useful software product. The project manager can feel that she has had a greater impact on a product than by merely working on a small, specialized piece of it.

TIP: Expect the unexpected as a project manager.

My first project management job was exciting. I moved into a private office for the first time, and had a telephone with multiple lines and lighted buttons and an administrative assistant down the hall. I can remember having to solve some problems that weren't in my job description. One of the first challenging problems given me by my boss was to convince a small group of software engineers to wear shoes to work. I tried the usual logical arguments—it is unsafe to walk barefoot in the office, you may drop something on your foot, and so on. The problem finally resolved itself as winter approached and temperatures dropped, making it uncomfortable to go barefoot.

You might ask how you get to become a good project manager. Managing many projects over time obviously will improve your skills, and the techniques and tips I've described should become second nature as you practice them. But this will not help the neophyte project manager, possibly managing his first project. Many companies will not tolerate project managers' mistakes, and a poor performance on the first project may eliminate the possibility of doing a second project. Software engineers interested in becoming project managers should seek to develop leadership skills outside of their normal work tasks. This could involve participating in company committees or task forces or activities outside of work, such as leadership positions in civic or religious clubs.

Within their project teams, software engineers interested in project management should seek roles in which they are exposed to project management tasks. This could include functioning as a team leader (Chapter 5) or as an apprentice to the project manager. An apprentice to the project manager could get to manage the project when the project manager is not in the office or could manage some specific aspects of the project, such as monitoring schedule progress, or could manage a subset of the project, such as a subsystem or a remote development site.

As with most skills, practice helps, and the skill will grow over time. For example, if you are uncomfortable giving presentations to groups of your peers, seek opportunities inside and outside of work to give practice presentations. Doing so in low-risk situations will prepare you to give project status presentations to your management when you become a project manager. You'll be better equipped to focus on communicating the key issues of your project rather than expending nervous energy on the mechanics of your presentation.

8.7 Summary

This chapter has offered some guidelines concerning the role of the software project manager. Software project management can be a rewarding career for engineers who enjoy making decisions based on multifaceted, often conflicting, factors. Table 8.2 summarizes the primary tasks and skills of the successful software project manager.

Table 8.2 *Role of the Project Manager.*

Task	Description	Desired Skills
Create a project vision	Communicate a vision of successful project completion	Marketing, business climate, technology trends, experience from earlier projects, communications, goal setting, consensus building
Direct, coach, and mentor	Be directive, function as a mentor to inexperienced team members, or function as a coach to more experienced team members, depending on the situation	Communications, empathy, technical
Make decisions	Make timely decisions concerning the project so as not to hold up the work progress of team members	Global analysis, communications, trade-off analysis, business climate, political climate
Coordinate	Coordinate the necessary communications among team members and provide organizational support to avoid wasting the time of team members	Time management, organizational, communications
Work with team members	Interact with all team members, especially the chief architect	Team building, team member, communications, consensus building, interpersonal, social, intercultural

PART four

Implementing

Trade-Offs and Project Decisions

On the IS2000 project, we knew that meeting our development schedule was critical to the success of the company. As a result, many of the decisions we made were biased toward achieving the schedule within the overall time frame that was allocated. With such a bias, other trade-offs—concerning quality, functionality, and cost—were sometimes shortchanged. As a project is implemented, the project manager must attempt to balance schedule, quality, functionality, and development cost while always keeping in mind the goals of the project.

EVERY day you attempt to implement a project, you will need to make trade-off decisions that affect the progress and outcome of the project. I cannot teach you how to make the right decisions, since that depends on the situation. In many cases, you will not know whether or not a particular decision was right until after the product has been released to the field. Over time, many of your decisions will become instinctual, based on your experience of what worked well or not on prior projects. I can suggest, however, that you recognize the reasons for your decisions, communicate those reasons to your team members and management, and keep a record of your decisions so that you can evaluate their impact in the future and reverse or modify them if necessary.

9.1 Using the Project Goals to Make Decisions

Chapter 7 discussed the importance of setting project goals, both to establishing the culture of the project and to recognizing when the project is successful. The successful project manager should always have the project goals in mind when making project decisions. If you are developing a product where quality is extremely important—such as safety-critical software or embedded software that is delivered in large quantities and is difficult to replace in the field (e.g., automobile controllers)—most of your decisions will consider quality factors first. That is, your decisions will first consider the impact on the potential quality of the resulting product. And when quality has the highest priority, you will more likely place less importance on schedule and cost. You may emphasize and communicate these goals as the basis for your decisions with statements like "We will not ship this product until our test results give us confidence that its quality is high."

Clearly stated, simple project goals that are well known by all members of the development team provide a framework for decision making. If your primary project goal is quality related, and most of your decisions consider quality first, the team will gain confidence in your ability to make consistently good decisions. Over time, team members will also consider the quality goal first when making their local decisions.

9.2 Managing Creeping Functionality and Architecture Drift

When implementing projects, project managers typically want to stick to the development plans they have painstakingly created when they planned the project. Unfortunately, things change and it is not possible to strictly implement the plan. In fact, flexibility is highly desirable, since quick decisions in making mid-course corrections to the plan will be necessary as business and environmental conditions change. This will occur while the product is being developed, for example, when new requirements surface, new design approaches are thought of, or team membership changes. However, the project manager must function as the gatekeeper for changes, ensuring that each proposed change to the plan is scrutinized and decided on. The project manager must play this role as the team's conservative, realizing all along that his development plans will change as soon as the team begins to follow it.

9.2.1 Creeping Functionality

One of the biggest reasons for changes to the project plan is a change in the requirements, or as I call it, *requirements churn*. Ideally, all the requirements should be known and prioritized during the requirements definition phase of the project. If this is the case, the developers can focus on developing the product to meet the known and unchanging requirements. However, this never happens. Some requirements surface only during development, since they are often not fully known in advance. Requirements shift due to changing market conditions. This type of *creeping functionality* can require more work than what you had planned. Also, requirements may change as the developers better understand the complexity of their proposed implementations for meeting certain requirements.

As the project manager, you need to manage requirements churn by addressing each change request as it occurs. The best way to do this is to associate a cost of implementation with each new or modified requirement. This forces product managers or your marketing counterparts to put priorities on every change they ask for. When they request a new feature, you will likely respond, "We would be happy to add that feature if it makes for a better product, but we will need additional staff to implement it or a few months added to the schedule." This helps train product managers to think about what they really need and what they can and cannot afford. It also makes you appear responsive to their requests while preserving some sanity for your team and sticking to the plan. On the other hand, the project manager cannot cost out the implementation of every new request so high that nothing different is ever done.

New ideas will inevitably surface that will yield a much better product. You must be willing to think as a business manager and evaluate the impact the new feature may have on the market success of your product. In some cases, you must be willing to throw out your existing plan and refocus your team on pursuing a new path. But this should be the exception rather than the rule. In many cases, the new feature can replace a lower-priority feature in your current plan. Thus, you'll likely be "horse-trading" one feature for another. If you document such decisions for both the product manager and the team members, you will be more likely to manage expectations down the road (see Chapter 4). Your release plan is a good project artifact to document the changes in major features you plan to release. Feel free to create new versions of the release plan and to distribute them to all team members. Since you will be replanning before each incremental release, this is a good time to document any changes so that no one forgets that the release and software development plans have changed over time.

9.2.2 Architecture Drift

Another plan that will likely change as the project is implemented is the architecture design. It is mainly the chief architect's responsibility to be the gatekeeper for the architecture, but as project manager you will need both to support his resistance and possibly to overrule his resistance, depending on the circumstances, as changes are proposed that may impact the project. As described earlier, the architecture design and requirements analysis should be done primarily at the beginning of the project, during the high-level design phase of the project. Remember the rule of thumb that this phase should last a few months (Chapter 2) and the recommended architecture design approaches, such as the four views [Hofmeister, Nord, and Soni 2000].

Over time the architecture will have a tendency to *drift* from its original vision of implementation. Some of this drift will be natural and inevitable as requirements and designs become better known. Some of it will be caused by not considering up front that your product may be part of a product line. New customers will possibly require new features that they may view as "special." Such concerns are best addressed up front by designing a product line architecture [Weiss and Lai 1999].

Again, real life will likely interfere with your nice plans, since requirements and architecture concepts will be missing up front, detailed designs may have an impact on the high-level design, and development team members will think of better ways to do things. The chief architect must carefully evaluate each requested change to the architecture. The project manager must evaluate the potential impact of each change on the project. The best way to keep track of changes is periodically to update the architecture design specification so that major changes are captured and communicated to the development team members. Such a document is a living document, in the sense that team members gain useful information about the architecture description that they can apply when they do their detailed designs. There is no need for the design to exactly match the implementation of the code in all cases. Rather, the architecture description document serves primarily as a communications tool for the developers, especially when development is occurring at multiple sites.

9.3   Taking Responsibility

One of the subtle aspects of project management is taking charge of the project without overpowering the individual development team members' freedom to make local decisions. A good way to take control visibly is also to take responsibility. This means that it becomes obvious to all team members that the project manager has taken responsibility for the outcome of the project. This can be shown via words or actions. The result is the belief by team members that the project manager cares about the project, the team members, the product, and the ultimate success of the project. Simply stated, the project manager demonstrates responsibility by taking an interest in the activities of the team members without doing their jobs for them. Responsibility also becomes visible when the project manager celebrates and appreciates the successes of the team members as they achieve milestones and successfully complete their tasks throughout the project.

Assuming the project manager has visibly taken responsibility for the project, it is also significant when each team member takes responsibility for his part of the project. Project managers love it when engineers make statements like "I cannot support the release of this software, since I've uncovered some serious bugs," which show passion for the product and indicate that the developers are engaged in their work. Such statements can also cause headaches for the project manager when he must overrule a developer's passionate statements. But if an open discussion occurs concerning the pros and cons of a specific decision, the right decision often will be made. I enjoy working with engineers who show passion for their work and am always suspicious of those who appear more apathetic. If they appear not to care about their work output, then maybe the quality won't be as good.

Project management responsibility also includes being responsible for the performance, actions, well-being, and career progression of your team members. This management approach can be compared to the view of the project manager (or engineering manager in a line organization) as the captain of a ship. If the ship is sinking, the good captain helps get everyone into the life-boats before he saves himself. For the software project manager this could include providing career guidance for individual team members and recommending them for promotions, bonuses, and the like when they have done a good job. To summarize: There are no bad software engineers, only bad software project managers.

At Siemens, occasionally there are management assignments where a manager leading a work group, committee, or task force is given the functional title of *der Pate*, which translates to *godfather* in English. I view this as a godfather-like role with the responsibility for the team and the well-being of its members. Over time, these relationships can mature into a mentoring type of role where the manager takes responsibility for the career progression of certain team members.

9.4   When to Accept or Reject Changes

As already indicated, you will tend to want to protect your plans from too many changes. Thus, you will function as a gatekeeper and analyze each change request as it comes up. These change requests come from many sources over the life of a project—from marketing for new feature requests, from the chief architect and development team members for design changes, and from system-testing for defect corrections. Furthermore, if you don't add new team members or if your business sales are not as strong as projected, your management (or your customer) may attempt to cut your development budget as the fiscal year progresses.

As a general rule, it's a good idea to scrutinize each requested change and offer some initial resistance. Too many changes will jerk your development team around too much, creating confusion about tasks, schedules, and project goals. You may be forced to create a special plan *du jour,* especially the last few days before a release, although this should be the exception rather than the rule. Accepting too many changes will create an environment where the development plan is not well known or understood, since things will be changing too frequently. Furthermore, you should communicate every significant decision about a change in project direction to all development team members, after it has been made.

Given that too much change is bad for the project, what criteria should you apply for accepting or rejecting change requests? In general, accept only those change requests that clearly improve the product from a cost, quality, or sales perspective or that improve the project from a schedule, cost, or efficiency perspective. To consider an extreme example, if a team member tells you she has an idea that will cut the time to market in half, don't respond that this disturbs your development plan. Rather, evaluate the merits and risks of the proposal. If it truly will cut the time to market in half without causing you to do something illegal or unethical or adversely impacting the project or product cost or quality, then throw out your current plan and implement the new plan. Still, you will need to do a careful analysis of the trade-offs involved with accepting the proposed change. Usually, great ideas that reduce time to market require additional investment, either for more people or for license fees for off-the-shelf product purchases. You will need to consider, for example, whether your company can support the additional investment. Often, spending additional R&D money to get a product to market more quickly will be a good investment if it results in additional sales or profits sooner and over the life of the product. You will need to define some possible outcome scenarios and run the numbers, or ask your financial analyst to look at whether the additional investment money is likely to be recovered in the future.

Fortunately, most organizations will also have some built-in resistance to change processes, so you will not always have to be the naysayer shooting down all the great ideas of the team members. Investments in many organizations need multiple signature approvals. Levels of control are put into place concerning **engineering change requests (ECRs)** and **engineering change orders (ECOs)**, depending on the progress of the product design. Many organizations with hardware development activities have **engineering review boards (ERBs)** for considering and deciding on implementation of ECRs. In hardware engineering, many of the ECRs are cost reduction related; i.e., if we make this change of component or design and we save x dollars per unit and produce y units, then we can save the company $x \bullet y$ dollars. Once the savings are understood, the ERB can decide whether to make the change or not, also depending on the engineering effort involved in implementing the change and any possible adverse consequences, such as decreased product quality or reliability.

For software projects, you can borrow some of the same processes that hardware engineering organizations use to help you adequately and consistently consider all the change requests. For example, you can establish an

ERB-like group that reviews the test results coming from system testing. This release criteria ERB can then evaluate each defect or change request as it is reported, and then decide if it should be corrected, deferred, or not acted on before release. In this way, you'll have a structured approach to consider all the change requests coming from system testing, evaluate the impact of each change, and then decide on whether the change should be implemented. Also, by establishing a process and committee for decision making, you will better reveal decision alternatives and differences of opinion for each change request.

When making technical decisions, the chief architect and the project manager should allow open discussions of alternatives until a set time. Then they make their decision and handle the next issue. The person closest to the implementation should have the strongest voice when making the decision. This is the "whoever has to code it decides" rule. Timely decisions are most important, since the lack of a decision can hamper the productivity of the entire development team. If a bad decision is made, it can often be changed later. The cost to making the changes resulting from a bad technical decision is often less than the cost of the productivity loss when multiple team members are forced to wait for a decision. Conversely, you'd like to delay decisions that are not needed by the team so that you have the most up-to-date information before making a decision. We call this general process "just-in-time decision making."

TIP: Try to recognize the reasons behind your gut reactions.

Another manager and I had the same reaction to a situation described by a development team member in an e-mail message. The team member explained that the product manager decided to leave out the feature he was working on for the next release. This particular feature had a fairly long list of reported defects associated with it, and the developer was struggling to get it to work. Our immediate gut reaction was that the developer was attempting to shirk his responsibility, i.e., to get out of doing the work to get the feature to operate reliably. On further discussion with the product manager, we realized that there were valid marketing reasons to drop this particular feature. But our initial reaction was one of disappointment that the developer didn't succeed in completing his task.

9.5   Ethical Decisions of the Project Manager

There are two types of change requests that the project manager should always reject: requests that cause the project manager or any team member to do something illegal and those that cause them to do something unethical. Such requests must never even be seriously considered. The risk of harm to the project, company, and individuals involved is too great.

There are many examples of project managers doing illegal actions for the benefit of their project, company, or development team, such as falsifying time sheets for government contracts and misrepresenting clinical test data for new medical device software. Every day you can read in the newspapers about industrial crimes (committed not just by software project managers) involving insider stock trading, unfair competitive practices, industrial espionage, Internet viruses, and the like. Such crimes will always be committed. But software project managers must guard against being so overzealous that they consider illegal actions. The risk is too high that such illegal actions will be discovered, and the project manager could end up in jail. In my opinion, no job is worth taking such a large personal risk. If your project fails, there are other project management opportunities at either your company or another. You can also always return to more technical work, function as a project leader, become a quality assurance support person, or the like. Your project's success is not worth any conceivable risk of a personal nature.

As a project manager, you must be familiar with and conscious of the various laws associated with managing the people on your project. In the United States, this includes laws associated with sex, age, religion, race, or nationality discrimination. You will need to be aware of unfortunate situations that can occur within social organizations like project teams. For example, for an incident of sexual harassment, you will need to take clear and timely action. Your first action for any such suspected incident will be to report it to your human resources staff. They will have training and expertise in handling such situations and will help you to follow the applicable laws and company policies.

The same guidelines apply to unethical actions. However, exactly what is unethical is not so clear. By my definition, an unethical action has the potential to harm someone, e.g., their career, reputation, personal life, livelihood. A general guideline for project managers when making decisions is always to ask what the right thing to do is. If a discovered defect has the potential to harm someone who uses your product, then correct the defect before you ship the product. Most of these decisions will be correct if common sense is applied, multiple people are involved in either making or reviewing the decisions, and there isn't a "win at all costs" culture instituted by the management of your company. A project manager has an ethical responsibility to do the best possible job within the constraints of his personal capabilities and the legal and moral constraints of the organization in which he works.

One of the more difficult ethical situations will be when you are faced with firing someone. As a project manager you may not have this responsibility, since line management might handle it. But you may provide inputs to line management concerning an individual's poor performance. If such negative inputs are provided off-the-cuff, i.e., without thinking about the circumstances and consequences of the feedback, you may do someone an injustice. Losing one's job can have significant emotional and financial implications. When you prepare for such a termination action, you must have reliable and measurable performance data built up over a period of time. Most companies define a warning or probationary period when new employees or employees with suspected performance problems are warned and monitored more closely, often by multiple managers. You also have a responsibility to ensure that your company gets good output and value for its human resources investment. Ignoring, hiding, or moving a problem employee among projects without any type of improvement or correction plan for the employee wastes company money.

At one time, I had a software engineer on one of my projects who clearly had no idea how to perform his tasks. His performance was significantly lower than anyone on the team, and the other team members recognized his lack of technical competence. (Often, other team members will observe a performance problem before you do.) It became clear to me that this individual needed to be removed from the project and the software engineering organization. When confronting this individual about the possibility of losing his job, he appeared almost relieved, and we quickly began discussing career alternatives. This individual realized that software engineering might not be the best career alternative for him. After he left the company, he kept in touch with me and reported on his progress in his new career. This particular termination situation worked out well, but such performance discussions often elicit emotional reactions, denials, defensiveness, and so on, that need to be overcome before the individual realistically looks at the next career step. Of course, these performance and career-related job mismatches are given more time and responsibility on the part of the manager than the no-tolerance type of termination situations, such as for illegal substance use or sexual harassment in the workplace. Your human resources department will have clear guidelines established regarding these no-tolerance situations.

> **TIP: Frequently remind yourself that it's only a job.**
>
> When you are caught up with the challenges of software project management, it's important not to take your work too seriously. Your job is not worth hurting your health, family life, friendships, and so on. Always be willing to walk away from your project if the pressure becomes too severe or you find yourself doing things you are uncomfortable with. Try not to worry too much about the things that you cannot control—natural disasters, honest mistakes, company politics, policies.

9.6 Summary

This chapter provided some guidelines on how to make trade-off decisions as your project is implemented. Your decisions concerning what modifications to your software development plan you will accept or reject will depend on the specific situation. I hope that you will make decisions consistent with achieving the project goals and that you will always reject any changes that may be illegal or ethically wrong.

CHAPTER 10

Incremental Development

On the IS2000 project, we knew that there was no way to implement all the features requested by marketing within the time frame and development team size we were constrained by. Incremental development gave us the alternative of defining feature releases that we could review with marketing and implement a little at a time. Not only did this help us negotiate feature priorities with marketing, but it helped organize the development sequence and provided an initial set of limited functionality that marketing was willing to sell as a package. Having a software architecture and component development estimates provide the project manager with the information necessary to implement an incremental development.

I HAVE experienced planning and implementing projects using an incremental development approach, and I believe it is a good development practice for many software projects. Incremental development (also called *iterative development*) helps to reduce the risks associated with requirements churn, short time to market, usability, and quality, since the product is developed feature by feature. Since functionality is introduced to the product in increments, you can define snapshot-engineering releases and provide them to a testing function to incrementally test the product as it is developed. Once a subset of the desired functionality is operational, users can begin to test or use the software product.

Chapter 2 discussed release planning. For the types of projects that I have been involved with, much of the requirements analysis and architecture design is done in a high-level design phase, prior to development. Clearly, there will be changes to requirements and the high-level design as features are designed and implemented during each increment. But most of the development team effort during each increment will be involved with detailed design, coding, and unit testing. As a rule of thumb (see Section 2.5), the time between incremental releases should be eight weeks or less. While the developers are preparing the next release, the system testers are examining the most recent incremental release and providing test results to the developers so that quality can be improved while the product is being developed.

10.1   Baselining the Software Development Plan

Part Two discussed how the project manager and the development team do not commit to implementing a development schedule until the architecture design is complete and the bottom-up estimates are done for each component identified in the design. In fact, the development schedule, documented within the **software development plan** (SDP), is detailed enough only for the first increment, and then you redo it or baseline it for each following release at the beginning of the increment. Thus, you create new versions of the SDP for each incremental release. In practice, you usually generate two versions. The first version is a "proposed" version that the development team can comment on, and the second version is the committed-to plan for implementing the next increment.

The effect of this approach to incremental development is that project planning continues as the product is being implemented. When baselining the SDP, the project manager is taking into consideration what may have changed since the last plan was made, what was achieved or omitted, what risks need to be addressed, and what adjustments must be made to the staffing or project organization. The new baselined version of the SDP is actually a short-term plan for the next eight or so weeks of development, assuming you follow the rules of thumb. Shorter incremental projects are easier to plan and manage than longer and larger projects. The baselined SDP also can function as a communications vehicle to identify any major changes affecting the project. If a new serious risk emerges as part of the current development increment, you can identify it in the baselined SDP for the next increment. You can define tasks and assign staff to help mitigate the risk in the next increment, e.g., developing a prototype of a particularly risky feature for marketing to evaluate.

Multiple versions of the SDP for each increment are not meant to change the overall project goals, major milestones, or product functionality. However, during real-life projects, things change, and baselining the SDP before each increment helps to identify the changes and allow for the additional planning during development to accommodate the changes. By creating multiple versions of the SDP, you can document project changes throughout development. This is particularly useful after you complete the current project, perform a postmortem audit on the project, and then start the planning for your next project. The SDP also helps refresh top management's memory when they remember only the delivery dates and not the functionality promised or the planning assumptions that went into projecting the dates.

10.2 Build Planning and Management

Chapter 2 showed you how to use the *build plan* for generating the schedule and the SDP. As part of baselining the SDP for each incremental release, you will add to the build plan for the intermediate builds to be achieved for the next increment. You may have to move some features that did not get successfully implemented from an earlier increment to the next increment. You may have to redo some features from a prior increment for a future increment. You also may have planned some prototype feature implementations in prior increments that you will now have to replace with production-quality code or code that implements different functionality.

After completing the initial build plan, you will be creating new versions of it prior to baselining the SDP at the beginning of each increment. Your build plans will likely implement very little visible functionality in the beginning. In fact, the first increment should probably serve primarily as a prototype of the architecture (vertical slice). In later builds, you will add functionality, feature by feature, focusing earlier on infrastructure components and most of the easier features, except for high-priority features with perceived high implementation risk. You should implement such difficult-to-implement, high-priority features in earlier increments, since the entire project's success could be jeopardized if they are unsuccessfully added at the very end of the development.

The *release plan* provides a framework of feature sets and targeted release dates. You will also update this before each increment. You will likely negotiate the feature set with your product manager for each increment. After the proposed SDP is circulated, you will probably need to modify the release plan to reflect reality, for example, who is available to work on which features, what has to be redone, which code is prototype versus production quality.

As you get closer to delivering the product to real users, you will need to put more emphasis on quality improvement when you baseline the SDP and plan these later incremental releases. In general, it's difficult to work on bug fixes and new features at the same time. The risk of side effects increases as you add new features to the system. You will become frustrated, because you seem to move backwards rather than forwards when something that worked before no longer works due to changes that affect the infrastructure or that break things. Thus, you should plan some of the final incremental releases mainly as bug-fixing releases. Although you did some testing and fixing as part of earlier increments, it's a good practice to focus on quality improvement and fixing as many bugs as possible during the last increments. Release criteria and techniques to manage the test and fix activities during these later builds are discussed later.

10.3 Getting Everyone Involved

When implementing a development project, it's important to get everyone involved in planning, striving for success, and achieving milestones along the way. It is uncomfortable for a project manager to feel that he is leading but that not everyone is following, like the military officer who yells "Charge!," starts running up a hill defended by the enemy, and then looks around to find that no one is behind him. My approach to scheduling a project is to solicit buy-in from every development team member so that the project schedule becomes the team's schedule. In my experience, if a development team believes they can achieve the schedule, then they will. It becomes a self-fulfilling prophecy. Thus, the first version of the SDP for each increment contains a schedule, a "proposed plan" in which every team member identified in the schedule has a chance to look at his tasks and point out inconsistencies, problems, risks, and so on. In some cases, these problems are real and the schedule needs to be adjusted. In some cases, the issues need to be negotiated or risks need to be mitigated by other means (e.g., add a second person to a task that has to be done by a particular date).

The way to respond to the proposed schedule is for each team member to provide feedback to the project manager on any problems and then to generate a "personal schedule" that identifies the tasks he will perform each week during the schedule. It becomes the team member's "personal commitment" to meet the schedule to the best of his ability. Most people try their hardest to meet commitments they have made to their management and other team members. If no feedback is given to the project manager concerning the proposed schedule, he should assume it is OK, and the final schedule, with any suggested and negotiated modifications, becomes the project team's commitment to management to deliver a product on the identified milestone date.

Remember: The release delivery date is a hard, fixed date. The details and intermediate milestones will likely fluctuate as the product is being developed. After all, it is only a plan and plans become much clearer as they are implemented. What is most important is that status is reviewed every week and team members are forthcoming with information so that the plans can be modified, if necessary, to ensure the delivery date. Also remember that all projects slip a week at a time, but if you know it when it happens you may still be able to recover. What isn't good for the project is when team members don't identify problems or wait until the end of the development increment to reveal them.

10.4 Tracking Progress

Chapter 6 discussed the use of the development status teleconference to track projects that are developed at multiple sites. Even for projects being done at a single location, there is a need to track project progress weekly. Get into the habit of comparing progress with the baselined development plan every week to give yourself the opportunity to introduce corrective actions to stick close to the plan without falling more than a week behind on your schedule. Some slips cannot easily be corrected, when unexpected events occur or much more work is required to achieve a task than was originally planned. But if you have a good idea of where everyone on your medium-size project is with respect to accomplishing their tasks, you can often move people around to support each other in achieving most of the tasks on time. Usually, if you are implementing your development schedule and meeting the release milestones, many other project variables, like the development budget, will also track your plan.

There are basically two ways to track progress, and I support doing them both every week. One way is through personal inquiry. This can be achieved by a "management by walking around" style, where you informally ask everyone on the project how things are going. This is practical only for medium-size projects in one location where you personally know all developers and their primary assignments. For larger projects that require some type of management hierarchy, you can still apply the personal inquiry approach to your project team leaders and other key contributors. On one project, my chief architect would usually stop by my office on the way into and out of work for a short status report. This way I was able to give him my status or concerns while he was able to tell me how things were proceeding from his perspective. Having an office near the building entrance/exit is helpful with this way of tracking progress.

Another way to track progress is through weekly status meetings. This is similar to the development status teleconference, but in a conference room at one site. Team members get to state what they have achieved during the past week as compared to their personal schedules. They can also identify any problems that they can use support for and report information (e.g., lessons learned, possible risks, actions missing from the plan) that may be of interest to the entire team. If the status meetings are held at the same time almost every week and they are kept short, most team members will not find them too burdensome. The project manager must structure the meetings so that key status information will be reported, discussions requiring considerable time are taken offline, and shared lessons learned or problems are interesting to the majority of the team members. The project manager can also use the weekly status meetings to communicate overall project progress and the achievement of important goals and milestones. He can also use it to introduce new team members and communicate any changes to the development plan or high-priority tasks. Again, the weekly status meeting must be scaled depending on the team size and the availability of an appropriate meeting room. The goals and agenda for such a weekly status meeting are given in Table 10.1. We often would hold this meeting toward the end of the workweek so that if critical tasks must be completed, team members may plan to work on them over the weekend.

If you have to miss a weekly meeting due to travel or other constraints, it's probably good to ask a delegate to facilitate the meeting or have the team

Table 10.1 *Weekly Status Meeting Goals and Agenda.*

Purpose: To review development project progress and communicate information to the development team.

Outcome vision: Development status is known, and actions are identified for any mid-course corrections.

Customer: Project management and all team members.

Success criteria: Individual status is communicated, issues are raised, and follow-up actions are identified.

Timeline:
- Start and agenda review: 9:30
- General project status/information: 9:35
- Individual status reports: 9:45
- Issues requiring follow-up actions: 10:15
- Wrap-up and feedback: 10:25
- Complete: 10:30

members e-mail you a short summary of their progress and any outstanding issues. This helps create disciplined work habits within a regular routine. It also helps force the team members to keep track of their personal schedules and learn to bring up appropriate issues that you can respond to with possible corrections. In theory, with weekly reporting and some flexibility with your resources, you will never be more than a week behind your planned schedule. Unfortunately, this is not easy to achieve, since when someone doesn't complete her assigned task, you may not have the right skills to reassign it to someone else, and it can also affect the tasks of the other person. Normally, you don't have enough or the right types of people to help put out fires when they come up.

Both the personal inquiry and status meeting approaches will work well only if the project manager is good at not overreacting to bad news concerning project status. You want problems to surface in such meetings so that they are never more than a week old, giving you a chance to attempt to correct them. What you don't want is for someone to say every week that everything is going fine and then the week before the release you discover that progress is nowhere near the plan. For such individuals, you may also want to rely on the personal inquiry approach rather than just information received during the status meeting. If you consistently overreact to bad news, many team members will eventually avoid giving you bad news. While I'm not suggesting that you hide your emotions, I am advising that you avoid discussing deficiencies in someone's approach or work habits in the public forum of the status meetings. Clearly, a team member who consistently misses his personal schedule will have diminished prestige in your view, but you should discuss your personal dissatisfaction with his performance and any corrective or improvement actions one-on-one.

10.5 Incremental Testing

One of the advantages of incremental development is that it allows incremental testing. As each engineering release is frozen, it can be turned over to your system-testing function. I typically provide a limited set of release notes with the incremental release. These release notes contain lists of what has been changed since the last engineering release. This includes added features and corrected defects.

While system testing is testing the most recent engineering release, the developers are working on the next release. This allows development and testing to occur in parallel. It is convenient if the testing function can provide test results to development before the next incremental release is frozen. This way, defect corrections can be worked on and included in the next incremental release. As the incremental releases get closer to a production release that may be shipped to users, you can place more effort on defect correction and less on new feature development. A tight cycle of test, fix, and retest is necessary as the production release time gets closer.

Ideally, testers should be located as close as possible to the developers. This may be difficult when special hardware is required for testing or for global development, where the testers may be in another site than some of the developers. Quality can be achieved only by a quick test, fix, retest cycle that is done the last few days before the release. Automated testing helps support the quick turnaround times necessary for incremental testing [Dustin, Rashkin, and Paul 1999].

It's difficult to add new features and build quality into the software at the same time. Thus, it's important to have some test results toward the middle of the incremental build cycle. This way, the developers can spend much of their effort adding new features during the first part of the incremental build cycle and then focus more on fixing defects during the second part of the cycle.

TIP: Meet your incremental release milestone dates.

The best way for a project manager to impress his management is to ship on time. Incremental development helps achieve this. When you consistently meet your incremental release delivery dates that are scheduled less than eight weeks apart, your management will be very happy. Most software projects do not meet their release dates, and management often does not have good visibility into the progress of the development. As you make the schedule/functionality trade-offs during the last few days of the incremental release cycle, consider that your management and customers will likely remember that you shipped on time and not remember that some small feature was missing from the release.

10.6   Release Criteria Meeting

As you get closer to the target incremental release date, you will need to monitor progress daily rather than weekly. You will likely get into a daily cycle in which you review new and open defect reports in the morning and then decide which defects will be corrected and who will make the fixes. The assigned developers will work on the corrections for the defects that have been assigned to them. Later in the day, the fixes will be included in a new build of the system. Depending on the severity of the defects and if they stop testing progress, system testing may continue testing on the new build or remain on the last incremental release. The next morning you will again look at the new defects. You will repeat this daily cycle the last few days before a release until you decide that the quality level of the incremental release is sufficient so that you can freeze and then release.

One approach to managing the last few days before an incremental release is to use a release criteria meeting. This meeting reviews the test results and then decides on the severity of the defects and who will fix them. The meeting also reviews the status of ongoing corrections. For a global development team, the meeting will likely be conducted as a teleconference. The meeting should include the project decision makers (e.g., the project manager and product manager), a system testing representative, and key developers who are working on critical defects. Table 10.2 gives the goals and agenda for a typical release criteria meeting. The release criteria meeting should be held every day until the release is frozen. If your development process is mature enough, you may also use the meeting to identify the source of the defects. This information is valuable if you are considering applying more sophisticated process techniques, such as defect prevention analysis.

TIP: Create a top-10 bug list.

Unfortunately, testing cannot be avoided regardless of how good your architecture is. In addition to functional testing, you will also need to do usability and performance testing. Make a top-10 bug list of the most important open defects, to raise the visibility of defect correction in the project. Plan to spend some time during the incremental release cycle when only bugs are being fixed and new-feature development stops. Remember the rule of thumb that 40% of your effort will be involved in testing.

Table 10.2 *Release Criteria Meeting Goals and Agenda.*

Purpose: To review outstanding known defects in order to determine if and when to release.

Outcome vision: Decisions are made concerning which defects to fix and which to defer.

Customer: Project and product management and all team members.

Success criteria: Software quality is known, release criteria are satisfied, and a formal decision is made to release to system testing or to the market.

Timeline:
- Start and agenda review: 9:30
- New defects: 9:35
- Open defects: 9:55
- Other work: 10:15
- Wrap-up and feedback: 10:25
- Complete: 10:30

10.7 Tooling

There are certain software tools required to do incremental development. For incremental development across multiple development sites, the tools must be capable of being remotely accessed. Two critical areas of tooling are configuration management and defect tracking [White 2000].

Configuration management controls source code so that integration can be managed by the buildmeister and multiple engineers do not make changes to the same code at the same time. A good, reliable configuration management tool is required to make the almost daily integration builds involved with incremental development. For a distributed development team, that may be working in different time zones at different times of the workday, a configuration management system is required that can be reliably accessed by all the remote team members. If the tool or the server that contains the project source code is not functional, the progress of the entire team will be negatively impacted. When setting up and planning a new project, configuration management is an area where the project manager should obtain the best tools available.

A defect-tracking tool is not quite so critical as configuration management, but for incremental development to succeed, a good tool is necessary. Defects will be put into status categories (e.g., new, open, fixed, closed), priorities and fix assignments made, and notations added as corrections are investigated. Thus, this is a tool the project manager will use very frequently as incremental release dates get closer. Again, for a distributed development team, remote access to the defect database is necessary. Each developer must be able to view the defects that have been assigned to him for correction. The project manager must be able to query and sort the information in the defect database to help determine if release criteria have been satisfied (e.g., we'll ship when there are no open defects at a high priority).

10.8 Summary

I recommend incremental development as a good practice for most software development projects. It's rewarding to the development team and everyone associated with the project to see the product built up, feature by feature. It provides good visibility on the progress of development and gives the project manager many close milestones to measure overall progress. Testing can proceed in parallel rather than waiting until the end of the development. Assuming acceptable quality, the latest build can be frozen and used as an incremental release that can go to system testing and eventually to users of the product.

CHAPTER 11

Creating Visibility and Avoiding Surprises

I once worked in an organization where there were frequent surprises with respect to what features were committed for delivery to specific customers. In fact, I once ran into difficulty when I unknowingly informed a customer of the future development plans for a specific feature the customer had already paid for and was impatiently waiting for. In this organization, development schedules were not visible and salespeople often "sold" features that were merely research ideas or on the bottom of a long queue of "desired" features. From that point on, I learned that it's better to make your software architecture, development schedules, and status highly visible, since organizations that depend on you can plan accordingly and help avoid surprises.

Your project will run much more smoothly if everyone is aware of its progress and the possibility of surprises is minimized. You will want to have good visibility of the progress status of each team member. Your management wants to have visibility concerning how the overall project is progressing, with an early warning of potential problems that might jeopardize achieving the project's goals. Such visibility is even more important for globally distributed projects, where you will not have frequent personal contact with team members located at remote sites. Due to time zone differences, it may take a day to inform everyone of an impending problem.

In an ideal world, you will design the architecture and then implement the software product in accordance with the architecture and the development plan. But problems will come up that require modifications to both the architecture and the development plan. The likelihood of such problems will be described within the risk analysis. But problems you never thought of in advance will also surface from time to time. You will need to communicate these new problems and once you have identified a solution you will need to act quickly to get the project back to its existing plan or a new one. Your success as a project manager will be measured not only on how well you implement the development plan but also on how well you react to the surprises you cannot avoid.

11.1   Risk Management

Chapter 3 discussed how risk analysis builds upon the list of potential risks that come out of an architecture evaluation, such as ATAM, and the issues, strategies, and project strategy conclusions that come from global analysis. Figure 3.3, reproduced here as Figure 11.1, shows how risk analysis fits in the project planning process.

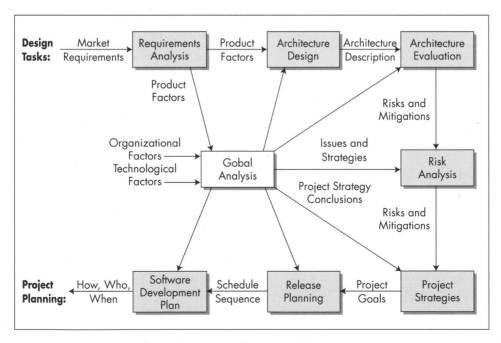

Figure 11.1 *How Risk Analysis Fits in the Project Planning Process.*

When implementing the project, you will carry out your risk mitigation actions as tasks scheduled in each incremental development cycle. You will adjust your implementation plans to compensate for the potential risks. For example, you may assign your best developer to a component that could be complicated to implement, or you may ask your chief architect to work closely with a developer who is struggling to keep up with the schedule.

As unexpected risks arise, you will need to modify your development plans. To anticipate the unexpected, you should keep some staff hours in reserve to help put out fires. For example, keep your chief architect off high-priority development tasks so that he can be made available to assist other team members when they experience difficulties or to look at fixing bugs that may affect the architecture design.

You may wish to use some of your personal time to mitigate unexpected risks or fight fires. You may need to roll up your sleeves and help solve unexpected problems or provide assistance to team members struggling with their tasks. If you believe that achieving adequate testing is a risk for the project, you may wish to run some of your own tests on the latest engineering release. Such testing activities will also give you firsthand information concerning your software quality, performance, and usability.

Although such efforts to help out with development will likely be viewed positively by team members, you must take caution not to spend so much time on development tasks that you ignore your project management responsibilities. This could hurt the overall progress of the project and thus create new and bigger fires to fight.

You also must take caution not to do someone's job for him. Taking on someone's task so that she can apply her efforts to a more important task may help project progress. But taking on someone's task because she is incompetent, lazy, or uncooperative would be inappropriate and could hurt overall team morale. Be careful you don't readily accept tasks from team members who rightly should be doing the work themselves.

For real-world projects, one of your most substantial risk areas will involve managing the migration strategies associated with replacing an existing product with the new product you are developing. Commonly, the migration plan brings up a number of risks you will need to pay attention to during development. For example, some of your development team members may be pulled back into working on the current product if an important defect is discovered during field use. To some extent your project may be dependent on the status of the current product. You may be planning to reuse parts of the old product in the new one. Quality problems may surface with this reused code, and you may need to replace it with new code or modify your staffing plan to supply more people with experience on the reused code. You probably will have addressed the migration plan when you did risk analysis as the architecture was being designed. But you will need to react to unplanned field events and the status of the current product maintenance team as you are implementing the new product.

11.2 Communicating Status and Issues

Just as you don't like surprises when project tasks are not completed successfully, your management will not like surprises associated with meeting your delivery dates. Missed delivery dates can negatively impact sales projections. When sales opportunities are missed, revenue is reduced and thus profits are also reduced.

You need to clearly communicate to your management the overall status concerning the progress of the project, and you need to bring up important issues that could negatively affect meeting your project's goals. Probably the most common of these issues that need to be communicated have to do with staff availability. When you have a development plan that anticipates a certain staffing level and the people are not available to work on the project, your schedule will likely slip. Such issues where you are depending on your management to provide something that is critical to the success of the project are the types of issues that must be communicated. Not only do you communicate the status concerning the issue, but you can also remind your management of the consequences if the issue is not resolved. For example, it would be appropriate to communicate that if two testers are not made available by the next incremental release date, you will not have good test data and thus quality may not be as good as planned.

Since you and the chief architect are the primary decision makers for the project, it is important for avoiding surprises that you keep track of which decisions have been made, which decisions need to be made, and which decisions are being changed. You will likely maintain some type of list indicating the decisions you have made and when you made them. Of course, you will also need a process for making decisions and forcing closure. This process will likely be coupled to how you track status, such as during the weekly status meeting. Maintaining a long list of issues that never seem to get resolved should serve as a red flag to your management that you are not adequately fulfilling your role as a primary decision maker.

Experiment with the way you provide status and issues information to your management. Different people absorb information differently, depending on the communication medium. For people who are visual learners you will need to provide status information using presentation charts and tables. When working with managers for the first time, pick a communication approach that is easiest for you in the beginning. For example, if it's quicker and easier for you to stop by your manager's office and give him an oral status report rather than taking the time to generate a written report, try that communication approach first. If you have trouble getting some of his time with the oral approach, or conversely if you spend endless hours in his office explaining too many details, you may want to switch to a written form of status communication. You may ask project managers who have more working experience with your manager what communication approaches worked best for them. Or you can ask your manager if there's any special format or frequency he prefers for receiving status information.

You should also filter status information so as to respect your boss's time. Too much detailed information on issues your boss cannot influence may provide fuel for lively conversation, but it will waste both of your time and not help the project progress. To some extent, the amount of information will correspond to the importance of the information. If you need to purchase something that was not in your original plan but is nevertheless critical to the success of the project, you should prepare enough detailed information so that the benefits of making the investment or the risks of not making the investment are clearly stated.

Experiment also with how you collect status information from your team members. Again, efficient, streamlined communications are the goal. The weekly status meetings described in Chapter 10 are a starting point.

11.3 Building Credibility with Management

As you implement your project, you will be providing status information to your management and raising issues that you will hopefully solve with the support of your management. You can build credibility over time with your management by providing information consistently and always doing what you say you will do. If your management believes that you successfully resolve most of the issues that arise, then when you bring up a really big issue, they will pay attention to it. If you consistently meet your delivery dates, then they will pay attention when you bring up an issue that can substantially affect the next release date. Consistency of communications and actions will build credibility over time. You will know this credibility is being established when your management requests less detailed status information and seems to respond better when you bring up important issues.

As a general rule it's often best to bring up some candidate solutions when you bring up a problem to your management. If you're anticipating a schedule slip, it's often good to also present possible solution scenarios, e.g., what might happen if you add staff or reduce functionality. Your management should support you and your project, but they should not make decisions for you.

TIP: Control the solution space when raising the visibility of potential problems.

We're often confronted towards the end of the fiscal year with what the impact may be of cutting project resources and expenses. This is one reason to spend your project budget funds early in the fiscal year. But when discussing such potential problems with your management, give them only those solution alternatives that are acceptable to you. If cutting your budget should not slip your development schedule from your point of view, then don't provide such a solution scenario. Rather, identify which features could be dropped as a consequence of cutting the development budget, and provide multiple functionality alternatives to choose from. Make sure to include among the acceptable alternatives the features you've been having trouble implementing, that have not yet been adequately planned or staffed, or that your development team does not find very interesting to implement.

11.4 Recognizing and Celebrating Success

Just as you bring up issues with your management as your project progresses, you should also bring up key accomplishments. Communicate to management and all development team members accomplishments, such as meeting engineering release dates, and celebrate all the major accomplishments. These celebrations can assume various forms, such as taking key team members out to lunch or ordering out for pizza. The form of the celebration will depend very much on your particular company and country culture. For example, Chapter 6 mentioned that some cultures prefer to discuss issues or problems rather than accomplishments. There will be differing local customs and laws concerning the use of alcoholic beverages.

The form of the celebration is not extremely important, assuming that you do not violate any local laws or company policies. What is most important is that the accomplishment be recognized, the team members are thanked for their efforts, and the team gets a short respite before they tackle the next major milestone. Your management will naturally enjoy hearing more about your successes than your problems. Remember to invite your management to as many celebrations as they have the time to participate in. Sometimes, they may even pick up the check for a celebration lunch. On the DPS2000 project, we often did a *demo du jour* to view the successful achievement of newly developed features.

TIP: Monitor your project's success by monitoring your waistline.

You will likely gain weight working on a successful development project. This is because many of the celebrations you throw as key milestones are met will involve food, such as team pizza and lunch parties. Furthermore, if you are working on a global development project, you will be traveling to the remote development sites, where you will also likely celebrate your project successes with meals. And you will probably meet with your team members and management during evening meals. As suggested in Chapter 6, you will attempt to get to know your remotely located colleagues outside of the normal work environment, probably while sharing food or drink. You should also monitor your physical and emotional health as your project progresses. Be aware of any effects that might be caused by long-term stress. If your project is not going well, you may find yourself becoming more irritable and impatient, which in turn could have a negative effect on your team.

11.5 Summary

Providing the appropriate visibility for your project and managing risks well will establish your reputation as a project manager. Only after completing a number of projects over many years will you be considered a "successful" project manager. But your day-to-day interactions with your management and your team will help establish your credibility as a leader. If your team and management have confidence in you as project manager, they will also likely have confidence that the project will succeed. Remember to celebrate your project's accomplishments and to spread recognition for achieving the key milestones to as many team members who deserve the credit.

CHAPTER 12

Staying Calm in the Heat of Battle

I once worked on a project whose delivery was tied directly to a major trade show. If we had nothing to demonstrate at the trade show, the company would be extremely embarrassed. Our product was the cornerstone of a suite of products, and we planned an announcement for a major corporate strategic thrust into a new business area. As you could imagine, the pressure on the development team was unbelievable, and team members were literally working around the clock developing the show release. After we successfully met this milestone and the team was reduced in size, many team members commented to me that my calm demeanor helped them get through the high-pressure environment.

PROJECT management is not always easy, particularly in the implementation phase of a project, when unexpected problems may arise. You and your team may need to struggle to keep up with your scheduled milestones and to stick to your development plan. You likely will have planned your project to be challenging to the development team to give your company a good return on its engineering investment. You will want your product to get to market as quickly as possible so that it can start producing revenue for your company.

Some weeks the pressure for meeting the project goals will make you feel like you are involved in a war against fate, your management, new technologies, or whatever obstacles hinder your project's progress. As you react to the stress of project management, your team members will be watching you. If you stay calm when things go wrong and maintain a basic optimism and confidence that you can achieve the project goals, the team will likely stay calm as well. If you panic, team members will also probably panic. Having a well-designed software architecture to implement can help maintain your optimism through the difficult times. This chapter offers tips for keeping your composure and optimism as you implement your project during stressful times.

12.1 Cheerleading, Micro-Management, and Discipline

As discussed in Chapter 7, each team member will need a different amount of support and direction depending on his experience level and the specific task he's working on. The project manager must be flexible concerning the amount of direction and support given, depending on the individual and situation. Similarly, you must be flexible concerning your management style and approach as you communicate to team members. If you overreact, you will be accused of being too excitable. If you underreact, you will be viewed as not caring.

The individuals on the team and the team as a group will respond differently to disparate types of communication styles. Some team members may prefer a direct, loud style of communication, while others may prefer a softer, more indirect approach. I once assisted a coach on a youth hockey team who during time-outs would yell at the players while pointing out what they did wrong and how they had to improve in order to win the game. For games in which the score wasn't close, he would have less to say. Often, some of the players would comment that they couldn't go back and play well without being yelled at. For this particular team, a loud communication style seemed to get the best results. As a project manager, you should be flexible with your communication style and experiment in the beginning about which style gets the best results. In the case of a software project, good results are achieved when the team members are strongly motivated to meet the goals of the project. The next few sections give some examples of communication styles you might try during the effort to mobilize your team members to best meet the project goals.

12.1.1 Cheerleading

A cheerleading type of communication style involves continual vocal encouragement to the team. When tasks and milestones are successfully achieved, there is much visible celebration and credit is given to the successful team members. This style works well at the beginning of a project, when the project manager is trying to boost the self-confidence of the development team members while trying to encourage and convince them that they can succeed. Cheerleading may be most appropriate for a project team that needs a lot of support. Cheerleading project managers are perceived as having a great interest in the team and its outcome. In many cultures, the team members generally appreciate the encouragement and interest of their manager. In other project cultures, the project manager as cheerleader is viewed suspiciously. The team, in this case, may view the manager as being naive or superficial.

Many project managers are cheerleaders even when its expression is not visible. You have developed a plan and during implementation are hoping the team will be able to successfully achieve it. Since you cannot personally do every task in your plan, you are forced to shout encouragement from the sidelines. Whenever a milestone is successfully met, you are thinking about how much better it is to communicate good news rather than bad news to your management, and patting yourself on the back that you planned a project that can indeed be successfully implemented. With incremental development (Chapter 10), your engineering release milestones will be fairly close together, so you have plenty of opportunities for cheering, encouraging, and celebrating good results.

12.1.2 Micro-Management

Micro-management works best when team members need a lot of direction and support. With this style you will "sweat the details" while becoming involved with the daily work of the development team members. You will need to micro-manage tasks that are very important to the outcome of the project. For example, depending on your project goals, you will likely want to micro-manage the tasks leading to the decision to release the product, since its quality can make or break its acceptance in the market. This is particularly true for products that have any safety-critical performance characteristics. You will want to know all the details in order to make the correct decisions concerning important project issues.

In some project cultures, the micro-manager is viewed as being intrusive. Some engineers may have the attitude "Why pay me to do a job when my manager is going to constantly interfere?" In such situations, the engineer may feel that the manager is "breathing down his neck" or "looking over his shoulder." Such scrutiny may be resented and the engineer may feel that the manager lacks confidence in his abilities to successfully complete the task.

In other situations, the micro-manager may be perceived as being "hands-on" and engaged with the project. The micro-manager will be more likely to answer any detailed questions about the project and the product architecture. This grasp of detailed information may impress his management.

Earlier I cautioned that the roles of the project manager and chief architect are critical to the successful outcome of the project. Clearly, for smaller projects these roles can overlap. But the micro-manager may have a tendency to assume other project roles. When this happens, he will have less time to devote to the project manager's role. This can have negative consequences on overall project progress.

12.1.3 Discipline

Discipline is necessary to stay on plan and meet all project commitments. The disciplined project manager has a good grasp of the details of the project plan, is well organized, and gives strong support to the development process. The disciplined project manager believes there is a correct way to do things and that there must be very good reasons to deviate from the development plan. The manager expects all processes to be followed as defined and all meetings to start and end on time. He expects team members to meet their personal schedules. Team members who deviate from the plan are the concern of the disciplined project manager, who may punish rather than reward employees not performing up to expectations.

On some projects, team members may view this style as inflexible. Other project teams may respect the project manager's consistent way of managing the project, viewing him as predictable, conservative, or fair.

TIP: Don't be a cry-wolf manager.

Some managers react strongly to every unexpected turn of project events. They may ask team members to work late into the evenings or on weekends to mitigate a perceived or actual risk. If this is done frequently, team members will be less willing to perform unexpected tasks. They will perceive that the manager is fabricating a *crisis du jour* to get them to give up large amounts of their personal time to perform tasks that he had not adequately planned. When a really big crisis comes up, they may not recognize its importance, and the manager may have difficulty getting them to respond .

12.2 Remaining Optimistic

As already discussed, certain management communication styles will work better depending on the situation and the project culture. Good project managers will apply different styles depending on how the project is progressing. The project manager and the chief architect need to have a vision of where the project and the implementation of the architecture are going. For a project to successfully meet its goals, both the project manager and the architect need to have a basic confidence that the project will succeed despite unexpected setbacks.

You will experience bad days as a project manager when progress stalls or goes in reverse. A common example is when defect corrections introduce side effects and break a feature that had been working in an earlier build. Despite these setbacks, the project manager will need to be almost unflappably optimistic that the project will complete successfully. This optimism is a basic attribute of leadership. If the project manager lacks confidence that the project will complete successfully, then development team members probably won't be confident.

Not all projects will be successful, and it is important that the project manager's optimism is not just wishful thinking. Project managers having doubts about the eventual success of their project need to determine whether they are merely having a bad development day or there are strong reasons why they will not meet their goals. If the bad days turn into a couple of bad weeks, the project manager should seriously consider modifying the project plan and announcing a change in project goals or direction. Again, having milestones that are close together will help the project manager determine the realism of his plan when compared with the project's rate of progress.

Optimism is a basic characteristic for the visionary part of the project manager's role. But every project and many of the team members will go through cyclical mood swings affecting the degree of optimism, depending on the phase of the project. Optimism will be generally high during the high-level design phase. Many new ideas are being discussed, plans are being made, and very few commitments have been made.

Optimism will also likely be high at the beginning of the development of a new incremental release. As the development within that release progresses, optimism will decrease as the developers wrestle with difficult implementation issues. The end date for the incremental release will draw increasingly closer and time pressure will increase on all team members.

The week before the incremental release date will be the low point for optimism. Too many loose ends will be dangling, and everyone will feel there is too much work to do in a short period of time. This is the point where the project manager's basic confidence has to be the strongest to get the team through the critical days before the release. The project manager sees the progress over the entire project, not just the narrow view of a developer chasing the last few defect corrections or feature additions. He needs to push the project to a successful conclusion of the current release within a few days. Here he may invoke a micro-management or directive style and help his team members realize which are high-priority tasks and which are not so that their useful output is greatest during the days before the release is frozen. The project manager will need to keep the team calm and centered as he makes the decision to release, and then get out of the way as the team prepares the final release. The team will experience a period of relief and accomplishment as the release is completed, and then go through a short letdown at the beginning of the next increment. Figure 12.1 gives a general plot of relative optimism and team member productivity over the time of a release increment cycle.

TIP: Avoid panicking when managing your project.

Your development team will watch your reactions to unexpected situations. If you panic, they also may panic. In the worst case, they will start thinking about abandoning the project if they think it won't succeed. If they leave unexpectedly, it will create further problems, since you will now have tasks that are not staffed. Although there will be many good reasons for you to panic, avoid revealing this to the team members. If you determine that the project goals are in jeopardy, you can replan, modify the goals, or take more serious actions to correct the situation. If you explain these plans calmly to team members, they

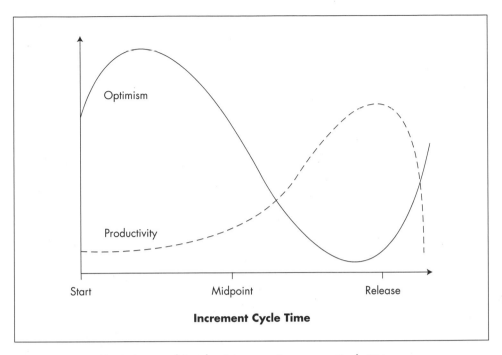

Figure 12.1 *Optimism and Productivity over Increment Cycle Time.*

most likely will support your modifications. Be especially aware of the impact of panic right before a release, when the productivity of the development team could plummet just when it should be highest. If you set your release dates for Fridays, you could always delay a release experiencing last-minute problems until Saturday morning, without jeopardizing your track record or reputation as a project manager.

12.3 Playing the Quality Card

There are certain times when the project manager should impose a higher goal on the project than "Let's not disappoint our management," usually when quality is most important. The project manager will have to demand that certain tasks get done in the name of quality (e.g., testing). He will also need to occasionally deviate from the development plan when quality criteria are not satisfied.

The difficulty with playing the quality card is that it is usually not clear when quality is good enough. The user perceives the quality of a product, and it is difficult for the project manager to determine in advance what a customer's perception will be. Thus, project tasks like testing are very important to help the project manager get an independent assessment of how good or bad the quality of a product is. As already stated, quality is often built through a test/fix/retest cycle toward the end of the project regardless of how good the architecture is and how many incremental releases were previously tested. This is often very hard work, and optimism will be at a low as new defects are discovered at the last moment. At this point the project manager has to be very disciplined in order to consider all the relevant data so that he makes the best decision concerning whether or not to release the product to a real user.

> ### TIP: Make quality a visible goal through your actions.
>
> I once worked on a project where every intermediate release milestone was met. The team's optimism and confidence was growing with each release, and the project manager was thinking alternately he was a brilliant planner or the plan was not challenging enough. As the team approached their most important release, i.e., the first one that would ship to customers, the mood of the project manager changed. He became obsessed with quality and wanted to micro-manage the system test data as it became available. For the production release, when quality was most important, he was willing to slip the release date a few days, whereas for every earlier release he had been much more disciplined. The message this manager gave the team by allowing the release to slip a few days was that quality is even more important than meeting schedule, and he was willing to take the heat from his management and deviate from his disciplined style in order to make the product better.

12.4 Providing Support and Removing Obstacles

The primary function of a good project manager is to provide support to his development team and remove obstacles that keep them from successfully completing their tasks. Thus, the project manager serves as a facilitator. The fewer obstacles each team member encounters, the more productive the overall team will be. Some of the project manager's time will thus be spent helping to increase the time available to other team members to accomplish their tasks.

Some of these obstacles will be significant, and the project manager can have a large impact on the productivity and morale of the team. An obvious example involves tools. Engineers are most productive when they have good tools to do their jobs effectively. For software engineers this includes computers and software. When an engineer reveals a problem in this area (e.g., her computer stopped working), you can affect team productivity directly by immediately reacting to the obstacle, either personally or through a support function that handles such needs.

With potential obstacles, a little time investment on the part of the project manager can prevent lost productivity. I think it's a good practice to share experience and discuss logistics *before* making business trips. When a team member is more comfortable working off site in a new environment, it often means she is more productive at that site. Usually, the project manager will have visited remote development sites before team members work there. Providing tips about which hotel is noisy or which is conveniently located near the office can help prevent obstacles and avoid loss of productivity.

12.5 Handling Problem Employees

Problem employees can negatively affect the morale and productivity of the other team members. Here the most important characteristic for a project manager to have is fairness. If the project manager gives the employees adequate warning, uses probationary periods, and consults the human resources department for guidance, he can feel justified in taking punitive actions against employees who are obstructing the team's progress. In some cases, the quickest solution will be to remove the problem employee from the project team. This is appropriate for handling skills mismatch, domain knowledge, or interpersonal problems. For more serious problems, the project manager may be justified in removing the team member from the company.

12.6 Emotions and Avoidance

By now you are probably wondering whether you could ever be a good project manager. You need to be able to adjust your communication style to suit the situation, remain optimistic even when things are going wrong, and apply quality as a guiding principle for deciding whether or not you should deviate from your plan. These are difficult things to focus on when everyone around you has lost confidence in you and your project and is predicting that the software will never work and will never be shipped.

It's important to realize that you cannot hide your emotions in such situations. If you are disappointed in your team's performance, you will probably tell them. If you have a problem employee on the team, you may have heated discussions with him until he fits in or you move him out of the project. Being a project manager does not require you to give up your humanity. I suggest, however, that you think a little before you react to a situation. If a big problem comes up that needs your response, think about it overnight before acting. Remember that your team members are "boss watchers" who will be looking at your reactions to determine their own level of comfort or discomfort with the project situation and future prognosis. You will regret emotional reactions such as berating a team member in front of other team members, especially if you react before all the facts are known. It's easy to suggest that you think before you react, but this is harder to do in the heat of battle. In some cases, team members will be waiting for an emotional reaction. Telling them they are all a "bunch of idiots" may be the appropriate emotional reaction for a specific situation, but don't expect such comments to increase productivity the next day.

There are also situations and decisions where the best course of action is to avoid any type of response or reaction. In many cases, a team member will bring up a problem or issue that he will solve in time himself. If you delay making a decision or indicate a time frame in which you will make the decision, often the team member will decide by himself how best to proceed. If you don't know how to solve a specific problem, it's OK to respond, "I don't know how to handle this. Let me think about it for a couple days and I'll get back to you." During that interim more facts may become available, new alternatives may appear, or the like. As long as you respond during the time period, thus meeting your commitment, most team members will accept a delayed response. Many of your decisions should also be tried out as proposals with other team members, before you commit to a solution. This decision-avoidance mechanism is called *just-in-time decision making*. In theory, later decisions will be better, because there will be more information available, as long as you do not exceed the need date for the decision. You also should be willing to reverse a decision if it turns out to be the wrong one. In this case, you admit you were wrong or describe the changes that have occurred and then proceed down a different path.

12.7 Quality of Work Life

In many cases, especially for a globally distributed project team, it may be difficult for you to remove environmental obstacles that get in the way of your team members' progress. But if you do have control over some aspects of the work environment, I suggest that you actively look for and act on improvements. There are some obvious things to improve that can have a big impact on your team's productivity. Development computers are one example. As your team uses faster computers and tools, in theory they will be able to work faster. I once worked in a company where there was a public paging system that was overused. Frequently during the day, everyone in the facility would be interrupted by page announcements for a single individual.

If you have some control over your physical plant, you might consider establishing a committee for improving the quality of work life. This is a more proactive version of the suggestion box, where each team member will be able to make suggestions about how to improve the work environment. You should select members for this committee who are motivated to improve the environment, interact well with most of the team members, and are willing to embrace change. You and your team will likely be together for as short a time period as you can plan in order to get your product to market quickly. You may as well make your time together as pleasant as possible. Some of your improvements to the quality of work life will not improve the team's short-term productivity directly. However, many team members will remember what you did to improve their work lives, and they will be eager to work on your projects in the future.

One more pleasant task that can be handled by the committee to improve the quality of work life is the planning of celebrations. Chapter 11 suggested that you recognize and celebrate your team's success in reaching key milestones, such as achieving release dates. Discussing the form and venue for team celebrations helps get more people engaged, is a fun topic to discuss, and builds the group spirit necessary for successful teams.

12.8 Summary

Project management will become stressful during certain natural points of the development cycle. Unexpected events will occur that you have not planned for and must react to. The project team will often look to the project manager for cues as to how to react in such situations. If the project manager stays relatively calm and practices a consistent communication style, the team will likely stay calm and let the project manager worry about resolving major issues. Over time, the team will increase their confidence in the project manager, and optimism will grow that the product will be successfully developed and delivered. The project manager's boss will also increase his confidence as the project manager deals with emergency situations and effectively communicates them. If all goes well, the project manager will participate in numerous parties with team members when they successfully reach their milestones.

PART five

Five

Measuring

Measures to Pay
Attention To

I've often noticed when working with new project managers that they easily get overloaded with the numerous details of the job and have many measures they attempt to pay attention to. As a result, they often spend their time on measurement data and tasks that are usually not very important. Not all quantifiable goals can be met. For example, a project manager may have to decide whether to meet his budget and miss his development schedule or exceed the budget and meet the development schedule. On the other hand, a project that is on schedule is usually under budget when it has been planned well. Unfortunately, many new project managers need to make a few mistakes to build up enough experience to know which measures they should pay attention to.

THIS book has provided some tips on planning a project, organizing the development team, and then implementing the plan. The final part of a project manager's job is to measure the progress of his project and the performance of the development team. This is not easily done, and there has been much research and discussion over the last 15 years on quantitative approaches to software project management; these are described in a number of books that discuss *software metrics*. Although for the experienced software project manager such metrics can become quite sophisticated, here we discuss a small number of measures that most project managers should pay attention to while managing their projects. By focusing on a small set of measures, the project manager can measure progress, determine how good a job has been done, and keep his development team focused on meeting the important project goals.

13.1   Global Metrics for Project Managers

In contrast to *global analysis* (determining design and project strategies by analyzing influencing factors) and *global development* (multisite product development), *global metrics* are high-level indicators that span multiple phases of a project [Moeller and Paulish 1993]. These are contrasted to *phase metrics,* which only provide insights into small parts of the project. Global metrics are of primary interest to the software project manager, since they give a high-level indication of the overall health of the project. We will describe five global metrics as examples that a project manager should pay attention to. These global metrics are commonly used within Siemens development organizations, as described in Moeller and Paulish [1993].

13.1.1   Size

Every software project manager should have some way of measuring the size of the product being developed. The project manager must have a sense of whether his product is "bigger than a breadbox" and how the current product might compare with prior products he has developed. This size is usually measured in lines of code or function points [Albrecht 1979]. Other units of size are the numbers of functions, subroutines, classes, modules, or subsystems.

Using lines of code versus other size measurements has always been controversial in the software metrics community. In fact, some advocates of the use of function points view the use of lines of code as a size measure as "irresponsible," saying it can lead to misuse and misinformation [Jones 1991]. In my experience, the use of lines of code is fine as long as most of the code for an organization's projects are in the same language. Clearly, comparing projects in different programming languages is not recommended. But where all the developers in an organization employ the same development tools and languages, and there are standards or scripts concerning how to count lines of code, this measure is a convenient way for the project manager to gain insight into how big his product is [Park 1992].

Lines of code as a size measurement will be used during the estimation of the schedule and effort (Chapter 2). As the product is developed using an incremental development process, it will be useful for giving the project manager a sense of project progress. In this way the project manager can evaluate the number of lines of code developed after each incremental release and compare it to the original size estimate. Toward the end of the project, lines of code will also help the project manager compare the resulting product with the one envisioned in the plan.

As already mentioned, estimating lines of code when planning your project is difficult. In my experience, estimates of lines of code made via a top-down approach tend to be smaller than those from a bottom-up approach. I believe this is because some value must be entered when considering each component of the architecture that needs to be estimated. Of course, some new components will be added to the architecture as development progresses. But some developers will reuse code rather than developing it from scratch. Thus, I support doing a bottom-up estimate once you have identified the modules and subsystems of the anticipated software architecture.

13.1.2   Schedule Deviation

One measure of process quality is schedule deviation—the difference between planned work time and actual work time divided by the planned work time, as a percentage. One rule of thumb in Section 2.5 states that the schedule deviation should be less than 20%. This means that a project planned for a 10-month development schedule should be accomplished within 12 months. Later, it was mentioned how important it is for a project to meet all its incremental release date milestones. In this case, you are striving for a schedule deviation of 0%.

The reason for raising the visibility of this measure is that so many projects miss their original schedules by 100% or more. By keeping this measure visible and following practices such as the weekly status meeting, the project manager has a better chance at keeping the project on track.

Remember that as each increment is baselined and planned, the goals of the project and the product's desired functionality can change dramatically. Thus, the envisioned original plan and the actual implemented plan may be quite dissimilar. But having a new version of the software development plan (SDP) for each baselined increment can help the project manager reconstruct the project history with respect to the decisions that were made for each baselined increment.

As a general practice, meeting development schedules should have high priority and visibility. Getting to market quickly and doing adequate and realistic market launch planning are easier when you know the development schedule and have faith it will be met. This is why I include schedule deviation as an important measure for the project manager to be concerned with.

13.1.3   Productivity

This metric takes the number of lines of code developed by the team for the product and divides it by the amount of effort applied, in staff-days. Thus, you typically see this measure reported in units of lines of code per staff-day. Typical performance values for this measure are in the range of 5–35 lines of code per staff-day [Moeller and Paulish 1993]. In case studies of Siemens software development organizations, project productivity measures were reported from 20.8 to 53.6 lines of code per staff-day [Paulish and Carleton 1994]. Larger projects tend to have smaller productivity values than smaller projects. This is due to the need for increased communications on larger projects.

To apply this metric, you must decide the time period over which to count. Typically, this would include the effort expended from the beginning of high-level design to the first customer shipment. Effort should include not only development tasks but also the effort expended for testing, reviews, project management, and documentation development. By keeping effort in units of staff-days, you will also have to be aware of issues involved with part-time team members and the different number of hours worked per staff-year per employee. Thus, your daily productivity rate may be very different than your team size suggests, and you will need to point this out to your management, who may have a "head count" number in mind for your project that is inconsistent with your productivity. You will also need to define how lines of code are counted; e.g., do you count reused lines of code? You will use a counting tool to consistently and automatically count lines of code per your definition.

If you are using lines of code per staff-day as a productivity measure you must apply it over the entire development time or within a development increment. For example, in the high-level design phase, when the architecture is being designed, no lines of code will be written. Thus, you cannot conclude that the architecture design team has no productivity. You will see later that you would measure progress using phase metrics for architecture design rather than a global metric like productivity.

Most metrics experts caution not to use measurement to evaluate the performance of individual team members [Austin 1996]. The fear is that if you were to define, for example, individual productivity measures for developers, they would distort the data to make themselves look good [Humphrey 1989]. For example, an individual subjected to personal productivity measures by his manager might write many lines of useless code that do not achieve the desired functionality. There have been recommendations concerning the use of personal software development processes [Humphrey 1997], but these measures are for the developer to understand and use for improvement. The personal measures are not generally shared with the developer's manager, hence the following tip concerning measuring the performance of individual team members.

> **TIP: Do not attempt to measure individual team members' productivity.**
>
> Although you will undoubtedly have opinions concerning the relative productivity of the individuals on your team, resist the urge to quantify an individual's contribution. Such measures will make team members nervous, and they will likely distort either their performance or the data used for the measure in order to "look good." Perhaps as software engineering matures as a discipline, standard measures for the performance of individual engineers will be defined. We sometimes compare measuring software engineers with rating baseball players. A baseball player with a .320 batting average who has hit 50 home runs in a season and has won a Golden Glove award is instantly recognized as an excellent player. We have no similar measures for software engineers. However, baseball is more than 100 years old, and maybe we just have not discovered a good set of measures for software engineers.

13.1.4   Defects

Counting defects is a simple way for a project manager to get a sense of the quality of the product being developed. A *defect* is an error in the software that produces an incorrect result for valid input. Other terms used with the same meaning are *fault, failure, bug*, and *error*. The count of defects can be tracked during different phases of development, for example, during unit-level testing, when you would expect to discover more defects than during system testing.

A simple way to track defects is to look at the number of defects identified by your defect-tracking system. For example, during the DPS2000 project, 270 defects were entered into the defect-tracking system, as six engineering releases were system-tested over a period of nine months. This number was relatively low compared to prior projects, which led the project manager to suspect alternately that product quality was relatively good and that system testing was not discovering enough bugs.

The defects metric is typically normalized by dividing the count of defects by the size of the product. Thus, you will find this metric usually stated as the number of defects found over a specified period of time (e.g., during system testing) divided by the number of thousand lines of code.

13.1.5 Customer Change Requests

A specialized type of product quality metric involving defect counts is the number of customer change requests. In this case, the unique change requests that result from customer use are counted over an arbitrary time period of one year after the first customer installation of the product. Most such change requests may result when a customer finds a bug that was not discovered during development or system testing. As in the case of the defects metric, the count is normalized by the size of the release, in units of change requests per thousand lines of code. Typical values for this metric can range from 0.3 to 1.6 defects per thousand lines of code [Moeller and Paulish 1993]. In case studies of Siemens software development organizations, customer change requests were reported from 0.008 to 0.36 defects per thousand lines of code [Paulish and Carleton 1994]. Again, field experience indicates that larger, more complicated software products tend to have more customer change requests than smaller, simpler products. Of course, a very poor-quality product that is not used by many customers could have a low customer change requests value, because not many people would bother to report the defects over the first year of field use.

TIP: Communicate in quantitative terms with your management.

I once received a phone call from the chief executive officer of our division asking me to stop by for a chat. This was the first time he had ever called me, and I quickly walked to his office, which was in a part of our office complex called "the land of Oz." We were working in the part of the facility called "Kansas." Sometimes the area where such corporate officers sit is called "mahogany row." I was ushered into his huge plush office and invited to sit down on the couch. After a brief conversation he asked, "How many defects do you think our product will have once it's shipped to customers?" Knowing we were shipping about 100K lines of code and that industry defect rates (i.e., customer change requests) at that time were averaging around four defects per thousand lines of code, I answered that I thought we would see about 400 defects after the product is delivered to the field. Well, he just about fell out of his big leather chair. He had no idea of the quality levels for software products at that time, and he now realized that a substantial software engineering staff would have to be kept in place to maintain the software. Although I was a bit disturbed by his surprise at my estimate, we had definitely communicated and he began to understand some of the realities of software-intensive businesses.

13.2   Phase Metrics for High-Level Design

The phase of a project when project planning and architecture design are done is the *high-level design phase*. Table 2.3 provided some rules of thumb for this phase. I believe that project managers should manage this phase of the project using mainly time-based measures. Although my software architect colleagues will likely disagree, I think that software architecture design is never completely finished. Even after a product is released and in a maintenance mode, there will still be change requests or defect corrections that may affect the software architecture. Thus, I believe that software architects should be given a time frame in which to "complete" their work. For example, Table 2.3 suggests that the high-level design phase last three months or less. If the design phase concludes with some type of review—e.g., an **Architecture Trade-off Analysis Method (ATAM)** evaluation—this will help set the milestones for the phase. Since some logistic planning is necessary to conduct an ATAM review for setting up reviewers, documentation, and meeting rooms, it is usually scheduled well in advance. The project manager can use this fixed date to help measure the progress of the design. If the ATAM review was scheduled three months in advance and the design team has been working six weeks on the design, then they should be approximately half finished. If the review is done and there are gaps in the design, these can be carried as action items for the next phase of design or during development.

Software architects will declare that high-level design is complete when there is enough description of the software architecture that it can be given to other team members to do detailed design on the modules or subsystems defined in the architecture. As a project manager, I've found this distinction between high-level and detailed design to be fuzzy. Thus, a project manager may declare that high-level design is complete when the design team has run out of time for doing such work. This is why I emphasize time-based measures and rules of thumb during the high-level design phase.

The other major measure of progress during the high-level design phase is associated with decision making. I have stated that the project manager should make project-related decisions and the chief software architect should make technical decisions. At the beginning of every new project there will be a long list of things to be decided concerning issues such as choice of hardware platform and software development tools. If the architect is aware of all the decisions that need to be made, he can sometimes defer decisions as long as the design accommodates the alternatives. But too many open issues will create uncertainty for the development team. From the point of view of the project manager, I prefer such platform, development environment, and tool selections to be made quickly and relatively early. Too often, I've observed design teams waste time discussing the pros and cons of various development tools rather than spending most of their time on the architecture design. Thus, for the high-level design phase, the project manager has to track progress on the high-level design and the various decisions that need to be made before development begins.

13.3 Cost-to-Completes

A useful measure of project status and progress is the *cost-to-complete*—an estimate of the remaining amount of work anticipated to complete the implementation of all components identified in the software architecture design and estimated during the bottom-up cost estimates (Chapter 2).

A simple way to prepare a cost-to-complete estimate is to periodically update the bottom-up estimation spreadsheet (see Figure 2.7) generated during project planning. You can periodically (e.g., quarterly) modify the data in the spreadsheet to reflect the anticipated hours remaining for each component for design, coding, and unit-testing effort. For example, for a component that has been designed but not yet coded or tested, you would enter a zero for the design effort and then update the anticipated efforts for coding and unit-testing.

An example segment of a cost-to-complete spreadsheet is given in Figure 13.1. For the "Execution context" component, the total effort is zero, since at the time of this example cost-to-complete this component development had been completed. Note that since this is only part of the overall spreadsheet, the values in the totals row are bigger than the sums of the numbers shown.

You can also periodically update the lines of code estimates for each component identified in the software architecture, add new components, or delete components that may no longer be implemented. Thus, by comparing the cost-to-completes with the original bottom-up estimation spreadsheet, you can identify changes to your original plans and assumptions.

By subtracting the total number of anticipated hours of the most recent cost-to-complete from the prior estimate, you can calculate the amount of work that has been accomplished. If you compare this with the number of people you applied to the project over the time period between the estimates, you can get a measure of whether your team is making progress as compared to your plan. If

	Code Size	Design Effort	Code Effort	Unit Test	Total Effort
Study mode	600	320	400	360	1080
Execute with old data	700	80	200	120	400
Language tables	1000	5	40	40	85
Check in and check out	1800	0	20	40	60
Example templates	0	400	300	120	820
Tariff calendars	1400	120	160	160	440
Execution context	500	0	0	0	0
Search object	2000	0	20	40	60
Totals	101900	3237	4532	3640	11309

Figure 13.1 *Example Cost-to-Complete Spreadsheet Segment.*

many hours were expended but the cost-to-complete did not reduce accordingly, your team may be inefficient or they are working on tasks not associated with implementing the components. To some extent, progress on a project is nonlinear, but with an incremental development approach you should start to see cells of the spreadsheet go to zero as later cost-to-completes are estimated.

You will also use the cost-to-completes to keep your management informed of your overall progress. Management sometimes has a "convenient" memory. For example, they may remember an end date for a project but forget that the project was not staffed as planned. One reason the cost-to-complete estimate did not reduce as much as anticipated is that staff was not added to the project as planned. You can also do quick calculations concerning the end dates of the project. For example, your schedule may reflect a limited number of development months remaining, but your cost-to-complete is much larger than the number of hours you could apply to the project based on your current team size and the remaining schedule time. Such quantitative assessments will help you communicate any warning flags that must be raised concerning the progress of the project.

A cost-to-complete is not the only way to measure project progress. Many sophisticated techniques, such as **earned value (EV)** [Fleming 1983], have existed for a long time for any type of project. For software projects you will want to use measures that are easy to calculate and have meaning in your environment. Other progress measures you might consider include comparing the number of lines of code implemented to your original estimate, comparing the number of features that have been implemented with the requirements specification, and comparing the number of builds or engineering releases implemented to the planned number.

13.4   Engineering Budgets

No engineering manager has ever met his budget. Rather, you must decide if you will go over budget or under budget while trying to come as close as possible to your original target. Such engineering budgets are usually determined for the fiscal year, and changing them is often next to impossible.

In Siemens, we usually want to get as close as possible to our target budget without exceeding it. However, there may be good reasons for you to exceed your budget as market or project conditions change. You may wish to accomplish more than you had planned (exceed expectations), or your original budget may have been underestimated. Exceeding your budget while missing your development targets is never a good practice.

You will likely come in under budget if you did not staff the project according to plan. Most software engineering budgets will very much be driven by labor costs. Material costs will typically be much lower as compared to a hardware-engineering project. Travel costs may become significant for global developments where team members are working off site, but will still be much less than the labor costs. You may need to consider software tool license fees, but you may also apply them as an organization or one-time expense rather than as direct project charges.

As stated earlier, you should buy the best computing equipment you can afford. Typically, computers will be capitalized rather than expensed. In general, you should attempt to obtain the best computers and software tools available for your development team, since their cost will be returned with increased development team productivity.

Budgets are typically tracked on a monthly basis. Time sheets will often be used to capture the labor costs, which will be the biggest part of your budget. If you are meeting your staffing plan and your schedule milestones, your project expenses will likely be close to your budget. There will be some seasonal deviations when vacations cluster, usually in the summertime and at the end of the calendar year. But if your project is progressing well, you do not need to pay much attention to your budget until a few months before the end of the fiscal year. At that time you could do a forecast of where your expenses will end up at the end of the year by multiplying the number of people you have on the project by the remaining workdays and your average labor rate. If your forecast is higher than your budget, you can tweak things to come closer to plan by deferring new hires, deferring any unnecessary purchases, or not deferring planned vacations.

13.5 Watching the Test Results

Earlier, the defects metric was identified as a useful way for software project managers to evaluate product quality. You will likely be counting the defects and reviewing the list of new and open defects every day, especially during the period prior to a release. You'll also be watching the system test results to see how serious the bugs are. You'll hope that no high-priority defects are discovered just before the release, which will force you to stop the release or slip your schedule.

Thus, the system-test results will be an area where you increase your scrutiny as the release date approaches. Every morning you will check your defect-tracking system to see if any significant bugs were discovered during the testing of the prior night. You will be interested to see if the rate of finding new defects is increasing or decreasing. You will track the assignment of fixes of bugs to see if the number of open bugs is decreasing while the number of fixed bugs is increasing. By examining the defect-tracking system database, you'll be able to print out reports that summarize the testing status at the time. If your rate of new defects is growing, the list of open defects is getting longer, and you still have high-priority bugs on the open list, it's probably not a good idea to release the software.

Watching the test results daily is probably the best way to evaluate the quality of the product you plan to ship to customers. You can also spend some of your personal time as either a test team member or a more informal tester so that you can get firsthand experience concerning the quality of your product.

13.6 Summary

In the spirit of middleweight software development processes that are driven by software architecture, I suggest you track a small set of highly visible metrics that evaluate the performance of your project and the quality of your developing product. Having a small set of metrics to pay attention to not only helps focus your attention on the important measures of your project, but also helps focus the attention of your team members on the important goals of your project. As you become a more experienced project manager, you can experiment with more sophisticated measures. Through this experimentation, you will develop rules of thumb that seem to work well for the types of projects you deal with. Almost instinctively, you will apply these rules of thumb to your project and project team members so that warning flags will go up when things don't seem quite right. By reacting to your internal warning flags, you will hopefully be able to pull your project quickly back on track when things go wrong. But, in the beginning, make sure you have a good grasp of the basic measures, i.e., your product size, quality, schedule deviation, and team productivity. If you meet your scheduled release dates and stay within your budget, you should have opportunities to manage many interesting projects in the course of your career. At some point, you may even get a user's feedback about how much he liked using your product, rather than just counting customer change requests.

What Is a "Good Job"?

My biggest frustrations as a project manager have occurred when I knew that our development team did a good job and produced a good product, but the product still had no significant impact in the market. In some cases, this was because the sales force was not ready to sell the product or they didn't understand the potential of the product. After a while, I tried to stop worrying about things that I couldn't control. If your development team meets the goals you establish at the beginning of the project, including successfully implementing the architecture that was envisioned, this is reason enough to celebrate your success.

As you measure the progress of your project and reflect on the accomplishments of your development team, you will likely be asking yourself, "How good a job did we do?" It's probable that your management will be asking the same question. As stated earlier, the success or failure of a project often reflects on the perceived performance of the project manager. Although there may be no real correlation between your project's success and your abilities as a project manager, it's clearly better for your career to be associated with good projects rather than bad ones. You may be asked to take on very difficult assignments that your management is aware of, or you may not be able to control many aspects of your project or business. But when your performance evaluation is done, it's more comfortable to have managed a successful project.

This chapter offers suggestions for how to measure whether or not your project is successful. Quantitative assessments would be helpful, but there will be many other variables. For example, using the schedule deviation metric (Chapter 13), you may be able to claim that you met every planned release date. But if customers do not like the product you delivered to them, meeting your development schedule may not be so important.

14.1 Trading Off Among Schedule, Functionality, and Quality

I have emphasized that project management is involved with trade-offs. You can establish goals at the beginning of a project, but every day you will need to make decisions that often appear to contradict the goals. The most common set of trade-offs will involve schedule, functionality, and quality. The decisions you make to achieve your goals in these three areas will likely determine the outcome of your project. Too much emphasis on one area to the detriment of the other areas will likely hurt the overall project.

It's easy to identify projects that are unsuccessful. They are delivered late, do not meet the functionality desired by users, and contain bugs that are discovered by the users. Project managers may make excuses like:

* I was never given the right people to staff the project.
* Marketing oversold the product's functionality to customers and made commitments we couldn't meet.
* We met our budget and schedule but had to cut back too much on desired functionality.
* We didn't allocate enough time for testing.
* My initial concerns with the aggressive schedule were not listened to.

Clearly, it's not my intent to provide handy excuses to project managers who do not meet their project goals. But keeping balance, focus, and visibility on the trade-offs among schedule, functionality, and quality will help ensure that the project turns out to be successful. Identifying the priorities among these goals will help guide the development so that good decisions are made.

> **TIP: Anticipate that your product will be used more than you expect.**
>
> I frequently buy gasoline from the same service station, which is on my way home from the office. This station, as well as others in the area, uses a credit card authorization terminal that I was responsible for developing before I worked for Siemens. The design for this particular product was created approximately 20 years ago, and it has been in the market for about 16 years. I'm always surprised to see this product in daily use after so many years. In fact, the attendants often let newer versions of this terminal sit idle while they continue to use the older (more reliable or familiar?) product. At the time, I didn't think of us as having done a particularly good job developing this product. The fact that the product has been successfully used for such a long time allows me to rate this particular project as successful, even though what I remember most are all the technical and organizational problems we had to overcome to get it to market.

14.2 Defining Project Success

You cannot easily meet all your project goals in all areas of schedule, functionality, and quality. Although I very seldom have seen a project that meets all its goals, I am suspicious that projects that meet all their goals may not have had challenging enough goals to start with. I would define project success for projects that meet their goals in at least two of the three areas of schedule, functionality, and quality. An example successful project would meet its schedule, provide most of the functionality planned (e.g., 90% to 95% of the planned features), and show good quality in both system testing and the field (e.g., few or no serious defects discovered in the field).

Considering our basic set of global metrics presented in Chapter 13, there are other factors that relate to a project's success that are not so easy to quantify. Although our example successful project quantifiably met its schedule, maybe the team was exploited or driven too hard. For example, would you consider a project successful if its business goals were met but multiple team members ended up with stress-related health problems or left the company as a result of poor morale? Thus, defining project success may not always be easy.

But from my experience, a project that is successful in meeting its goals in two of the areas of schedule, functionality, and quality is rare and should probably be viewed as an overall success. For such projects, I also suggest that some project funding be allocated for a team celebration that recognizes its success.

> **TIP: Don't confuse project performance with individual performance.**
>
> Although there will always be a tendency to correlate successful projects with successful performers, it is important to distinguish personal performance from your project's performance. I once was discussing an individual's performance during an appraisal, and I was generally dissatisfied with his accomplishments. Without thinking, I mentioned that many defects were discovered during his code inspections, which indicated a general sloppiness in his work. The fact that I was paying attention to code inspection reports got back to other team members, and it significantly hurt the value of future inspections, since authors and reviewers were now afraid to discover too many defects. Poor performers can sometimes be lucky to be assigned to a successful project. Be careful to distinguish the relative contributions of all the team members, and don't necessarily assume that if their project was successful, they all did a good job.

14.3 Measuring Team Members' Contributions

As a project manager, you will be asked to measure the relative contributions of the members of your team. Your line manager may be responsible for generating the performance evaluation documentation, determining salary adjustments and bonuses, and conducting the evaluation. But even if you are not directly responsible for performance evaluations, your line manager will inevitably solicit your inputs concerning an individual's performance on your project. You will tend to measure your team members using the same goals as for your project—i.e., did they meet their schedule dates, did they implement the functions desired, did they develop high-quality code? However, you also will consider many soft factors that are not easy to quantify—e.g., do the team members communicate effectively, do they have a positive attitude concerning the project, do they work well together and support each other, can you rely on them?

Many individual performance appraisals follow a **management by objectives (MBO)** format and life cycle. With MBO, you jointly identify and discuss the objectives of the individual at the beginning of the review period or the end of the prior review period. An example project-related objective could be that the individual will meet the milestone dates specified in the project schedule for tasks assigned to him. Typically, there may also be objectives not directly related to project goals, such as improving writing skills and learning a new technology. At the end of the appraisal period (e.g., one fiscal year), the manager will evaluate how well the objectives were met. There will also be evaluations of areas without specific objectives that the organization thinks are important to reinforce. For example, a research organization may attempt to evaluate the employee's contribution in the areas of papers published or innovations (e.g., patent disclosures).

As part of your evaluation process, you may also be asked to rank the relative contributions of the team members. This is not easy to do, since the team members may have contributed in very diverse roles. For example, how do you compare the contribution to the project and performance of the chief architect with that of the buildmeister? Rankings tend to have more senior-level contributors at the top, since they can often contribute more to the project due to a wider range of experience and skills. One way to generate a ranking is to compare individual team members in pairs, and then to determine whom you would miss more if they were suddenly to leave the project. To compensate for the more junior members of the team, you could give them some extra consideration for potential and also establish lower expectations for their contributions due to their lower salary grade. But the bottom line is that salary adjustments will be driven to a large extent from your rankings. People you perceive as having made a greater contribution to your project will more likely be given greater monetary rewards.

14.4 Rewards

Inevitably on every project the subject of rewards for individual and team contributions will come up for discussion. This is usually a complicated philosophical discussion about what is an adequate reward for members of a successful project and how team members can be motivated to meet or exceed their project's goals. Often the subject will be raised by well-meaning managers, who will ask the project manager during project planning, "What can we do to get the team to work more to get done quicker?" From the manager's perspective, spending a little money on team or personal incentives to get additional sales when a product gets to market sooner may be a good business investment. But from my experience as a project manager, such incentives will only cause problems. Initially there's the problem of defining who will get the incentives and what will be offered, based on the delivery date achieved. But the bigger problem is that such incentives can distort the balance among schedule, functionality, and quality and perturb the project goals. If someone tells you they will give you more money to get your work done early, schedule will very likely pop to the top of your personal priorities at the expense of quality and functionality. You will also be very disappointed if you do not meet the earlier delivery dates, and there will likely be some unpopular and unfortunate individual who holds back a release due to discovered defects.

I'd much prefer to set milestones that are more likely to be met while providing adequate functionality and quality. I prefer these milestones to be public and to be well-known by everyone in the organization. If there's a serious defect discovered at the last minute that delays the release, so be it. This is a reasonable trade-off between schedule and quality, and missing the release date by a couple days will not adversely affect the financial incentives of all the team members.

If such incentives are viewed as bad and disruptive to project goals, what types of rewards are good to suggest? My preference is for rewards that recognize team members and that are somewhat unexpected. For these types of rewards, you would budget some money to be allocated to team members as the project situation develops. If the project goals were not met, you would probably use this money to help reduce your overrun when milestones are missed. When things go well or even better than planned, you would use this money as a thank you and recognition for good work. This recognition can be in the form of team rewards or individual rewards, depending on the circumstances.

As an example, let's consider a project team that meets its first three engineering release milestone dates with the functionality that was promised over a six-month period. For this case, you could take some of your budgeted reward money and give it to all the team members as a public recognition and thank you. You could also give rewards to a few team members who you felt made a significant and possibly unexpected contribution to meeting the project goals. In this case, you would keep the individual rewards private. In either case, you are reinforcing that meeting schedule and functionality are important to the success of the project, and you are showing appreciation for the effort expended. Part of the appeal of this approach is that the reward is mostly unexpected, and therefore often more appreciated by the team members. For the earlier delivery date incentive example described earlier, the team members will often already have spent their incentive money, even though they do not meet the earlier date specified by the manager hoping for an earlier market entry.

As you plan rewards for team members, there is often much discussion as to whether they should be public or private. Public rewards should include everyone on the project team or be given to subteams whose performance others in the organization should emulate. A problem with public rewards is that some team members will get rewarded for minimal contributions just because they were on the team. A worse situation is when subteams are publicly rewarded but you exclude someone from the team reward either on purpose or by accident. Private rewards are usually easier to determine and control, provided that the project manager realizes that no information is ever completely secret in a project. Private rewards typically affect a smaller number of team members, but may have a bigger impact on the individuals involved.

I have seen incentive situations that work well under special circumstances. One situation may be during a facility closing or to support a product that is near the end of its lifetime. In these cases, you hold out the incentive as an inducement for the employee to remain with the company to perform the task assigned over a specified period of time. If it is known that a product must be supported or a plant must stay open until the end of September, say, incentives can be specified to keep people on board. For this case, a lump sum of money is paid if the employee agrees to stay with the company and perform the specified task until the agreed-on date. If the employee leaves the task or company earlier than the end of September, then this incentive money is forfeited. This usually works well, since the time period is specified in advance and the employee can make definitive plans concerning what he will do after he completes the task.

14.5 Staff Turnover

One indicator of whether or not your project is successful may be determined by your staff. Team members who are enduring a difficult or unsuccessful project may show their displeasure by leaving the company. We call this "voting with their feet." The *staff turnover* metric will often give an overall idea of whether or not team members are enjoying their project work. The staff turnover metric is defined as the number of team members who have left in the last 12 months divided by the staff size 12 months ago, as a percentage [Paulish and Carleton 1994]. In an economy that is not in recession, some staff turnover is good, for team members may find promotion opportunities, change career goals, and so on. But high staff turnover creates major headaches for project managers and the organization overall. Project managers suddenly find themselves with tasks that are no longer staffed. Critical skills may walk out the doors of the company. It is expensive for the organization to identify and qualify candidates to replace the people who have left.

In some situations the staff turnover is high due to layoffs caused by difficult business conditions. Such downsizing usually has negative consequences for projects that must continue after the layoff. Team members often lose confidence in the organization and become fearful that they too may lose their jobs. The surviving team members may have to take on the additional tasks of their colleagues who have been removed from the organization. Such an environment makes the job of the project manager even more difficult.

One of the biggest effects of layoffs or high staff turnover is that software projects lose their continuity. Every software product that is released will need to be maintained as long as customers continue to use it. It's always convenient to have the original developers of the product within the company so that difficult customer change requests can be addressed, if necessary. Software process improvements tend to take lots of time to implement, as lessons learned from one project are applied to the next project. When staff turnover is too high, the organization will continually restart their software process improvement activities and most likely make slower progress than if the software engineering staff is available to implement the improvements.

Staff turnover depends on the business climate and the culture of the organization as well as on the success or failures of specific projects. We have observed in Siemens that software engineers in Germany tend to stay with their organization longer than engineers in similar organizations in the United

States. This is perhaps culturally driven, but having a stable workforce is a big advantage when domain knowledge is required to develop new products.

14.6   Summary

As a project manager, you will need to evaluate and measure what a good job is, both for your project and for each of your development team members. You may attempt to do this quantitatively, but there will be many additional factors to consider. Simply stated, if your project or individual team members meet their goals, then they have done a good job. Meeting all of the goals is unrealistic, but meeting only a few of the goals cannot be considered good performance.

PART six

Case Studies

IS2000

THE Imaging System 2000 (IS2000) has been used extensively as an example project in this book. For us, it was a very interesting project that initially ran into problems, was restarted under difficult business conditions, and ultimately has proven successful. At last count, more than 600 IS2000 systems have been installed in the field, and the business division responsible for it has been profitable, in part due to the product's sales success. Many of our techniques were "proven" on the IS2000 project, and we have been able to replicate its success on subsequent projects. This chapter summarizes some of the major project management challenges as the IS2000 was being designed and developed.

15.1 Background

We first became involved with the IS2000 project when the management of the company developing it became frustrated with the poor development progress. Scheduled milestones were missed without a good understanding of when they might be completed in the future. We participated on review teams formed to evaluate the project's practices and technical approach. As expected, and similar to many other projects, deficiencies in project management and design were uncovered. It also became obvious at the time that the current product line was losing market share. The loss of profitability created severe morale problems throughout the organization, and staff turnover became significant at all levels of the organization.

Thus, the project situation quickly moved from concern to crisis. The new product (IS2000) was needed quickly, since the current product was losing sales. The IS2000 project manager and key staff members left the company. We found ourselves quickly moving from roles of reviewers or consultants to team members as company management asked us to help stem the impending crisis. As a result, we took over responsibility for project management, the software architecture, and the software development over a critical eight-month period. Within the constraints of this difficult business situation, the company management was willing to apply new design and management techniques, as long as it moved the IS2000 quickly forward to the market.

Over the years, the amount of software in this company's products has increased in size and complexity, often replacing more costly hardware subsystems. A cross-functional team had been established to define the marketing requirements for the IS2000, and the requirements were well understood by most team members. The software engineering staff had been trained in object-oriented methods and C++, and prior software development projects had been implemented in C.

15.2   System Overview

Figure 15.1 presents the IS2000 system overview. The IS2000 acquires raw image data from a probe and then displays the data as it is being acquired. The image data is stored as it is acquired. It can be displayed and processed, both on the user control panel of the IS2000 and on remote imaging computers that are networked to the IS2000. Since the probe is mounted on a moveable mechanical structure, collision detection interference calculations are performed for safety.

Due to severe restrictions on the development team size and the desired time to market, new functionality implementation of the IS2000 was restricted mainly to the acquisition computer and its interface with the probe. Data display and processing reused the existing product code to a large extent. This was achieved using a loosely coupled architecture where the new functions and many of the existing functions would coexist on two different computers that were connected. The IS2000 was packaged as a new product line, although much code was reused from the existing product line.

After the new architecture was designed, the IS2000 was implemented in approximately 74K lines of C++ code. The development took approximately

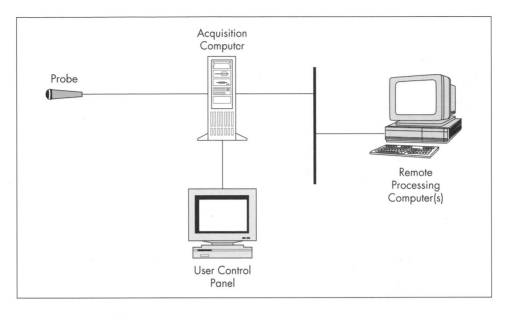

Figure 15.1 *IS2000 Imaging System Overview.*

13 months, and 10 staff-years were applied with a peak team size of 13 engineers. Our software development plan, which we made using the architecture centered software project planning (ACSPP) approach, had a 12-month development schedule. Thus, the implementation missed the schedule plan by one month, for a schedule deviation of approximately 8.3%.

The project met its goals, and the new product line was well received by the market. The temporary project management and technical team were replaced with permanent new staff when it became clear that the development would be successfully completed. The new staff members are still in place, and they have made substantial enhancements to the product line, both for new features and new variations of products.

15.3   Project Planning

Many of our project planning and architecture design approaches were first applied to the IS2000 project. We had the opportunity to design and plan concurrently with the result that the project plan was derived from the software architecture.

15.3.1   High-Level Design

For the IS2000, the original team was developing the product without having an acceptable software architecture in place. Thus, the project was restarted and a new software architecture design was developed using a small design team. Team members not involved directly with the high-level software architecture design were given tasks to investigate new technology alternatives, prototype certain parts of the architecture, become trained on new technologies, and so on.

The design team used the four-views approach to describe the new software architecture. Global analysis was applied, although at this time the term *global analysis* was not in common parlance, and factor tables and issue cards were not used. However, the design team was careful to document the factors influencing the design decisions that were being made. Many of the design decisions and resulting project strategies were driven very much by the need to get a product to market quickly.

A big part of the effort for the design team was to explain and review the architecture with all the other development team members. The architecture description became a communication mechanism between the design team and the development team. This was important for the future success of the development, since the development team had to understand and support the new architecture. The four-views approach was helpful for providing the architecture description.

15.3.2   Top-Down Schedule

While the design team was working on the architecture, I (as the project manager) was working on the first top-down schedule estimates using lines of code and Cocomo. The first top-down estimates helped clarify the problem that the development team and the company would be facing. The effort estimates compared with the desired development schedule indicated that there were not nearly enough developers currently in the organization to achieve such a plan. This put additional importance on our efforts to look at reuse alternatives and further analyze the requirements in order to reduce the potential scope of the development. There clearly wasn't enough time or people to achieve the product that was desired. The full set of requirements was fairly well known, since there were existing older products similar to the IS2000 that were already being sold. These factors drove us toward reuse alternatives. The strategy eventually selected was to reuse part of the existing product system within the new architecture. In fact, the user control panel and remote processing computer(s) from Figure 15.1 utilized parts of the current products. This helped reduce the scope of the development effort to the acquisition computer.

15.3.3   Release Plans

We spent many hours discussing the relative priorities of the desired feature list with our marketing counterparts. The key to defining a successful release plan was to identify the minimal feature set that could be sold in the market. From that list, we could define an even smaller list of features so that some limited amount of functional in-house and beta system-testing could be performed. We looked not only at how features could be released and thus the sequence in which they would be developed, but also at the sequence that software components would be developed. We kept the release increments small, and we used the first release to implement a vertical slice of the software architecture. This vertical slice helped "validate" the architecture, and it helped build confidence concerning the architecture within the development team.

15.3.4   Bottom-Up Estimates

Another way in which we got the development team to learn and support the new software architecture was through the bottom-up cost estimates. We provided training to all the members of the development team who would be involved in generating the bottom-up cost estimates for each module. We gave an overview of the architecture to the estimators. It described the estimation process, including the purpose for the four-hour "paper design" and instructions on how to fill out the estimation spreadsheet forms.

After the four-hour paper design and the estimation form were completed, the design team reviewed each estimate before submitting it to the project manager. In some cases, the design team reviewed the estimate and the paper design with the development team member who generated it. The project manager collected all the estimation forms and summed up the total estimates for lines of code to be developed, and effort for detailed design, coding, and unit-level testing. The additional effort for system testing, documentation generation, project management, configuration management, integration, and the like was added to the bottom-up estimate to get the total anticipated effort for the project. We compared this effort estimate with the effort obtained from the top-down analysis.

15.3.5   Project Schedule

Since the time to market was so critical for the IS2000 project, we were very careful with creating the development schedule. All the information needed was available. This included the effort estimates for each component, the release plan, the top-down schedule from Cocomo, and the anticipated project organization. We also had access to a project administrator in the organization, who helped integrate the IS2000 schedule with other project schedules in the organization. We used Microsoft's Project to develop, communicate, and later track the schedule.

We reduced the development time by reducing the scope of the development through reuse of the existing products. We also took steps to increase the size of the development team and/or replace current team members who would leave the company. At the time, Siemens was investigating how software could be developed using software engineers in India. Although we didn't subcontract any development work outside of our facility, we began to bring in Indian software engineers to staff some of the tasks within the schedule.

15.3.6   Software Development Plan

We took the software development schedule, the proposed project development organization, the definition of responsibilities, and a list of some of the key risks and integrated all this information into the software development plan (SDP). This document summarized when, how, and with whom the software would be developed. This document became our commitment to our management to develop the product within the given schedule with the staffing plan identified. Thus, the document required detailed review by each development team member and our management. Upon such review and eventual approval by management, the development schedule was published and maintained by the project administrator. He updated and made public the schedule and its achievement every month of the 13-month development project.

15.3.7   Personal Schedules

After the SDP was approved and distributed, we asked members of the development team to generate a personal schedule identifying their milestones for each week within the first development increment. We asked team members to submit their personal schedule to the project manager. The personal schedule was in the form of a list of activities planned to be accomplished for each week. Some discussion was held with selected team members when the personal schedule appeared to conflict with the schedule in the SDP. Although not the case with this project, in some situations the personal schedules could cause a change in the development schedule. An example is when an individual's vacation schedule interferes with the expected milestones to be achieved in the SDP.

We reviewed the personal schedules weekly with the development team staff. In most cases, this was accomplished in the weekly status meeting, which we held on Friday afternoons. But, for conflict situations that might require modifying staffing assignments, we would meet one-on-one with the developer or with his team leader.

15.4   Project Management

There were a number of significant project management challenges associated with the IS2000 project and the company business and organizational climate at the time. These would be described mainly as organizational influencing factors that the temporary project manager had to address, but there were also many technological and product factors that the temporary chief architect and the architecture team addressed. We restarted the architecture design to a large extent, and selected new technologies to replace many of the choices of the prior management team. Thus, in many ways we scratched the current project plan and developed new plans along with a new architecture.

Initially, the project management took on a sense of urgency or crisis management. Within crisis management, a project manager becomes more directive and less supportive. Support will decrease, since decisions need to be made very quickly in order to stabilize the situation, restart the project as quickly as possible, and then make forward progress on the development of the architecture and implementation of the new project plan. Credibility is established once the plan starts to be successfully implemented and the new milestones are successfully met. In such situations, the project manager does not have time to build consensus as each decision is made.

This management style can often drive additional staff members from the company, who now realize that they have less influence on the future direction of the project than they did before. Coupled with the overall poor morale due to the difficult business situation and the fact that the management of the company was also changing, one of the major project management challenges was to keep enough of the core team members together long enough to initiate the restart of the project. One management technique in such a crisis management situation is to hold daily morning status meetings with the core team members, which we did. In this way, the core team members at least felt they were being kept informed of the new decisions being made. One of the challenges for the new management team was to identify who was important for the future success of the project so that they could be included within the communication and decision inner circle.

Part of the success of the new management team was based on the fact that they were temporarily applied to the project. Thus, there was no need to build friends and supporters, worry about long-term issues, or be concerned with building up organizational infrastructure. A temporary team can focus on the project and technical issues required to turn around the project, without the usual political constraints associated with a long-term commitment to the organization. Part of the charter of the new, temporary team was to recruit, interview, and hire permanent replacements for themselves and other staff and management members who had left the company. This brought in "new blood," which also helped stabilize the situation and demonstrated a corporate resolve to move the project and company to a better situation.

Another challenge was to build the morale and self-confidence of the team. We held weekly team status meetings, not only to gather information but also to build some awareness of team spirit. New team members were introduced to the existing team. Weekly progress results (the meetings were held on Friday afternoons) were reviewed, and the crisis situation began to become more routine. We held one-on-one "getting to know you" meetings to establish some personal rapport with each team member and also to explain the new set of project goals. We planned some social activities for the team members and solicited individuals who could organize and suggest such events. Through these events, the team was gradually built up again, after having been close to disbanding during the crisis situation.

One of the most difficult project management challenges was to buy time for the architecture design team to create and document the architecture so that we could then replan the project. Management had become frustrated by the inability of the prior project team to meet their milestones and predict how long development tasks would take. Now the new project management team was saying to company management that we couldn't know the size and duration of the project until we had time to create an architecture design. The temporary nature of the new project management team and the lack of a direct reporting relationship to the company management made it easier to say, "I don't know yet how long this development will take; I'll let you know when I've done the appropriate analysis to make a realistic plan." The unstated agreement within this response was "If you don't accept my conditions, feel free to find someone else to do the job." Such unstated agreements, of course, are beneath the surface of any project manager's relationship with his management, but in this specific crisis situation the project manager was much freer to do things his way.

The pressure to get quick information about the anticipated development schedule was related to the fact that the product had to get to market quickly to stem the financial losses associated with the current product. This implied that not only was a quick answer desired, but it also had better be the right answer. If we found no solutions, the entire financial viability of the business was at stake. Thus, the project goals were clear, and creative solutions were required to get the product to the market quickly using the existing team plus any new hires or contractors that could be absorbed within the time frame required. We made some calculations to quantify the loss in revenue for each month the product would be late. This information helped reinforce to the team members the importance of meeting the development schedule.

The fact that the project was stopped and then restarted created some challenges with managing the existing development team. Usually, architecture design is done with a small team. The design team members can then move into team leader roles for implementing the major subsystems of the architecture. The architecture design team is kept small so that progress doesn't get bogged down with too many communication paths. The chief architect must mediate different opinions and approaches to avoid a "too many cooks in the kitchen" effect. In the case of the IS2000, the development team was already in place. Team members not part of the small architecture design team needed to be given productive work during the period when the architecture was being developed. Writing large amounts of production code while the architecture didn't exist would be counterproductive and frustrating to the team members. Thus, we needed to define prototyping and investigative tasks for these team members to do to support the architecture design.

This was a challenge to maintain efficiency, but there were many tasks that needed to be done to support the architecture concepts being designed (via prototyping or analysis) and to investigate technology alternatives that might be used in the development (e.g., software tools, platforms, methods).

15.5   Lessons Learned

We learned many lessons from the IS2000 project, especially about dealing with people in a crisis situation. But we also experienced firsthand the dependencies between architecture design and project planning. When described well, software architecture becomes a communications basis for all the team members and their management. Since the architecture represents a vision of what will eventually be implemented, it is important to share this vision with everyone that is or will be involved with the project. For the IS2000, the description and communication of the vision to be implemented were critical to restarting the project. Architecture is equally important to new projects. The product implementation vision can be described in the conceptual architecture view, and other views of the architecture help make the implementation more concrete to the development team. Once the architecture communication is initiated, many ideas come from the team members concerning trade-offs, design decisions, and implementation approaches. This dialog is important for the team to build a common understanding of where it needs to go in the future development.

Having the opportunity to do project planning in parallel with designing the new architecture gave us insights into how the project plan should be driven by the architecture. The architecture describes the structure of the system to be implemented. We found that using the architecture, especially the definition of the software components to be implemented, was a good way to plan the schedules, organization, and development cost estimates for the project. Having the team members become involved in estimating the work needed to design, implement, and test their components was a good way for them to learn about the architecture. It also helped them buy into the development schedule rather than the earlier schedules, which were viewed as a fabrication by the project manager. A structured way for the team members to contribute to the project planning helped increase the realism of and commitment to the resulting software development plan.

Another primary lesson we learned from the IS2000 project was the critical nature of the project manager/chief architect relationship. Having been in these roles on earlier projects, we often felt the loneliness associated with making many decisions that may or may not turn out well. Since technical decisions affect the project planning, and vice versa, having a two-person team that can discuss the implications of decisions is extremely useful. We had to make decisions quickly due to the need to get to market quickly. The environment and short time frame made it difficult to review a proposed technical or project direction decision with many members of the development or management team. But, the project manager and the chief architect could review proposed decisions as they came up, with minimal overhead. Thus, decisions were made quickly, but not totally within a vacuum. Furthermore, the sheer number of decisions that had to be made or remade, as in the case of the first attempt at the development, made it impossible for one individual to make all the decisions. A division of concern among technical issues versus projcct issues seemed to be a natural split of responsibilities, with an up-front realization that such decisions would depend on one another.

CHAPTER 16

DPS2000

THE Data Processing System 2000 (DPS2000) is a software system for acquiring and processing meter data, from electrical, gas, and water meters. The meter data is stored and processed so that billing determinants can be calculated for periodic transfer to a billing system. The billing system generates the bills for energy or resource consumers. The DPS2000 architecture design and development project were planned and managed using many of the techniques described in this book. The development was done at four sites in three countries. The resulting product is currently being successfully sold and distributed.

16.1   Background

In 1999, we initiated the design of a software architecture (called Athena) for meter data-acquisition and -processing central stations. A product line architecture was required since multiple application packages were envisioned in order to support future business needs. In addition, existing product architectures were being evaluated for supporting the envisioned application packages.

Historically, these existing product platforms were often modified and tailored toward customer specific requirements within project engineering centers located throughout the world. As a result, such proliferation of platforms and products was occurring that it was difficult to bring new features back into the baseline product. Furthermore, there was a strong trend toward deregulation in the power distribution industry that was believed would cause changes in requirements as well as new business opportunities.

A meter data-processing central station collects data from electric, gas, and water meters connected via telephone lines and other media. The meter data is stored and processed. The type of processing depends on the type of consumer using the resource and its contractual agreement with the supplier of the resource. Thus, many different types of software applications must run on the DPS2000 platform. For example, the processing software for commercial consumers using electricity would be quite different than that for residential water consumers. Furthermore, control functions are provided. For example, commands are sent out to high-power utilization equipment when load must be shed during high demand periods. Modern electric meters can provide measurement data as often as once a minute, which allows *tariff agreements* to be specified between energy consumers and providers such that the price of energy varies with the time of day, the week, and the year and also the amount of energy used. The DPS2000 performs calculations on the meter data, the results of which are typically sent to a utility's billing system.

Five initial application packages were planned for implementation on the Athena platform. These ranged from meter data acquisition through calculation and reporting to load management control and payment systems implementation. The application requirements were quite diverse and required a high degree of flexibility from the product line architecture design. The first two applications were supported directly by the architecture, since their development was initiated shortly after the architecture was designed and reviewed. At the time of the architecture design, marketing requirements specifications existed for the first two applications but not for the other three applications.

A high-level design team was formed consisting of five engineers with a mixture of domain and architecture design expertise. A chief architect was appointed, and the team began the architecture design by analyzing the marketing requirements, developing the conceptual architecture, investigating applicable development technologies, and some simple prototyping.

16.2 Global Analysis

Early on during the high-level design, a global analysis was completed for the DPS2000. The global analysis considered factors that would influence the design, grouped into categories of organizational, technological, and product influences. Analysis of the influencing factors resulted in a set of design strategies that have been used to guide both the product line architecture design and implementation of the application packages.

16.2.1   Organizational Influencing Factors

Organizational factors such as schedule and budget apply only to the product currently being designed. Other organizational factors, such as organizational attitudes, culture, development site(s) location, and software development process, can impact every product developed by an organization.

An example of an organizational influencing factor for the DPS2000 was that the technical skills necessary to implement the application packages were in short supply, since prior products had been Unix-based with local user interfaces and marketing required new products to be Windows-based with Web-based user interfaces. The resulting strategy to address this influence was to bootstrap and exploit expertise located at multiple development sites and to invest in training courses early in the development. Also, a second level of design specification documentation was developed at a level lower than the high-level design. This system design specification concentrated on describing the interfaces between major subsystems of the architecture so that it was easier to parcel out subsystem development to a remote software engineering site.

Another organizational factor was that company management wanted to get the product to market as quickly as possible. Since the market was rapidly changing, it was viewed as critical to quickly get some limited features of the product to potential users so their feedback could be solicited. Our strategy to address this factor was to develop the product incrementally so that scheduled release dates were met even if some features were missing from the release. Thus, for the DPS2000, project schedule took priority over functionality. A build plan was developed for each engineering release identifying the sequence for adding functionality. The project functionality and schedule were baselined after each engineering release. We found that a six-week to eight-week development cycle for each engineering release worked well for the development team to provide a reasonable set of features that could be tested and evaluated.

16.2.2   Technological Influencing Factors

Technological factors limit design choices to the hardware, software, architecture technology, and standards that are currently available. But technology changes over time and products must adapt, so the architecture should be designed with flexibility in mind.

An example of a technological influencing factor was that a distributed object broker was necessary for meeting the scalability and availability requirements within a distributed hardware configuration. The strategy selected to address this factor was to use Microsoft COM throughout system development.

Another technological factor was that we knew that our database system would change over time. Marketing specified that Oracle 8 be used for the DPS2000. But we knew that new database versions would become available and that certain customers would likely prefer vendors other than Oracle. Thus, we designed a layer in the architecture so that we could isolate and encapsulate the database for anticipating that these requirements would change in the future.

16.2.3   Product Influencing Factors

Product factors include features of a product as well as qualities like performance, dependability, security, and cost. These factors may be different in future versions of the product, so the architecture should be designed to support the anticipated changes.

An example of a product influencing factor was that to support a product line architecture, the DPS2000 graphical user interface (GUI) must be able to accommodate many different types of users for different applications. The strategy selected to address this factor was to implement the GUI as a Web-based GUI so that additional flexibility could be achieved as new applications are added and location independence could be achieved for the various user populations.

Another factor was the anticipated performance of the system. The DPS2000 was intended for industrial and commercial applications where thousands of meters would be handled. It was never specified to address residential market requirements where meter data for millions of consumers would be required. However, we knew that a scalable distributed platform would be necessary to meet these potential unknown market performance requirements. Furthermore, the primary purpose of the DPS2000 is to perform the calculations on meter data before they are sent to a billing system. Again, we anticipated that a scalable distributed platform was necessary to meet unknown calculation time requirements.

As is the case for any product line architecture, but especially one that will be sold into a changing market resulting from deregulation, a high degree of flexibility is necessary as an overall design goal in order to have a chance at anticipating meeting new, unspecified requirements. Unfortunately, this means that the architecture may be considered "overdesigned" for the simpler nearer-term applications, but the flexibility will be necessary to extend the life of the product line. In an organization with limited software development resources, application packages will be developed mainly sequentially, and thus the product line architecture will necessarily be required to live for many years.

16.3 Product Line Design Strategies

Design strategies determine the priorities and constraints of the architecture and help identify potential risks associated with the implementation of the software system. As a result of the DPS2000 global analysis, we identified 24 design strategies that we believed could address the influencing factors. From these 24 design strategies, we derived six major conclusions that we used as guiding principles for the Athena architecture design and resulting development.

- *Reuse the current data-acquisition system.* The architecture design shows the new data-processing system loosely coupled to the existing acquisition system with well-defined interfaces and separate data storage (Figure 16.1). This saves development time, since code for handling communication protocols and meter setup need not be redeveloped or ported. Basic system utilities, such as the message/alarming system, are used by all subsystems.
- *Reuse third-party software wherever possible.* A design strategy was followed to attempt to use third-party tools whenever possible. Furthermore, most of these tools came from a single vendor, Microsoft, which helped reduce tool selection decision and training time. An innovative approach was implemented to use Excel as a several-purpose computation engine.
- *Replace the functionality of the current product with the new product.* We used the current product's functionality to determine the basic requirements and features of the new product. This helped simplify requirements definition and testing. We added innovative new features to the new product to distinguish it from the current product.

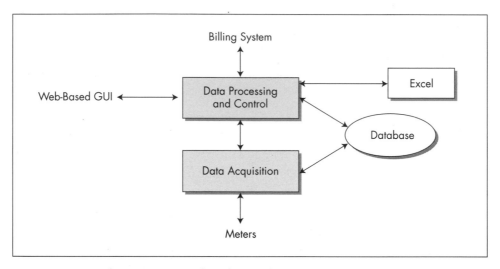

Figure 16.1 *Athena Conceptual Architecture.*

- *Design the DPS2000 as a software product.* New software technologies and business models were evolving at the time we started designing the DPS2000. By developing a purely software product, newly emerging business models [e.g., e-commerce, **application service providers (ASPs)**] could be investigated and offered as potential solutions to a deregulated market with new requirements.
- *Web-based GUI.* All interactions with the DPS2000 we designed to be performed using a Web-based GUI. This has been implemented within a three-tiered architecture. GUI development effort and the process of incremental releases are simplified. From a marketing point of view, the Web-based GUI enables location-independent access to the system and a high degree of flexibility to network and scale the system using intranets or the Internet. The three-tiered architecture provides a structure for adding future applications as business objects.
- *Multisite development.* The lack of sufficient technical skills at a single location was an influencing factor that we addressed by setting up a multisite development at four sites in three countries. This put constraints on the design so that components could be more easily distributed for development at multiple locations, and the development environment and tooling we set up for multiple locations.

While implementing the DPS2000 project, we used these six major project strategy conclusions to guide the development. Our only major deviation from these guidelines was associated with reusing third-party software. We always attempted to use third-party software but quickly found out that in a small number of cases the software didn't meet our requirements, did not function as expected, had quality problems, or created incompatibility problems with other components. In one case, we reversed our decision to use a third-party software component and replaced it with our own in-house software. In retrospect, this was the correct decision, but of course we had to maintain the component we developed. However, having the project strategy conclusions highly visible made us aware when we were considering deviating from them. This helped and supported our decision making during the DPS2000 project.

16.4 DPS2000 Architecture

The Athena high-level software architecture we designed using the four-views approach: conceptual, module, execution, and code [Hofmeister, Nord, and Soni 2000]. The architecture was reviewed using the Architecture Tradeoff Analysis Method (ATAM)[1], which was developed at the Software Engineering Institute (SEI) of Carnegie Mellon University (CMU) in Pittsburgh [Kazman et al. 1999].

We also analyzed the architecture to provide inputs to the project's development cost and schedule estimation. With the architecture-centered software project planning (ACSPP) approach, the software architecture design document was a primary input to the top-down and bottom-up project schedule and effort planning processes. From this we generated an incremental development build plan so that product functionality was built up, feature by feature, within engineering releases that were system-tested until the functionality and quality were adequate for beta testing with prospective customers.

The software architecture of Athena is based on a three-tiered model (user interface tier, business logic tier, and database tier), so new metering applications can easily be added in the future at the middle, or business logic, tier (Figure 16.2). The user interface tier consists of a set of Web pages, a Web

---

1. ATAM is a service mark of Carnegie Mellon University.

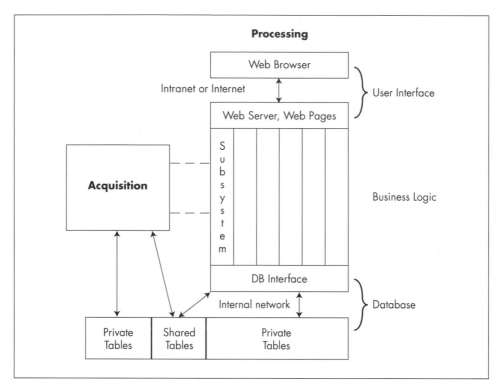

Figure 16.2 *Three-Tiered Architecture.*

server, and a Web browser for interaction with the user. The business logic tier is a group of subsystems that defines the business logic. The database tier contains the database interface, database tables, and database procedures. The business logic subsystems use the database interface or call database procedures to obtain and manipulate data in the database tables.

Customer accounts are managed through the consumer tree subsystem design, where the relationships among master accounts, accounts, contracts, and consumers are described in a tree structure (Figure 16.3). Each node in the tree contains active elements, such as meter proxies, calculations, reports, and tariff agreements. Scheduled events are maintained at each node so that a daily schedule is automatically generated and loaded to the meter data-acquisition subsystem from the consumer tree subsystem.

The Web-based GUI (top tier) provides marketing, implementation, and cost advantages. User capability is simplified and empowered through the use

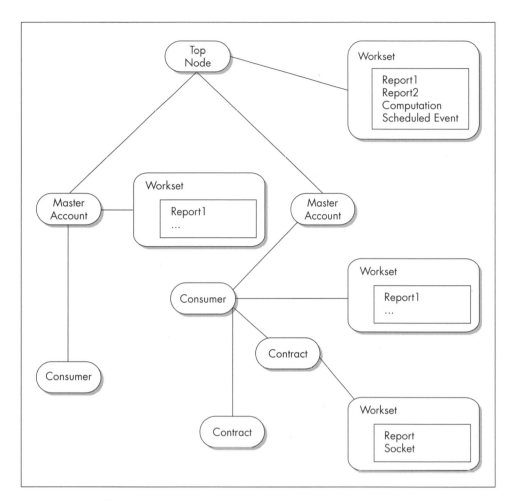

Figure 16.3 *Consumer Tree.*

of templates. Operators of the DPS2000 can manage the system (depending on their security profile) from a Web browser on any client computer connected to the Internet or their intranet. The architecture is designed for scalability, since multiple users can access the system simultaneously, with customer data segmentation and checkin/checkout capabilities for avoiding conflicts.

Microsoft Excel is used as a general-purpose load profile computation engine. This provides both power and ease of use, since most users already have experience using Excel spreadsheets for calculations. The relationships among meter proxies, calculations, tariff agreements, and reports are managed using a mapping description notation that allows simple to complex calculation schemes for generating load profiles and billing determinants.

16.5 Project Planning

We planned the DPS2000 software development as a sequence of incremental engineering releases with increasing functionality. The first release consisted of a "vertical slice" through the architecture layer diagram, which functioned as a prototype of the architecture. The last planned release was the first set of functionality that would be sold as a package to a customer. We also planned alpha and beta releases that were tested by an in-house system-testing function or by lead users. The project schedule we structured such that while in-house testers or users are testing a release, the development team is working on the next release. The cycle time for these incremental releases depended on the times needed for testing and feature development as well as on business constraints, such as when the first set of useful functionality is needed by customers. For our global multisite development, we found a six-week to eight-week cycle time between incremental releases to work best. The release plans were also driven by the dates of trade shows, at which time a new release with the latest functionality is required. We suggest fixing the release dates and release cycles and then fitting in the functionality for each release, depending on the bottom-up estimates and what makes sense for functionally testing the software as a set of user-visible features.

The incremental release process was also a result of our global development process. We found that one of the best means of communication was via the system itself. Only after parts of the DPS2000 were prototyped was it possible to fully understand and discuss the requirements. Perhaps this is because the operation of the system itself became a common language for us all. Incremental releases also encouraged the developers to quickly learn and start using new technologies, since they needed to learn enough to be able to implement even partial functionality.

With consultation from marketing and project management, a build plan was completed detailing which product feature would be incorporated in which engineering release. From the build plan, a software development plan (SDP) for each release was made. The SDP contains individual task assignments, schedule, sets of features, dependencies between features, risks, and test plans.

Like the architecture, the SDP is a communications vehicle, and thus it must be simple enough to be understood by everyone on the team. Also, it is better for the engineers to plan the details of their work in their personal schedules rather than for project management to schedule everything for them. This is especially true for multisite development, where the developers must be flexible and responsive to the work going on at the other sites.

During the planning process for each incremental release, drafts of the proposed schedules and task assignments were circulated to the team members. The first version was distributed as a proposed development schedule and staffing plan to get feedback from all the team members. We would often receive feedback from the team members, such as "This feature cannot be achieved in the time frame planned," "Joe is better qualified for this task than I am," and "I have vacation or training planned during these weeks." Based on this feedback, we would develop and distribute a second version of the plan, which contained the "final" schedule committing the release dates and desired feature set.

We found that a clear division of development responsibilities was very important to the team members. The SDP represents a commitment by the project team to develop the software product within the schedule and staffing requirements described.

We have found that a description of the overall project goals is useful and should be stated in the software development plan. An example statement of project goals is: Quality will have higher priority than schedule, which will have higher priority than functionality. Such a statement of project goals helped the project manager make the inevitable trade-offs that must be decided right before a release. It gave guidance in answering the last-minute questions, such as "Should I slip schedule to put in a few more features?" The project goals are important to explicitly state for a global project team, since we observed cultural biases concerning qualities such as timeliness, perfectionism, quality, openness, and transparency.

16.6 Project Management

Each development site had a local manager to manage the team members at that site. There was also an overall project manager and a project manager for each software application package development. Thus, there was overlapping management responsibility for achieving the project goals. These managers had to negotiate individual work assignments, for example, if an individual planned to work on multiple application packages in parallel. The overall project manager resolved conflicts that couldn't be handled at a lower level. In practice, many of these types of staffing conflicts surfaced when the proposed software development plan was distributed for feedback.

The chief architect was responsible for decision making and resolving technical conflicts for the application package. Analogous to the overall project manager, there was an overall technical manager. In practice, key technical decisions that affected the overall project goals were reviewed with the project and technical management, before they were implemented.

A responsible engineer was assigned to each subsystem who designed and implemented it for the DPS2000. The team members, who generally wanted clear division of responsibilities and ownership of subsystem code, strongly supported this approach.

Project status tracking was done during weekly teleconferences. Each team member was encouraged to report on his development progress and to raise information or issues to be shared with other team members.

16.7 Lessons Learned

We were pleased with our experience implementing the first two application packages using the Athena software architecture. Some team members viewed the development of a system design specification as an unnecessary step that delayed the start of the application packages implementation. However, new development team members working on both the current and new application packages have successfully used this specification. It has been critical for partitioning work packages across the four development sites. We have observed that integration of the various subsystems has gone remarkably smoothly when the subsystem leaders are brought together in one location.

We've had good experiences with our approach to incremental development. Publishing the **Uniform Resource Locator (URL)** for the test system in Switzerland enables all team members and their management to watch the progress of the development as new features are continually added. This was a big morale boost for the team, since everyone was aware of the rapid progress being made after the high-level design phase was completed and development began. The first engineering release was an implementation of a vertical slice through the architecture. This helped validate the architecture and gave the development team the confidence and understanding of the architecture to be able to implement the future engineering releases.

At the end of the planning phase for each incremental release, each team member has a personal schedule with weekly milestones for the components that he is responsible for developing. In addition, there is an overall project schedule, monitored by the project manager, that identifies how the components are allocated to the incremental releases. The development team members have developed the schedules to a large extent, and thus their ownership of these schedules is relatively high. Business management, marketing, service, system testing, and sales can refer to the SDP and the release plan to see when functionality becomes available in the various incremental releases.

Since we put priority on meeting scheduled release dates and traded off functionality and quality as necessary, the development team successfully achieved every release date. This helped build up the credibility of the development team with management, since they knew that a new set of functionality would be ready for validation testing by the dates that were planned and committed to at the beginning of the baselined engineering release cycle. Fortunately, our quality remained relatively high throughout the development, so the trade-off between meeting schedule and quality was never seriously challenged.

The DPS2000 software product line architecture is designed to be very flexible and expandable, to handle a wide variety of applications. This is a primary design requirement, since the power distribution industry is rapidly changing as a result of worldwide deregulation. The diversity of our development team members, with their differing skills and experience, has helped us achieve a flexible design that is better suited for the world market.

Conclusions

I HAVE provided a number of tips and two case studies for managing software projects by using software architecture as a central artifact for driving the planning, organizing, implementing, and measuring of a project.

17.1 Sharing Best Practices

One of the major and long-standing frustrations of any researcher in software engineering is the relative lack of experiments. Many researchers disapprove of the term *software engineering* since the practices used for the production of software often seem more like an "art" than "engineering" or "science." Clearly, software engineering lacks the formalism, rules of thumb, mathematics, physics, methods, and history of other engineering disciplines, such as electrical, civil, and mechanical engineering.

The tips provided here are based on anecdotal experiences and can be classified as best practices found to work within an environment for the types of products we produce, for the size of the projects we work on, applied over a limited period of time, etc. Thus, I've provided many disclaimers along with a request to the reader to try practices that have worked for us with the belief that they may be helpful to others.

The preface states that our industry is not well known for producing good-quality software on schedule and on budget. In fact, there are many well-publicized problems associated with software systems, such as the

Therac-25 accidents [Leveson and Turner 1993], the Denver Airport baggage-handling system [Appleby 1994], and the Mars Polar Lander. Unfortunately, there are many other failed software projects that received no publicity when they did not meet their goals. Many of these failures were never analyzed as to cause. They are often simply forgotten. In fact, it's often the rule rather than the exception that software products are delivered behind schedule and with major quality problems.

Part of the difficulty with software experimentation is that software development is a labor-intensive activity extending over many months or years. Experiments with students with small software development tasks rarely simulate a real industrial environment. Many of the projects I have worked on have a one-year development plan. If you add the time required for high-level design, project planning, downtime between projects, and so on, then experienced software project managers, like myself, may get an opportunity to manage four to five projects per decade. Coupled with the fact that many projects have development times longer than one year and the rapid changes in software technologies that have occurred over the last 20 years, then very few software project managers have more experience than I do.

In my opinion, the only way to make substantial progress to better manage software projects is to share best practices. This is being done in many organizations that are willing to learn from their successes and their mistakes. If the majority of the staff stays at the company for an extended period of time, these best practices are spread around new projects and improved and adapted over time. Many organizations lack the size, discipline, history, and stable workforce to internally share best practices effectively. This is why it is important to publish such best practices, and I welcome the opportunity to share experiences with software project managers around the world.

I have described middleweight processes that seem to work for medium-sized projects. The next project that we are considering applying architecture-centric software project management to is a relatively large product development. Preliminary plans are considering a team of approximately 400 people located in five development sites in five countries across three continents. It is estimated that approximately 1 **million lines of code (MLOC)** will be developed. When we apply our project management methods to this project, it will be a good test of the scalability of our approach. Undoubtedly, our methods will be adapted and improved as we apply them to larger projects. If this is our next project and I'm still employed after using our methods for the next few years, I would be pleased to share our best practices with my fellow project managers.

17.2 Benefits

I have suggested initiating high-level architecture design and project planning prior to committing to a development schedule and involving large numbers of developers. The software architecture, as a primary artifact, becomes central to managing the project. Risks are better understood when they are analyzed from a technical and project view while using techniques such as global analysis. The architecture helps define the project organization. In today's global economy, it is likely that global development will occur when the project organization is split across multiple countries, possibly in different time zones. The project manager and chief architect must work together as a decision-making team for the project while many trade-off decisions are made and possibly remade as the development progresses.

Not only must the project manager worry about technical issues, but he must also worry about the people-related aspects of the project. The best people possible must be obtained, and they will require varying amounts of direction and support as the development progresses. The project manager and chief architect must strive to provide enough support to make the development team as productive as possible, since the first company to market with a new product often captures the largest market share.

Probably the biggest benefit to applying the architecture-centric practices described herein is that projects become more predictable. Using our architecture-centered software project planning (ACSPP) technique along with incremental development driven by the software architecture, I cannot remember the last time we missed a release date. When ACSPP is used to generate a software development plan that is driven by the architecture design and release increments are limited to a four- to eight-week development cycle, it becomes much easier to meet your planned release dates. The development is broken down into smaller increments that are easier to plan and manage. You may end up missing a few features, but the majority of features will be there, and you've planned the releases such that they contain testable subsets of functionality.

We've also experienced the benefit that our software quality is much higher than earlier projects, since each incremental release is being tested when it's available rather than having all the validation testing at the end of development. This requires some planning by the project manager and chief architect to make sure that the development team has adequate time in the next increment to fix defects discovered from the prior increment. But once a team has some experience developing a few increments, the process works remarkably well.

Consistently meeting release dates helps establish the credibility of a project manager with his management. When such credibility is established, it makes for much more productive and constructive planning discussions for future projects. In organizations where this credibility is not present, there may be mistrust concerning what can and cannot be realistically achieved. Without this trust, project managers may engage in extravagant padding of their estimates, and business management may try to intimidate project managers to commit to meeting schedules that are unrealistic. Such practices tend to hurt the organization over time and have contributed to project manager burnout.

Although I'm sure there is some disagreement depending on individual preferences, I generally believe that software engineers like working within the type of planned project that is driven by the architecture. As I have stated, a project manager has certain obligations to his development team. Projects will never be implemented as they are planned. But the lack of planning will always frustrate a development team when it requires team members to do rework or be unproductive due to lack of definition or direction. Also, plans that are too detailed and micro-managed will frustrate team members, since the team will have less freedom and be less able to make their own trade-off decisions. If the goals of the project and design strategies are well known to all the development team members, the team is more likely to make the correct trade-off decisions.

17.3 Summary

I hope you will find useful the suggestions, tips, and methods that I have described for architecture-centric project management. The biggest reward for any engineer is to see his products being used by other people. Many people in the course of their daily lives may use the software systems that you develop. Very specialized customers for special applications may also use them. They may be applied to perceived "important" applications, such as for medical equipment and safety-critical applications. Regardless of the application, every user is special to the software development engineer. Software engineers will continue to tolerate bad project managers when they continue to have the chance to create software products that impact people's lives in the real world. But a little bit of planning based on an architecture design that represents a vision of the product to be implemented goes a long way in achieving a productive and motivated project development team that meets the project goals. I wish you good luck on your next project.

PART seven

Appendix

Appendix: Useful forms

THIS appendix contains forms you may find useful as you attempt to apply the techniques described in this book. You can easily set up these forms as spreadsheets or tables within your engineering documents.

Generic Factor Table: Organizational Factors.

Organizational Factors	Flexibility and Changeabilty	Impact
O1: *<Factor category>*		
O1.1: *<Factor category>*		
<Description of factor>	*<What aspects of the factor are flexible or changeable?>*	*<Components affected by the factor or changes to it>*
O1.2: *<Factor category>*		
<Description of factor>	*<What aspects of the factor are flexible or changeable?>*	*<Components affected by the factor or changes to it>*
O2: *<Factor category>*		
O2.1: *<Factor category>*		
<Description of factor>	*<What aspects of the factor are flexible or changeable?>*	*<Components affected by the factor or changes to it>*
O2.2: *<Factor category>*		
<Description of factor>	*<What aspects of the factor are flexible or changeable?>*	*<Components affected by the factor or changes to it>*

Fill-in Factor Table: Organizational Factors.

Organizational Factors	Flexibility and Changeabilty	Impact
O1:		
O1.1:		
O1.2:		
O2:		
O2.1:		
O2.2:		

Generic Factor Table: Technological Factors.

Technological Factors	Flexibility and Changeabilty	Impact
T1: <Factor category>		
T1.1: <Factor category>		
<Description of factor>	<What aspects of the factor are flexible or changeable?>	<Components affected by the factor or changes to it>
T1.2: <Factor category>		
<Description of factor>	<What aspects of the factor are flexible or changeable?>	<Components affected by the factor or changes to it>
T2: <Factor category>		
T2.1: <Factor category>		
<Description of factor>	<What aspects of the factor are flexible or changeable?>	<Components affected by the factor or changes to it>
T2.2: <Factor category>		
<Description of factor>	<What aspects of the factor are flexible or changeable?>	<Components affected by the factor or changes to it>

Fill-in Factor Table: Technological Factors.

Technological Factors	Flexibility and Changeabilty	Impact
T1:		
T1.1:		
T1.2:		
T2:		
T2.1:		
T2.2:		

Generic Factor Table: Product Factors.

Product Factors	Flexibility and Changeabilty	Impact
P1: <Factor category>		
P1.1: <Factor category>		
<Description of factor>	<What aspects of the factor are flexible or changeable?>	<Components affected by the factor or changes to it>
P1.2: <Factor category>		
<Description of factor>	<What aspects of the factor are flexible or changeable?>	<Components affected by the factor or changes to it>
P2: <Factor category>		
P2.1: <Factor category>		
<Description of factor>	<What aspects of the factor are flexible or changeable?>	<Components affected by the factor or changes to it>
P2.2: <Factor category>		
<Description of factor>	<What aspects of the factor are flexible or changeable?>	<Components affected by the factor or changes to it>

Fill-in Factor Table: Product Factors.

Product Factors	Flexibility & Changeabilty	Impact
P1:		
P1.1:		
P1.2:		
P2:		
P2.1:		
P2.2:		

Generic Issue Card.

<Name of the Architectural Design Issue>
<Description of the issue>
Influencing factors: <Influencing factors that affect this design issue and how they influence it>
Solution: <Discussion of a general solution to the design issues, followed by a list of the associated strategies>
Strategy: <Name of Strategy> <Explanation of the strategy>

Generic Issue Card.   (*continued*)

Strategy: <Name of Strategy>

<Explanation of the strategy>

Related Strategies:

<References to related strategies and a discussion of how they are related to this design issue>

Fill-in Issue Card.

Influencing factors:

Solution:

Strategy:

Strategy:

Related Strategies:

Generic Summary of Strategies.

Issue	Influencing Factors	Applicable Strategy
Name of design issue	Factor list	Strategy name Strategy name Strategy name
Name of design issue	Factor list	Strategy name Strategy name Strategy name
Name of design issue	Factor list	Strategy name Strategy name Strategy name
Name of design issue	Factor list	Strategy name Strategy name Strategy name

Fill-in Summary of Strategies.

Issue	Influencing Factors	Applicable Strategy

Component Design Summary Estimations

Name and Version:
Estimator:
Date:

Component Name	No. of functons, objects, widgets	Confidence	Complexity	Code Size	Design Effort	Coding Effort	Test Effort	Assumptions
Interface Groups (AP)								
Interface Group 1								
Remaining Groups								
Classes/Data Structs								
Obj A or Struct List A								
Remaining Objs/Strcts								
GUI: Windows								
Window 1								
Remaining Windows								
GUI: Event Handlers								
Window 1								
Remaining Windows								
Other Subcomps								
Subcomp 1								
Open Issues								
Open Issue 1								
Total								

Software Component Estimation Form.

IS2000 Bottom-Up Cost Estimation
Major work packages

	Confidence	Complexity	Code Size	Total Effort (hours)	Total Effort (staff-years)
Versioned Object	3	5	2000	720	0.3938731
Study Management	3.2	3.4	600	1280	0.7002188
Check In and Check Out	3.7	3.3	1800	1320	0.7221007
Templates	3	5	1000	2400	1.3129103
Schedule Maker	1	5	19500	2920	1.5973742
GUI	2.8	3.6	18300	4960	2.7133479
Communication System	3	4	500	640	0.3501094
Probe Interface	3	3	11500	1580	0.8643326
HW Diagnostics	4	3	400	250	0.1367615
Flat Panel Display	4	3	700	800	0.4376368
All Other functions			20000	3500	1.9146608
Totals			76300	20370	11.143326

Estimation Summary Sheet (Also Cost-to-Complete Form).

	ER1	ER2	ER3	R1	R2+
Schedule Maker					
Search Consumer Tree for Scheduled Events	✓			✓	
Create a Schedule	✓			✓	
Handle Report Events	✓			✓	
Handle Acquisition Events		✓		✓	
Optimize Acquisitions					✓
Handle Set Parameter Scheduled Events		✓		✓	
Display and Manual Update of Schedules			✓	✓	

Build Plan.

Acronym List

ACSPP: architecture-centered software project planning

ANSI: American National Standards Institute

API: application programming interface

ASCII: American Standard Code for Information Interchange

ASP: application service provider

ATAM: Architecture Trade-off Analysis Method

BCS: British Computer Society

CASE: computer-aided software engineering

CDR: critical design review

CM: configuration management

CMM: capability maturity model

CMU: Carnegie Mellon University

Cocomo: Constructive Cost Model

CORBA: Common object request broker architecture

COTS: commercial off-the-shelf

CPU: central processing unit

CRS: component release specification

CSA: Computing Services Association; Canadian Standards Association

DB: database

DBMS: database management system

DCOM: distributed component object model

DDD: detailed design document

DLL: dynamic link library

DLOC: delta lines of code

DMA: direct memory access

DRM: defect removal model

DSP: digital signal processor

ECO: engineering change order

ECR: engineering change request

EDP: electronic data processing

EEPROM: electrically erasable programmable read-only memory

ER: engineering release

ERB: engineering review board

ESPRIT: European Strategic Programme for Research and Development in Information Technology

EV: earned value

FDA: Food and Drug Administration

FP: function points

FPA: function point analysis

FRS: feature release specification

GA: global analysis

G/Q/M: goals/questions/metrics

GUI: graphical user interface

HLD: high-level design

HLDD: high-level design document

HW: hardware

I&C: instrumentation and control; industrial and commercial

IEEE: Institute of Electrical and Electronics Engineers

IPC: interprocess communication

ISDN: Integrated Services Digital Network

ISO: International Standards Organization

IT: information technology

J2EE: Java 2 Enterprise Edition

KLOC: thousands of lines of code

KPA: key process area

KPR: known problem report

LAN: local area network

LOC: lines of code

MBO: management by objectives

MLOC: million lines of code

MR: modification request

MRS: marketing requirements specification

MTBF: mean time between failures

MTS: Microsoft Transaction Manager

MTTF: mean time to failure

MTTR: mean time to repair

MS: Microsoft

NASA: National Aeronautics and Space Administration

NLOC: net lines of code

OMG: object management group

PBX: private branch exchange

PC: personal computer

PCG: product control group

PCS: project control system

PLA: product line architecture

PLC: programmable logic controller; power line communications

PMW: project manager's workbench

POIM: planning, organizing, implementing, measuring

PPP: product planning process

PR: problem report

PROM: programmable read-only memory

QA: quality assurance

QC: quality control

QFD: quality function deployment

QM: quality management

R: release

R&D: research and development

RAM: random-access memory

RCS: revision control system

RMI: remote method invocation

ROOM: real-time object-oriented modeling

RPC: remote procedure call

RUP: Rational Unified Process

SCCS: source code control system

SCR: Siemens Corporate Research

SDP: software development plan

SEI: Software Engineering Institute

SEL: Software Engineering Laboratory

SOAP: Simple Open-Access Protocol

SPR: software problem report

SQE: software quality engineering

SRS: system requirements specification

SW: software

TQM: total quality management

TR: test release

UI: user interface

UML: Unified Modeling Language

URL: Uniform Resource Locator

V&V: verification and validation

XML: eXtended Markup Language

Bibliography

Albrecht, A., "Measuring Application Development Productivity," *Proceedings* of the *Joint Share/Guide Symposium*, 1979. pp. 83–92.

Albrecht, A. and Gaffney, J., "Software Function, Source Lines of Code and Development Effort Prediction: A Software Science Validation," *IEEE Transactions on Software Engineering*, Vol. SE-9, No. 6, 1983. pp. 639–648.

Appleby, C., "Bugs Still Biting Denver Airport," *Informationweek*, August 22, 1994, p. 24.

Austin, R., *Measuring and Managing Performance in Organizations,* New York: Dorset House, 1996.

Austin, R. and Paulish, D., "A Survey of Commonly Applied Methods for Software Process Improvement," Tech. Report CMU/SEI-93-TR-27, ESC-TR-93-201, Software Engineering Institute, Carnegie Mellon University, Pittsburgh, PA; 1993.

Bache, R. and Bazzanna, G., *Software Metrics for Product Assessment*, New York: McGraw-Hill, 1994.

Bass, L., P. Clements, and R. Kazman, *Software Architecture in Practice*, Reading, MA: Addison-Wesley, 1998.

Beck, K., *Extreme Programming Explained: Embrace Change,* Boston: Addison-Wesley, 2000.

Beck, K. and Fowler, M., *Planning Extreme Programming*, Boston: Addison-Wesley, 2001.

Boehm, B., *Software Engineering Economics*, Englewood Cliffs, NJ: Prentice-Hall, 1981.

Boehm, B. and DeMarco, T., "Software Risk Management," *IEEE Software*, Vol. 14, No. 3, May/June 1997, pp. 17–19.

Boehm, B. et al., *Software Cost Estimation with Cocomo II*, Upper Saddle River, NJ: Prentice-Hall, 2000.

Booch, G., Rumbaugh, J., and Jacobson, I., *The Unified Modeling Language User Guide*, Reading, MA: Addison-Wesley, 1999.

Brooks, F., *The Mythical Man-Month: Essays on Software Engineering*, Reading, MA: Addison-Wesley, 1975.

Buschmann, F., Meunier, R., Rohnert, H., Sommerlad, P., and Stal, M., *Pattern-Oriented Software Architecture: A System of Patterns*, Chichester, UK: Wiley, 1996.

Card, D. and Glass, R., *Measuring Software Design Quality*, Englewood Cliffs, NJ: Prentice-Hall, 1990.

Coad, P., *Java Modeling in Color with UML*, Englewood Cliffs, NJ: Prentice Hall, 1999.

Cobb, R. and Mills, H., "Engineering Software Under Statistical Quality Control," *IEEE Software*, November 1990, pp. 44–54.

DeMarco, T. and Lister, T., *Peopleware: Productive Projects and Teams*, New York: DorsetHouse, 1987.

Dicks, D., *Ticking Along Free: Stories About Switzerland*, Basel: Bergli Books, 2000.

Dreger, B., *Function Point Analysis*, Englewood Cliffs, NJ: Prentice-Hall, 1989.

Dustin, E., Rashka, J., and Paul, J., *Automated Software Testing: Introduction, Management, and Performance*, Reading, MA: Addison-Wesley, 1999.

Fagan, M., "Design and Code Inspections to Reduce Errors in Program Development," *IBM Systems Journal*, Vol. 15, No. 3, pp. 182–210, 1976.

Fenton, N.*, Software Metrics: A Rigorous Approach*, London: Chapman & Hall, 1991.

Fenton, N., Whitty, R., and Iizuka, Y., *Software Quality Assurance and Measurement: A Worldwide Perspective,* London: International Thomson, 1995.

Fleming, Q., *Put Earned Value into Your Management Control System*, Columbus, OH: Publishing Horizons, 1983.

Fleming, Q. and Koppelman, J., *Earned Value Project Management*, 2nd ed., Upper Darby, PA: Project Management Institute, 2000.

Florac, W. and Carleton, A., *Measuring the Software Process*: *Statistical Process Control for Software Process Improvement*, Reading, MA: Addison-Wesley, 1999.

Fowler, M., "Put Your Process on a Diet," *Software Development*, Vol. 8, No. 12, December 2000, pp. 32–36.

Fowler, M. and Highsmith, J., "The Agile Manifesto," *Software Development*, Vol. 9, No. 8, August 2001, pp. 28–32.

Fowler, P. and Rifkin, S., *Software Engineering Process Group Guide*, Technical Report CMU/SEI-90-TR-24, Software Engineering Institute, Pittsburgh, PA, 1990.

Fowler, M. and Scott, K., *UML Distilled: A Brief Guide to the Standard Object Modeling Language*, 2nd ed., Boston: Addison-Wesley, 2000.

Gamma, E., Helm, R., Johnson, R., and Vlissides, J., *Design Patterns: Elements of Reusable Object-Oriented Software*, Reading, MA: Addison-Wesley, 1995.

Gilb, T. and Graham, D., *Software Inspection*, Reading, MA: Addison-Wesley, 1993.

Gill, G. and Kemerer, C., "Cyclomatic Complexity Density and Software Maintenance Productivity," *IEEE Transactions on Software Engineering*, Vol. 17, No. 12, December 1991, pp. 1284–1288.

Gomaa, H*., Software Design Methods for Concurrent and Real-Time Systems*, Boston: Addison-Wesley, 1993.

Gomaa, H., *Designing Concurrent, Distributed, and Real-Time Applications with UML*, Boston: Addison-Wesley, 2000.

Grady, R., *Successful Software Process Improvement*, Upper Saddle River, NJ: Prentice-Hall, 1997.

Grady, R. and Caswell, D., *Software Metrics: Establishing a Company-Wide Program*, Englewood Cliffs, NJ: Prentice-Hall, 1987.

Highsmith, J., *Adaptive Software Development: A Collaborative Approach to Managing Complex Systems*, New York: Dorset House, 2000.

Hofmeister, C., Nord, R., and Soni, D., "Describing Software Architecture with UML," *Proceedings of the TC2 First Working IFIP Conference on Software Architecture (WICSA1)*, Boston: Kluwer Academic, 1999, pp. 145–159.

Hofmeister, C., Nord, R., and Soni, D., *Applied Software Architecture*, Boston: Addison-Wesley, 2000.

Humphrey, W., *Managing the Software Process*, Reading, MA: Addison-Wesley, 1989.

Humphrey, W., *A Discipline for Software Engineering*, Reading, MA: Addison-Wesley, 1995.

Humphrey, W., *Introduction to the Personal Software Process[sm]*, Reading, MA: Addison-Wesley, 1997.

Humphrey, W., *Introduction to the Team Software Process[sm]*, Boston: Addison-Wesley, 2000.

Jackson, M., *Software Requirements & Specifications: A Lexicon of Practice, Principles, and Prejudices*, Reading, MA: Addison-Wesley, 1995.

Jacobson, I., Christerson, M., Jonsson, P., and Overgaard, G., *Object-Oriented Software Engineering: A Use Case Driven Approach,* Reading: MA: Addsion-Wesley, 1992.

Jeffries, R., Anderson, A., and Hendrickson, C., *Extreme Programming Installed*, Boston: Addison-Wesley, 2001.

Jilek, P., Moeller, K., and Paulish, D., "The Use of Software Metrics for Software Development," *Proceedings of the Ninth World Conference on Computer Security, Audit, and Control*, London: Elsevier Advanced Technology, 1992.

Johnson, J., "Turning Chaos into Success," *Software Magazine*, Vol. 19, No. 3, December 1999/January 2000, pp. 30–39.

Jones, C., *Applied Software Measurement*, New York: McGraw-Hill, 1991.

Jones, C., *Assessment and Control of Software Risks*, Englewood Cliffs, NJ: Prentice Hall, 1994.

Jones, C., *Software Assessments, Benchmarks, and Best Practices*, Boston: Addison-Wesley, 2000.

Kazman, R., Barbacci, M., Klein, M., Carriere, S., and Woods, S., "Experience with Performing Architecture Tradeoff Analysis," *Proceedings of the 21st International Conference on Software Engineering*, New York: ACM Press, 1999, pp. 54–63.

Kopper, E., "Swiss and Germans: Similarities and Differences in Work-Related Values, Attitudes, and Behavior," *International Journal of Intercultural Relations*, New York: Pergamon Press, 1993, pp. 167–184.

Kruchten, P., "The 4+1 View Model of Architecture," *IEEE Software*, Vol. 12, No. 6, 1995, pp. 42–50.

Kruchten, P., *The Rational Unified Process: An Introduction*, Reading, MA: Addison-Wesley, 1999.

Kuvaja, P., Simila, J., Kranik, L., Bicego, A., Saukkonen, S., and Koch, G., *Software Process Assessment and Improvement: The Bootstrap Approach*, Oxford: Blackwell, 1994.

Leveson, N. and Turner, C., "An Investigation of the Therac-25 Accidents," *IEEE Computer*, Vol. 26, No. 7, July 1993, pp. 18–41.

Leveson, N., *Safeware: System Safety and Computers,* Reading, MA: Addison-Wesley, 1995.

McCabe, T., "A Complexity Measure," *IEEE Transactions on Software Engineering*, Vol. 2, November 4, December 1976.

Moeller, K. and Paulish, D., *Software Metrics: A Practitioner's Guide to Improved Product Development*, London: IEEE Press, 1993.

Moitra, D., "India's Software Industry," *IEEE Software*, Vol. 18, No. 1, January/February 2001, pp. 77–80.

Musa, J., Iannino, A., and Okumoto, K., *Software Reliability: Measurement, Prediction, Application*, New York: McGraw-Hill, 1987.

Park, R., *Software Size Measurement: A Framework for Counting Source Statements*, Technology Report CMU/SEI-92-TR-20 or ESC-TR-92-020, Software Engineering Institute, Carnegie Mellon University, Pittsburgh, PA, 1992.

Paulish, D. and Carleton, A., "Case Studies of Software-Process-Improvement Measurement," *IEEE Computer*, Vol. 27, No. 9, September 1994, pp. 50–57.

Paulish, D. and Greenberg, M., "Athena: A Software Product Line Architecture for Meter Data Processing and Control," *Proceedings of the Software Product Lines Workshop*, 2000, pp. 35–40.

Paulish, D., Nord, R., and Soni, D., "Experience with Architecture-Centered Software Project Planning," *Proceedings of the Second International Software Architecture Workshop (ISAW-2)*, New York: ACM Press, 1996, pp. 126–129.

Paulk, M. et al., *The Capability Maturity Model: Guidelines for Improving the Software Process*, Reading, MA: Addison-Wesley, 1995.

Putnam, L. and Myers, W., *Measures for Excellence: Reliable Software on Time, Within Budget*, New York: Yourdan Press 1992.

Rising, L. and Janoff, N., "The Scrum Software Development Process for Small Teams," *IEEE Software*, Vol. 17, No. 4, July/August 2000, pp. 26–32.

Royce, W., *Software Project Management: A Unified Framework*, Reading, MA: Addison-Wesley, 1998.

Selby, R., Basili, V., and Baker, F., "Cleanroom Software Development: An Empirical Evaluation," *IEEE Transactions on Software Engineering*, September 1987, pp. 1027–1037.

Shaw, M. and Garlan, D., *Software Architecture: Perspectives on an Emerging Discipline*, Englewood Cliffs, NJ: Prentice-Hall, 1996.

Sherman, W., Paulish, D., Klinger, M., and Liao, W., "Scenario-Driven Software Design," *Electronic Design*, Vol. 43, No. 22, October 24, 1995, pp. 67–80.

Soni, D., Nord, R., and Hofmeister, C., "Software Architecture in Industrial Applications," In *Proceedings of the 17th International Conference on Software Engineering*, New York: ACM Press, 1995. pp. 196–207.

Thayer, R., *Software Engineering Project Management*, Los Alamitos, CA: IEEE Computer Society Press, 1997.

Weiss, D. and Lai, C., *Software Product-Line Engineering: A Family-Based Software Development Process*, Reading, MA: Addison-Wesley, 1999.

White, B., *Software Configuration Management Strategies and Rational ClearCase: A Practical Introduction*, Boston: Addison-Wesley, 2000.

Williams, L., Kessler, R., Cunningham, W., and Jeffries, R., "Strengthening the Case for Pair Programming," *IEEE Software*, Vol. 17, No. 4, July/August 2000, pp. 19–25.

Index

The SEI Series in Software Engineering

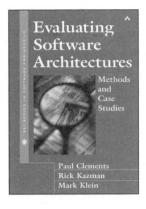

Evaluating Software Architectures
Methods and Case Studies
Paul Clements, Rick Kazman, and Mark Klein

This book is a comprehensive, step-by-step guide to software architecture evaluation, describing specific methods that can quickly and inexpensively mitigate enormous risk in software projects. The methods are illustrated both by case studies and by sample artifacts put into play during an evaluation: view-graphs, scenarios, final reports—everything you need to evaluate an architecture in your own organization.
0-201-70482-X • Hardcover • 240 Pages • ©2002

Software Product Lines
Practices and Patterns
Paul Clements and Linda Northrop

Building product lines from common assets can yield remarkable improvements in productivity, time to market, product quality, and customer satisfaction. This book provides a framework of specific practices, with detailed case studies, to guide the implementation of product lines in your own organization.
0-201-70332-7 • Hardcover • 608 Pages • ©2002

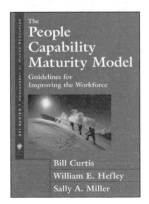

The People Capability Maturity Model
Guidelines for Improving the Workforce
Bill Curtis, William E. Hefley, and Sally A. Miller

Employing the process maturity framework of the Software CMM, the People Capability Maturity Model (People CMM) describes best practices for managing and developing an organization's workforce. This book describes the People CMM and the key practices that comprise each of its maturity levels, and shows how to apply the model in guiding organizational improvements. Includes case studies.
0-201-60445-0 • Hardback • 448 Pages • ©2002

Winning with Software

An Executive Strategy

Watts S. Humphrey

Watts S. Humphrey, drawing on his own extensive executive and management experience, shows corporate executives and senior managers why software is both a business problem and a business opportunity. He first demonstrates the critical importance of software to nearly every business, large and small, then outlines seven steps needed to gain control of a software operation and transform it into a professional, businesslike engineering function.

0-201-77639-1 • Hardcover • 256 pages • ©2002

Architecture-Centric Software Project Management

A Practical Guide

Daniel J. Paulish

Written for project managers and software architects, this book demonstrates how to draw on software architecture to design schedules, generate estimates, make scope decisions, and manage the team for a successful outcome. With case studies and examples based on practical experience, each cornerstone of effective project management is addressed—planning, organizing, implementing, and measuring.

0-201-73409-5 • Paperback • 320 pages • ©2002

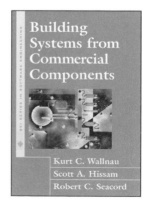

Building Systems from Commercial Components

Kurt C. Wallnau, Scott A. Hissam, and Robert C. Seacord

Commercial components are increasingly seen as an effective means to save time and money in building large software systems. However, integrating pre-existing components, with pre-existing specifications, is a delicate and difficult task. This book describes specific engineering practices needed to accomplish that task successfully, illustrating the techniques described with case studies and examples.

0-201-70064-6 • Hardcover • 432 pages • ©2002

CMMI℠ Distilled

A Practical Introduction to Integrated Process Improvement
Dennis M. Ahern, Aaron Clouse, and Richard Turner

The Capability Maturity Model Integration (CMMI) is the latest version of the popular CMM framework, designed specifically to integrate an organization's process improvement activities across disciplines. This book provides a concise introduction to the CMMI, highlighting the benefits of integrated process improvement, explaining key features of the new framework, and suggesting how to choose appropriate models and representations for your organization.

0-201-73500-8 • Paperback • 336 pages • ©2001

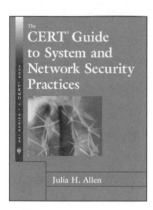

The CERT® Guide to System and Network Security Practices

By Julia H. Allen

The CERT Coordination Center helps systems administrators secure systems connected to public networks, develops key security practices, and provides timely security implementations. This book makes CERT practices and implementations available in book form, and offers step-by-step guidance for protecting your systems and networks against malicious and inadvertent compromise.

0-201-73723-X • Paperback • 480 pages • ©2001

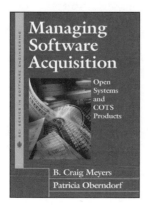

Managing Software Acquisition

Open Systems and COTS Products
B. Craig Meyers and Patricia Oberndorf

The acquisition of open systems and commercial off-the-shelf (COTS) products is an increasingly vital part of large-scale software development, offering significant savings in time and money. This book presents fundamental principles and best practices for successful acquisition and utilization of open systems and COTS products.

0-201-70454-4 • Hardcover • 400 pages • ©2001

Introduction to the Team Software Process℠
Watts S. Humphrey

The Team Software Process (TSP) provides software engineers with a framework designed to build and maintain more effective teams. This book, particularly useful for engineers and students trained in the Personal Software Process (PSP), introduces TSP and the concrete steps needed to improve software teamwork.

0-201-47719-X • Hardcover • 496 pages • ©2000

CMM in Practice
Processes for Executing Software Projects at Infosys
Pankaj Jalote

This book describes the implementation of CMM at Infosys Technologies, and illustrates in detail how software projects are executed at this highly mature software development organization. The book examines the various stages in the life cycle of an actual Infosys project as a running example throughout the book, describing the technical and management processes used to initiate, plan, and execute it.

0-201-61626-2 • Hardcover • 400 pages • ©2000

Measuring the Software Process
Statistical Process Control for Software Process Improvement
William A. Florac and Anita D. Carleton

This book shows how to use measurements to manage and improve software processes within your organization. It explains specifically how quality characteristics of software products and processes can be quantified, plotted, and analyzed, so that the performance of software development activities can be predicted, controlled, and guided to achieve both business and technical goals.

0-201-60444-2 • Hardcover • 272 pages • ©1999

Cleanroom Software Engineering

Technology and Process

Stacy Prowell, Carmen J. Trammell, Richard C. Linger, and Jesse H. Poore

This book provides an introduction and in-depth description of the Cleanroom approach to high-quality software development. Following an explanation of basic Cleanroom theory and practice, the authors draw on their extensive experience in industry to elaborate the Cleanroom development and certification process and show how this process is compatible with the Capability Maturity Model (CMM).

0-201-85480-5 • Hardcover • 416 pages • ©1999

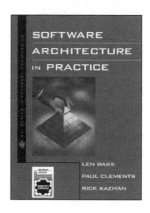

Software Architecture in Practice

Len Bass, Paul Clements, and Rick Kazman

This book introduces the concepts and practice of software architecture, not only covering essential technical topics for specifying and validating a system, but also emphasizing the importance of the business context in which large systems are designed. Enhancing both technical and organizational discussions, key points are illuminated by substantial case studies.

0-201-19930-0 • Hardcover • 480 pages • ©1998

Managing Risk

Methods for Software Systems Development

By Elaine M. Hall

Written for busy professionals charged with delivering high-quality products on time and within budget, this comprehensive guide describes a success formula for managing software risk. The book follows a five-part risk management road map designed to take you from crisis to control of your software project.

0-201-25592-8 • Hardcover • 400 pages • ©1998

Software Process Improvement
Practical Guidelines for Business Success
By Sami Zahran

This book will help you manage and control the quality of your organization's software products by showing you how to develop a preventive culture of disciplined and continuous process improvement.

0-201-17782-X • Hardcover • 480 pages • ©1998

Introduction to the Personal Software Process
By Watts S. Humphrey

This workbook provides a hands-on introduction to the basic discipline of software engineering, as expressed in the author's well-known Personal Software Process (PSP). By applying the forms and methods of PSP described in the book, you can learn to manage your time effectively and to monitor the quality of your work, with enormous benefits in both regards.

0-201-54809-7 • Paperback • 304 pages • ©1997

Managing Technical People
Innovation, Teamwork, and the Software Process
By Watts S. Humphrey

Drawing on the author's extensive experience as a senior manager of software development at IBM, this book describes proven techniques for managing technical professionals. The author shows specifically how to identify, motivate, and organize innovative people, while tying leadership practices to improvements in the software process.

0-201-54597-7 • Paperback • 352 pages • ©1997

The Capability Maturity Model
Guidelines for Improving the Software Process
By Carnegie Mellon University/Software
Engineering Institute

This book provides the authoritative description and technical overview of the Capability Maturity Model (CMM), with guidelines for improving software process management. The CMM provides software professionals in government and industry with the ability to identify, adopt, and use sound management and technical practices for delivering quality software on time and within budget.

0-201-54664-7 • Hardcover • 464 pages • ©1995

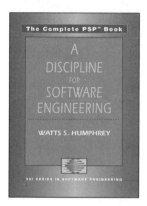

A Discipline for Software Engineering
The Complete PSP Book
By Watts S. Humphrey

This book scales down to a personal level the successful methods developed by the author to help managers and organizations evaluate and improve their software capabilities—methods comprising the Personal Software Process (PSP). The author's aim with PSP is to help individual software practitioners develop the skills and habits needed to plan, track, and analyze large and complex projects, and to develop high-quality products.

0-201-54610-8 • Hardcover • 816 pages • ©1995

Software Design Methods for Concurrent and Real-Time Systems
By Hassan Gomaa

This book provides a basic understanding of concepts and issues in concurrent system design, while surveying and comparing a range of applicable object-oriented design methods. The book describes a practical approach for applying real-time scheduling theory to analyze the performance of real-time designs.

0-201-52577-1 • Hardcover • 464 pages • ©1993

Managing the Software Process

By Watts S. Humphrey

This landmark book introduces the author's methods, now commonly practiced in industry, for improving software development and maintenance processes. Emphasizing the basic principles and priorities of the software process, the book's sections are organized in a natural way to guide organizations through needed improvement activities.

0-201-18095-2 • Hardcover • 512 pages • ©1989

Other titles of interest from Addison-Wesley

Practical Software Measurement

Objective Information for Decision Makers
By John McGarry, David Card, Cheryl Jones, Beth Layman, Elizabeth Clark, Joseph Dean, and Fred Hall

A critical task in developing and maintaining software-intensive systems is to meet project cost, schedule, and technical objectives. This official guide to Practical Software Measurement (PSM) shows how to accomplish that task through sound measurement techniques and the development of a software measurement process. It provides a comprehensive description of PSM's techniques and practical guidance based on PSM's actual application in large-scale software projects.

0-201-71516-3 • Hardcover • 256 pages • ©2002

Making the Software Business Case

Improvement by the Numbers
By Donald J. Reifer

This book shows software engineers and managers how to prepare the *business* case for change and improvement. It presents the tricks of the trade developed by this well-known author over many years, tricks that have repeatedly helped his clients win the battle of the budget. The first part of the book addresses the fundamentals associated with creating a business case; the second part uses case studies to illustrate cases made for different types of software improvement initiatives.

0-201-72887-7 • Paperback • 304 pages • ©2002